IMAGES
of America

CHELMSFORD REVISITED

I0807626

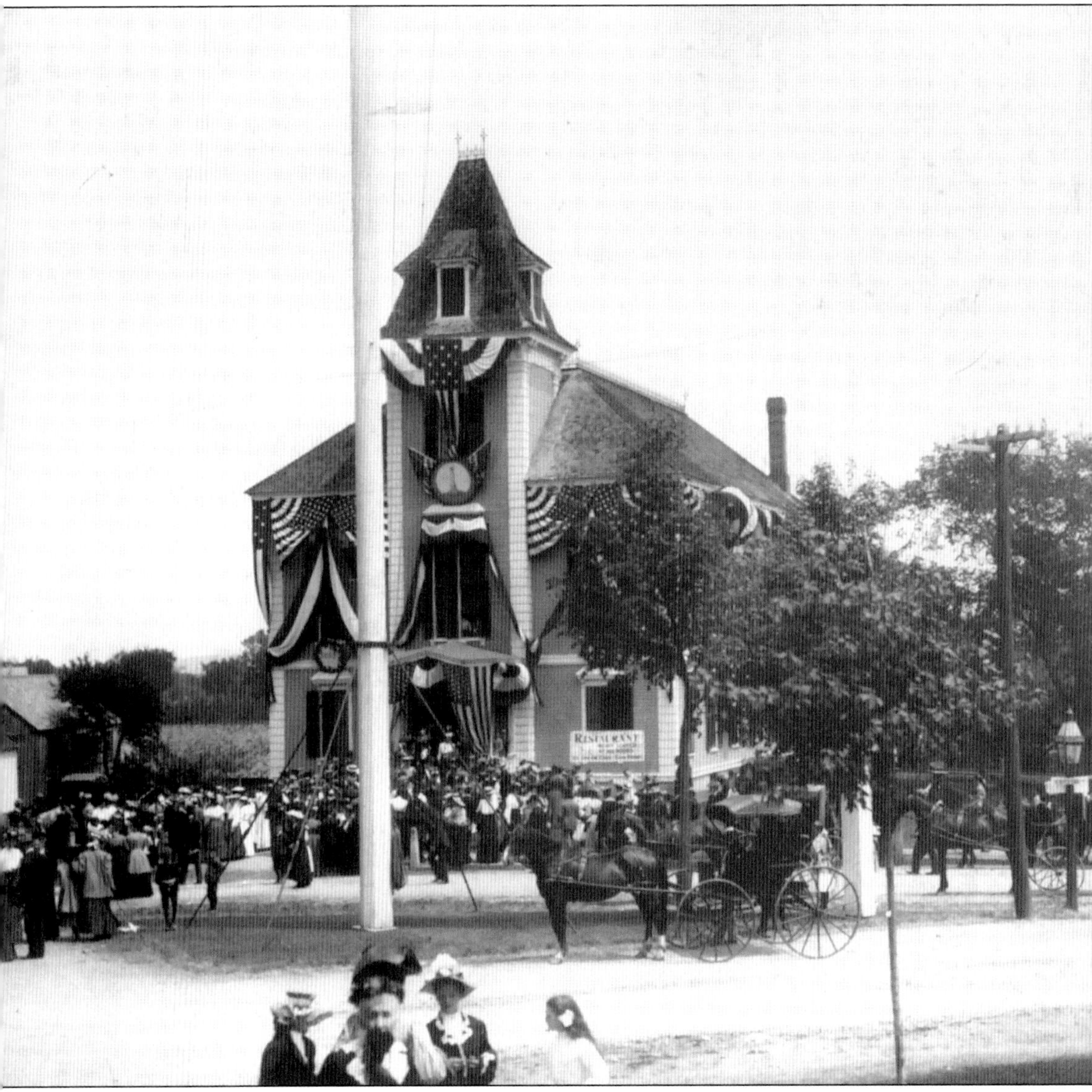

The town of Chelmsford celebrated its 250th anniversary in grand style over a four-day period from May 28 to 31, 1905. Simon Towle, who had already left a significant photographic legacy in Chelmsford starting around 1861, returned as the official photographer for the 1905 event at age 72. He captured this image on May 29 as the town hall was emptying out after 2:00 p.m. anniversary exercises. (Chelmsford Historical Society Collection.)

On the Cover: The Parkhurst family, posing around 1889 in front of their home at 78 High Street, operated the S.W. Parkhurst General Store in Central Square from 1880 to 1923 and owned the building until 1969. Pictured, from left to right, are G. Thomas, Willis B. (seated), Emma L., Martha J., Bertha A., and S. Waldo Parkhurst. (Chelmsford Historical Society Collection.)

IMAGES
of America

CHELMSFORD REVISITED

Fred Merriam for the
Chelmsford Historical Society

ARCADIA
PUBLISHING

ISBN 978-1-4671-2074-6

Published by Arcadia Publishing
Charleston, South Carolina

Printed in the United States of America

Library of Congress Control Number: 2013942516

For all general information, please contact Arcadia Publishing:
Telephone 843-853-2070
Fax 843-853-0044
E-mail sales@arcadiapublishing.com
For customer service and orders:
Toll-Free 1-888-313-2665

Visit us on the Internet at www.arcadiapublishing.com

This book is dedicated to the countless volunteers of Chelmsford who continually improve the quality of life in town and keep its heritage alive.

Contents

Acknowledgments

The undertaking of this book project would not have been possible without two organizations and their many volunteers who have diligently worked to preserve the town's historical heritage. Since its founding in 1930 at the Adams Library, the nonprofit Chelmsford Historical Society has cared for and organized the town's historical treasures and was the source of most of the photographs. The Chelmsford Historical Commission, established at the annual town meeting in 1966 under Massachusetts General Laws Chapter 40, Section 8D, "for the preservation, promotion, and development of the historical assets of the town," has provided a wealth of carefully researched information. In addition, several individuals contributed new information and photographs, some by request and some by happy coincidence, including the following: Louise Alden, Bill Bennett, David Brow, Richard Bump, Kevin Clarke, John Crawford III, Judy Fichtenbaum, Tim Fraize, Dana Gray, Eric Johnson, Sandy Parkhurst Johnston, Bill Johnston Jr., Kim MacKenzie, George Merrill, Ann Perham, Brad Perham, Donnie Peterson, Linda Prescott, Tina Sousa, Leona Sprague, Harry Taplin, Deb Taverna, and Becky Warren. Thanks also go to Tom Christiano, Linda Prescott, and Deb Taverna for proofreading the text.

Essential to any project is the support, encouragement, and understanding of family. I would like to thank my wife, Carol, a past president of the Chelmsford Historical Society, for sharing her opinions, making sure the necessary time was available, and keeping the household running in the present.

INTRODUCTION

The Chelmsford Historical Society has a wonderful collection of photographs and negatives dating back to the early days of photography. Sadly, not all of the original owners thought to label the subject matter on the back of the prints or on the packaging, so there are a number of excellent images in need of identification. One of the joys of this project was the detective work resulting in identification and location of unidentified people and places captured in crystal clear photographs and glass-plate negatives over a century old.

A mystery begging to be solved was the identity of the photographer behind the Royal Shawcross Collection, which is in the possession of the Chelmsford Public Library. Royal Shawcross was a historically minded former board of selectmen member residing in North Chelmsford from 1923 to 1980. He was too young to have taken the photographs in the library's collection. An e-mail exchange that started via the historical society website in June 2012 with Bill Johnston from Johnson City, Tennessee, led to the discovery that his family (descendants of George C. Moore) had prints that were similar in format, quality, and labeling to the Shawcross Collection. A flurry of detective work led to the conclusion that Simon Towle, working out of a studio on Merrimack Street in Lowell, was the photographer. Further checking showed that the stereopticon photographs of Chelmsford from the 1860s and 1870s in the Chelmsford Historical Society Collection and the official photographs for the 250th anniversary celebration in 1905 were also taken by Simon Towle. In an unexpected twist, Bill discovered that Simon Towle and George C. Moore were related.

As the chapter topics fell into place, it became evident that there were more than enough photographs from the east, south, and center sections of Chelmsford to complete this book. The Royal Shawcross Collection depicts North Chelmsford and West Chelmsford exclusively, and the historical society has many more unpublished photographs of the north and west sections, so a decision was made to cover North Chelmsford and West Chelmsford in a separate book.

It was a surprise that very little was known about the oldest house in Chelmsford, listed as being built in 1656 and located at 50 Hunt Road on the intersection with Littleton Road. In February 2013, Leona Sprague, a member of the Emanouil family, who had grown up in that house, shared some photograph copies of very old photographs the family had and wondered if they could be identified. Some detective work revealed that the family depicted outside the house and in a studio portrait was that of Civil War veteran George A. Byam. Two unidentified glass-plate negatives of this family in the Chelmsford Historical Society Collection now had meaning. In April 2013, an e-mail was received via the historical society website from Richard Bump, living north of Rockwall, Texas, stating that he is the great-great-grandson of George A. Byam and has extensive genealogy information on the Byam and Russell families in Chelmsford. The photographs are now well identified.

During the making of the Center Common chapter, there were not quite enough photographs available to build a story for the east side of the common, so that chapter was set aside. In early

May 2013, firefighters Donnie Peterson and Bill Bennett contacted this writer about publishing the fire department archives entrusted to their care. It was agreed that the archives would be published on the town website, but in the meantime, the wonderful photographs in that collection were exactly what was needed to complete the Center Common chapter.

In the Other Houses chapter, there is a wealth of information and photographs for the family of David Perham, founder of the Perham Cider Mill, but nothing on David C. Perham, who lived nearby on Westford Street. In late May 2013, Ann and Brad Perham (great-great-grandson of David C. Perham) of Walpole, Massachusetts, e-mailed the historical society stating that they were closing out Brad's father's house and asked if the society would be interested in the archives of Brad's grandfather Arnold C. Perham. This collection includes a large number of well-identified photographs including several Simon Towle stereopticon images of David C. Perham with his family and farm buildings. There are also many documents related to David's grandson Arnold C. Perham as a milk and meat inspector, fire chief, planning board member, president of the Chelmsford Historical Society, and member of the historical commission.

Several notable Chelmsford people had similar names. Rufus F. Emerson and Rufus W. Emerson were born within a year of each other and died within three years of each other. They were first cousins and their grandfather was Deacon Owen Emerson. An uncle named Rufus (no middle initial) died young at age 29—just months after the cousins were born in 1834 and 1835—so there may be a naming connection. Rufus F. was the father of photographer Arthur I. Emerson, and Rufus W. was the brother of James P. Emerson at 11 North Road and was married to Martha L. Parkhurst, a daughter of Baptist minister Rev. John Parkhurst.

"Deacon" David Perham and David C. Perham, 17 years younger, lived almost across Westford Street from each other. It turns out that they were third cousins with a common great-great-grandfather Samuel, according to information provided by Ann Perham. Deacon David's family lived in Chelmsford for many generations, while David C. came from New Hampshire and married Maria A. Byam from 19 Maple Road, now known as Red Wing Farm. Both David Perham families became powerful influences in the historical, political, and business lives of Chelmsford.

Amos F. Adams and Amos B. Adams, 12 years younger, were contemporaries. Amos F. left South Chelmsford at age 20 to work at the Quincy Market and found success in Boston as a commission merchant (buying and selling goods at a percentage of the sales price). He contributed to several worthy projects in Chelmsford, including the library named in his honor. Amos B. remained in Chelmsford, becoming a lumber dealer at the corner of Chelmsford and Fletcher Streets.

One

THE PHOTOGRAPHERS

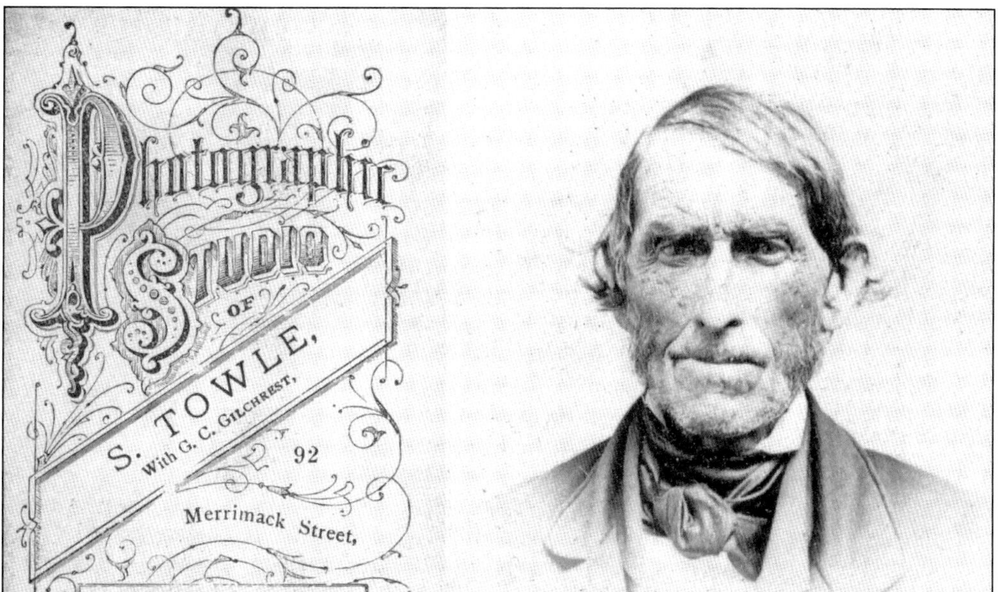

Simon Towle (1834–1910), a native of Buxton, Maine, was a professional photographer in Lowell starting in 1855 and then in Old Orchard Beach after 1893. Simon took many of the earliest stereo photographs of Chelmsford; extensive photographs during the peak of the mill era in North Chelmsford, which are now in the Chelmsford Public Library's Royal Shawcross Collection; and the photographs for the town's 1905 anniversary publication. (Tim Fraize.)

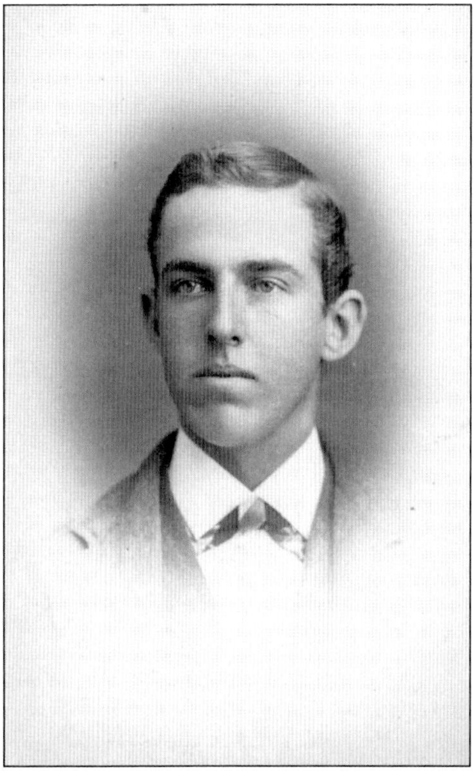

Arthur Irving Emerson (1860–1937) grew up at 41 Westford Street and worked as the head clerk in S. Waldo Parkhurst's store in Central Square. In 1893, he decided to make a career change and set up a professional photography studio in his parents' home. This carte de visite, or "visiting card," was taken around 1878 at the J.Z. Boomhower studio in Lowell. (Chelmsford Historical Society Collection.)

Using a remote pneumatic shutter control, Arthur I. Emerson took this family portrait around 1888 in the parlor of their home at 41 Westford Street. Pictured, from left to right, are his father, R. Francis; Arthur; mother, Adeline "Addie" D.; sister Susan M.; and brother Frank A. Emerson. Arthur took photographs of hunting expeditions with Chelmsford friends, so the fox fur on the floor is no doubt his handiwork. (Chelmsford Historical Society Collection.)

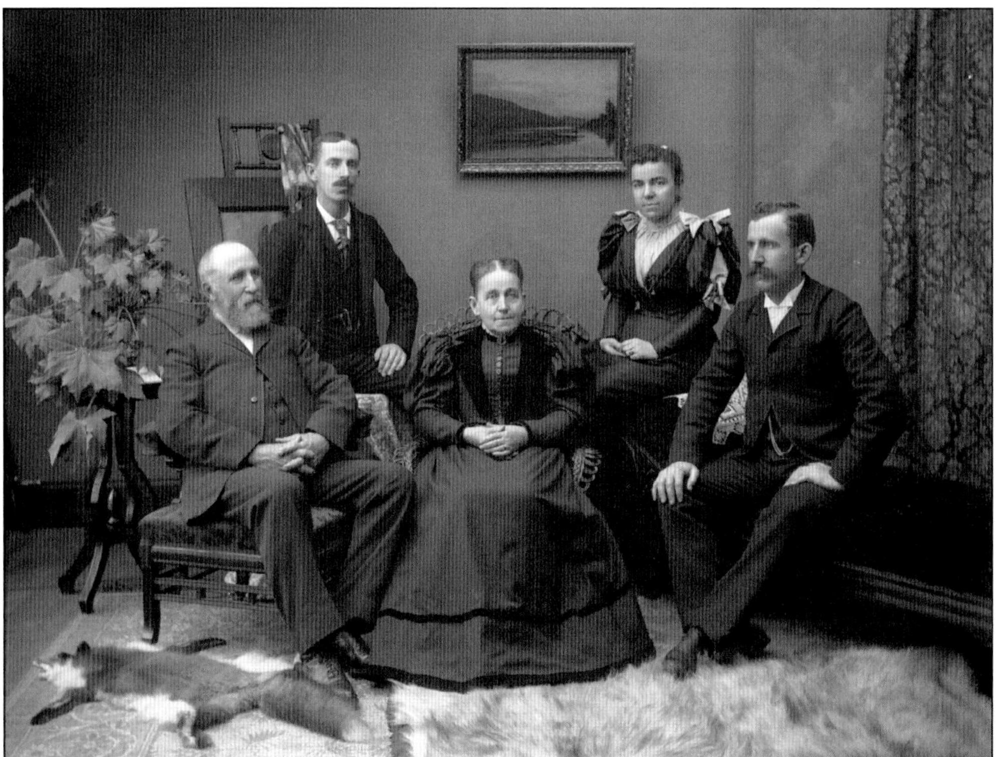

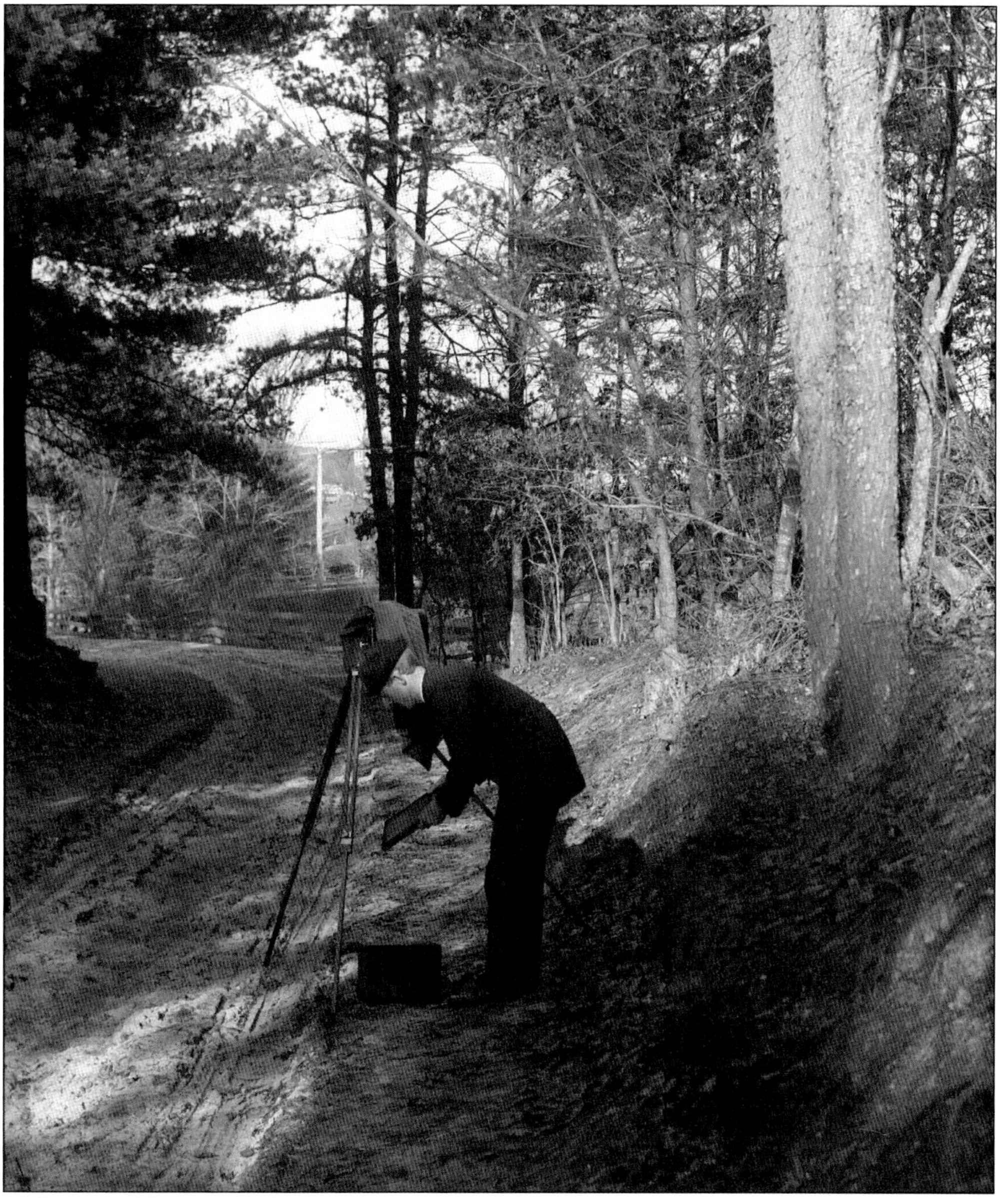

Willis B. Parkhurst took this photograph of Arthur I. Emerson and his view camera on a scenic road in 1889. This camera was capable of taking 8-by-10-inch, 5-by-8-inch, or 4-by-5-inch glass dry-plate negatives. Arthur is holding a light-tight case for an 8-by-10 negative. In 1837, Louis Daguerre developed the first commercially practical process for creating permanent images using a silver-plated copper sheet coated with silver iodide and developed with warmed mercury. The resulting image was a positive but was reversed left to right, and copies could not be made except by taking multiple photographs or using a multiple-lens camera. Daguerreotype photography was predominant from 1840 to the late 1850s. Simon Towle was a daguerrean artist in Lowell from 1855 to 1860. Ambrotypes, positive images on glass, were only popular from 1855 to 1865, and tintypes, positive images on sheet iron painted black and painted again with brown enamel after developing, started in 1856 and survived until 1900 as carnival souvenirs. (Chelmsford Historical Society Collection.)

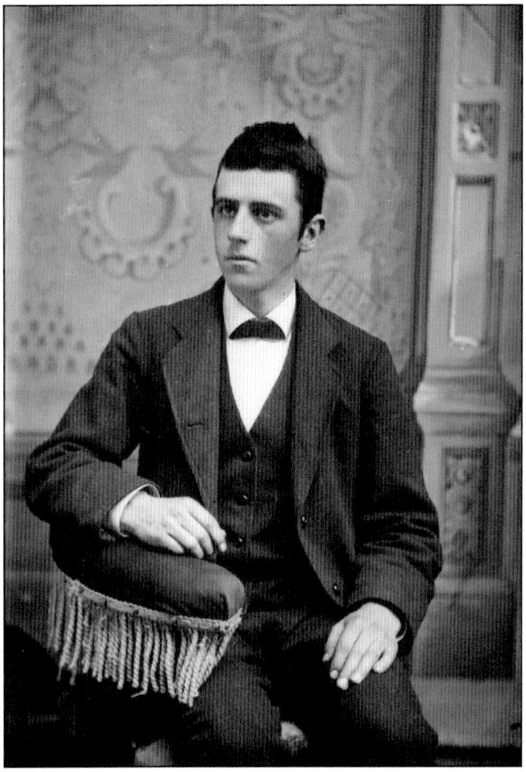

Willis Barrett Parkhurst (1865–1921) was the son of Central Square storekeeper S. Waldo Parkhurst and grew up at 78 High Street, where he lived all his life. He was a machinist at the Saco-Lowell Shops by trade and recorded images of his family and neighborhood using a view camera from 1888 to 1913. This tintype studio portrait of Willis was taken around 1883. (Chelmsford Historical Society Collection.)

Willis B. Parkhurst took this family portrait outside the family home at 78 High Street around 1889. Pictured, from left to right, are Willis; sister Bertha A.; mother, Martha J.; brother G. Thomas; sister Emma L.; and father, S. Waldo Parkhurst. Willis is squeezing the shutter bulb, and the air pressure carried through the pneumatic tube opens the camera shutter. (Chelmsford Historical Society Collection.)

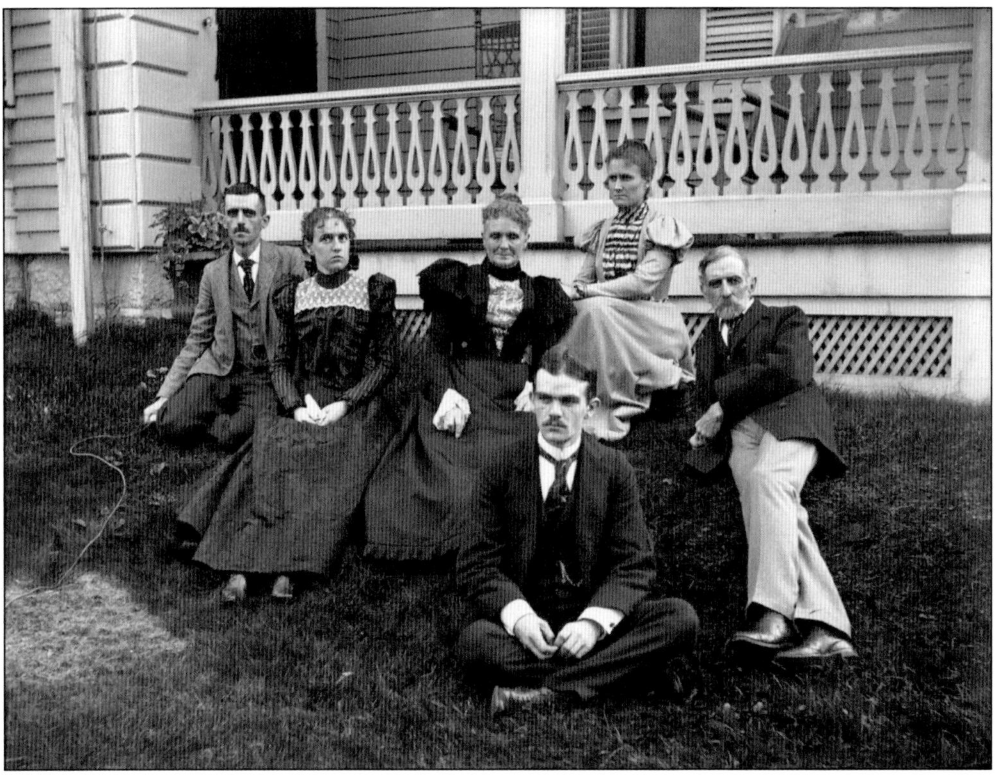

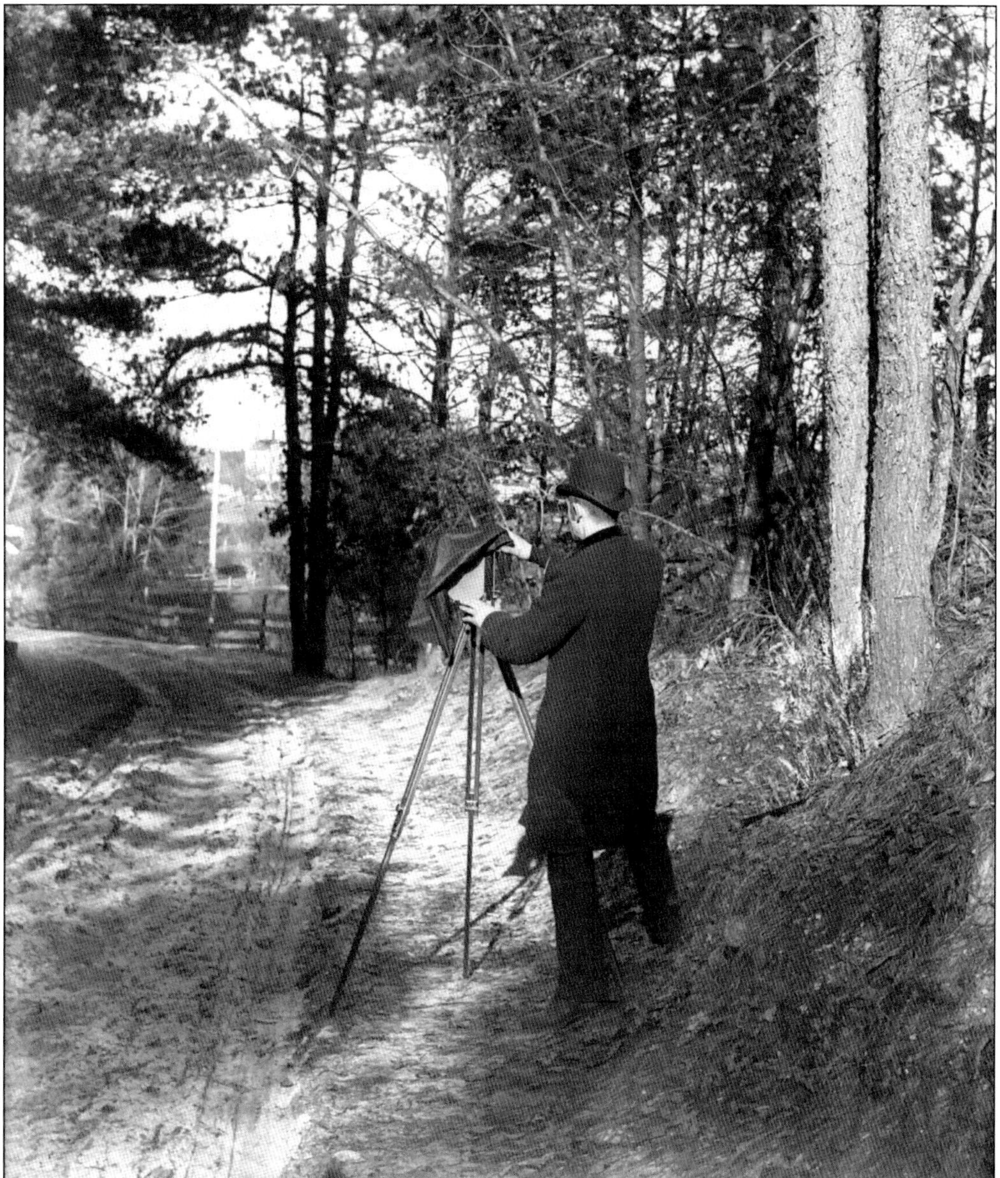

Arthur I. Emerson took this photograph of Willis B. Parkhurst and his view camera in 1889. Prior to 1851, there was no practical way to make high-quality copies from a single negative. From 1851 to 1871, a wet-plate process was used to produce a negative image on a glass plate. This process involved mixing chemicals including iodide, chloride, or bromide salts with silver nitrate and spreading this collodion mixture onto a glass plate in a portable darkroom before taking the photograph. The chemicals reacted to produce silver iodide, silver chloride, or silver bromide, which are unstable to light and chemically change when exposed. A developer solution was then used to reduce the exposed chemicals to metallic silver. The glass negative could be used an unlimited number of times to expose positive images on paper. By the time Willis and Arthur took up amateur photography in the 1880s, dry-plate glass negatives with a more practical shelf life were being produced and readily available at local photographic supply stores. (Chelmsford Historical Society Collection.)

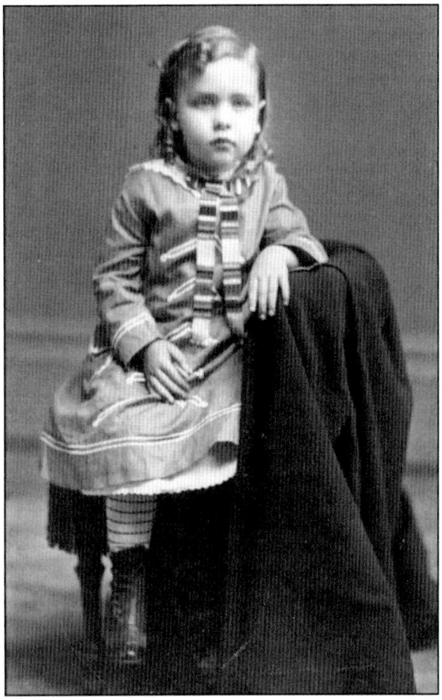

Winthrop Adams Parkhurst (1874–1963), the son of George A. Parkhurst, is shown in this June 1877 Boomhower carte de visite at the age of three wearing a dress, as was common practice in Victorian times for boys age three and under. The carte de visite format was introduced in France in 1859, starting a worldwide social trend then called "cardomania," a precursor to business cards. (Chelmsford Historical Society Collection.)

In 1901, Winthrop A. Parkhurst married Millie May Jefts and, soon after, purchased their home at 15 Acton Road. They had a daughter, Barbara A., in 1907 and a son, George A., in 1914. Flexible 3.25-by-4.25-inch celluloid negatives from an 1890s folding camera are a part of the Chelmsford Historical Society Collection. This c. 1908 photograph shows Winthrop holding Barbara. (Chelmsford Historical Society Collection.)

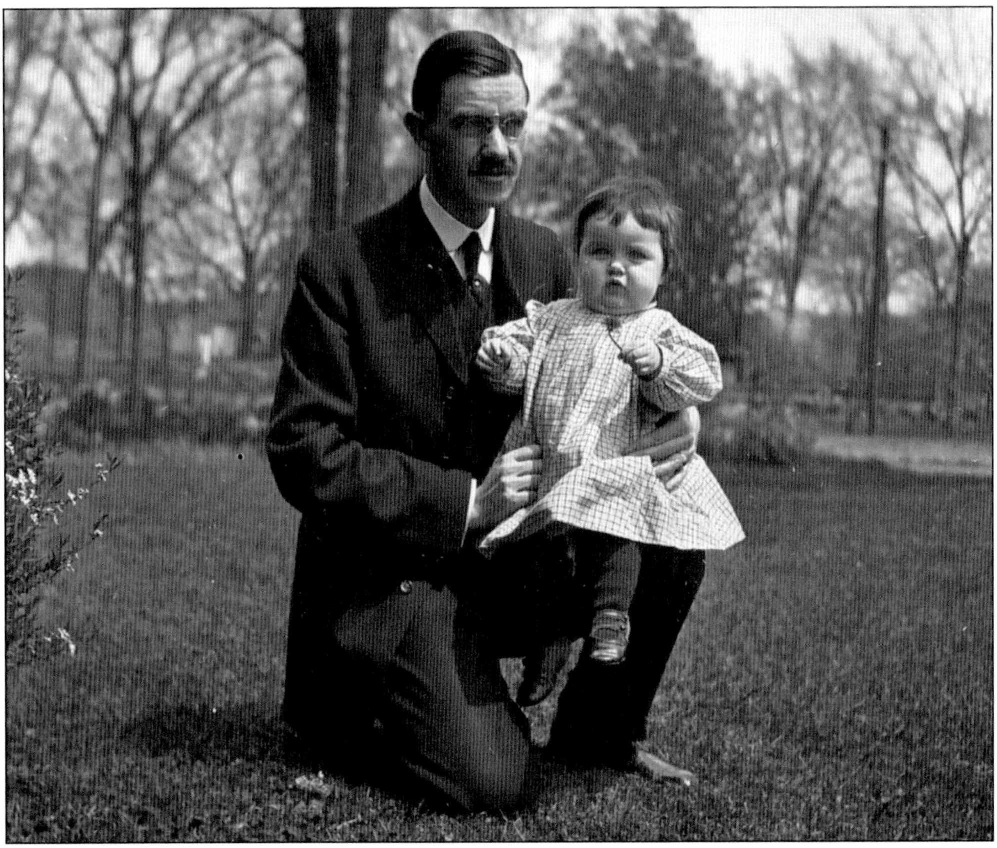

Two

Central Square

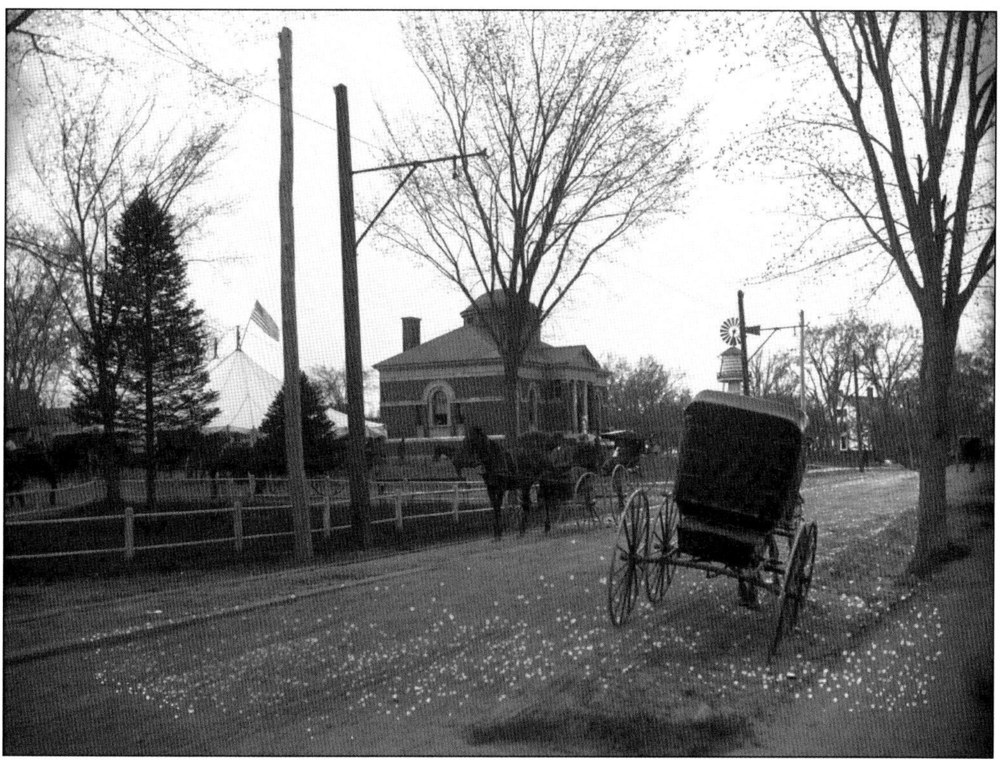

The trolley tracks heading south from Central Square, overhead wire, and the photographer's buggy are seen in the foreground on Adams Library's dedication day, May 8, 1895, as people were arriving at the tent to attend a dinner. The house of J. Adams Bartlett, who had donated a former vineyard on his property as a site for the library, is to the right of the large windmill. (Chelmsford Historical Society Collection.)

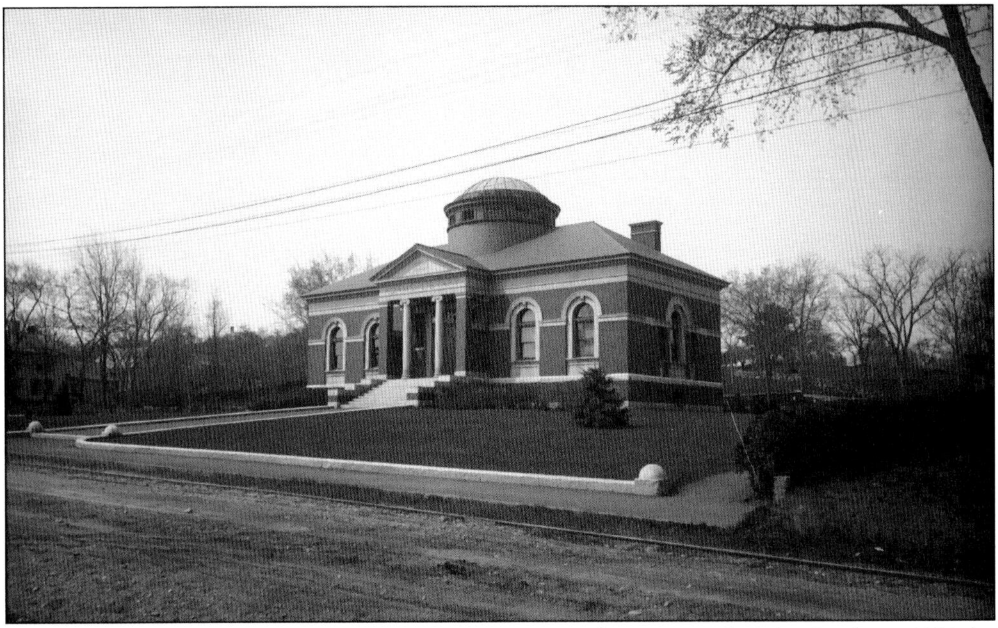

Amos F. Adams, a successful Boston commission merchant, provided the funds in 1894 for construction of the library. In 1899, he also donated the granite curbing and concrete sidewalks shown in this c. 1900 image. The house at far left was owned by carpenter, builder, and architect Jonathan Larcom. The brother of poet and author Lucy Larcom, Jonathan had constructed the town hall on North Road in 1879. (Chelmsford Historical Society Collection.)

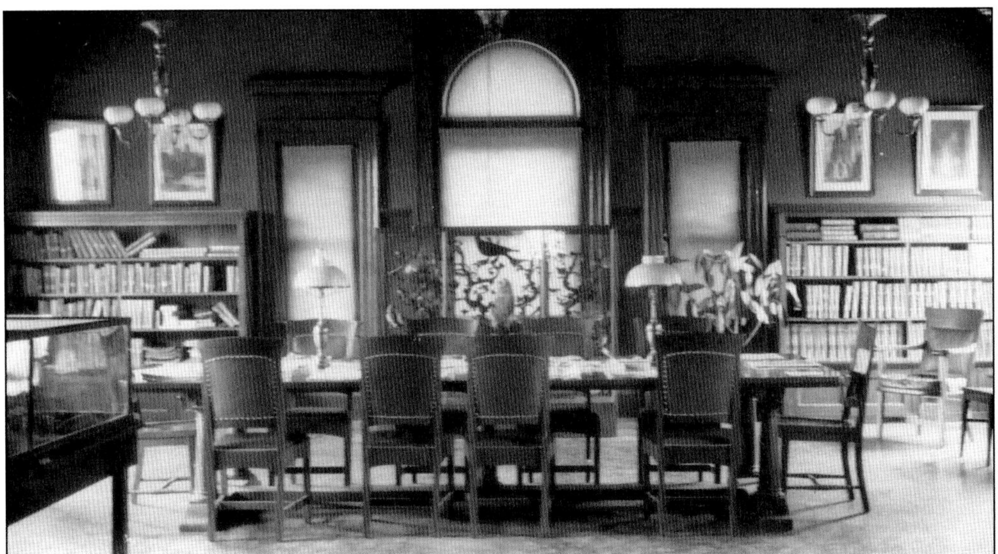

This photograph print shows the Adams Library reading room, with electric lighting and a display case for historical artifacts, in the early 1900s. The glass case with the stuffed bird collection was given to the historical society by the trustees of the Adams Library in 1981 and can now be seen in the Watt-Stevens Room at the Barrett-Byam House. (Linda Prescott.)

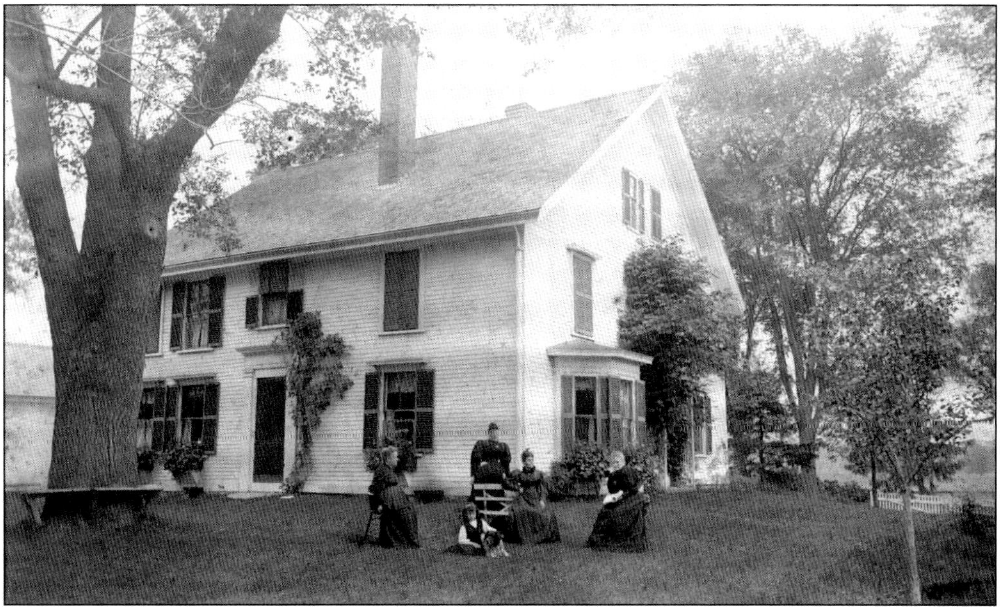

This 1892 photograph of 4 Bartlett Street shows, from left to right, Mary Greenleaf, Bertha G. Bartlett with Spot, Fanny Biden, Mary Biden, and Emma L. Bartlett. Emma L. was the wife of J. Adams Bartlett, and Greenleaf was her sister. The Bidens were family friends of the Bartletts. Not shown here are Emma L. Bartlett's daughters Mary Biden Bartlett, named for Mary Biden, and Emma M. Bartlett. (Chelmsford Historical Society Collection.)

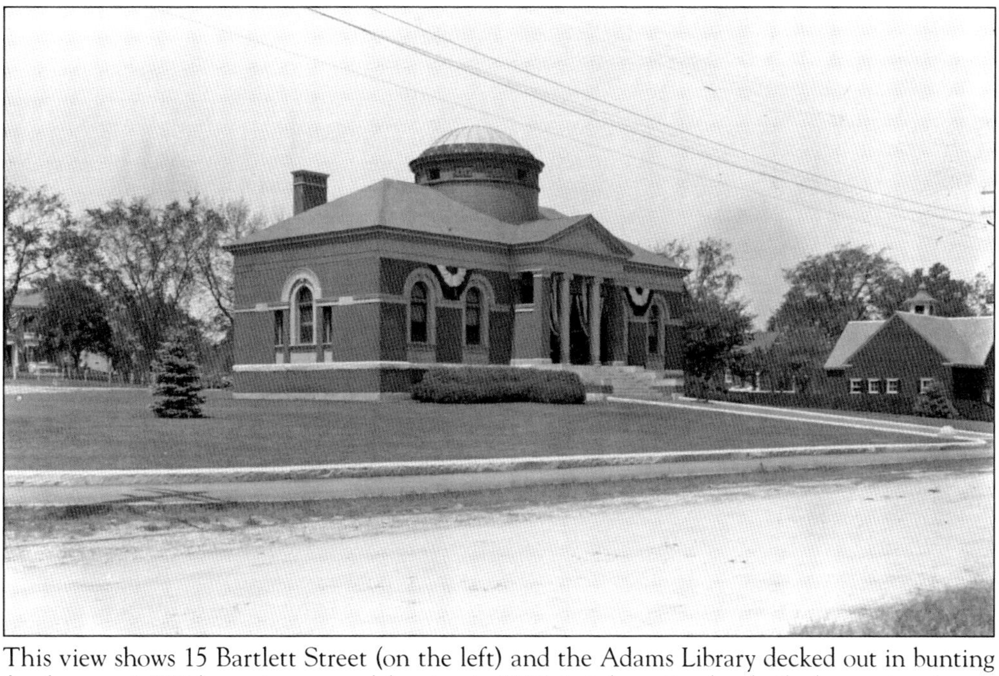

This view shows 15 Bartlett Street (on the left) and the Adams Library decked out in bunting for the town's 250th anniversary celebration in 1905. J. Adams Bartlett built the carriage house at right for his daughter Mary Biden (née Bartlett) Scoboria in 1904. The Scoborias' house was moved in 1997 to Ann's Way, and the carriage house was torn down in 1998 for expansion of the library. (Chelmsford Historical Society Collection.)

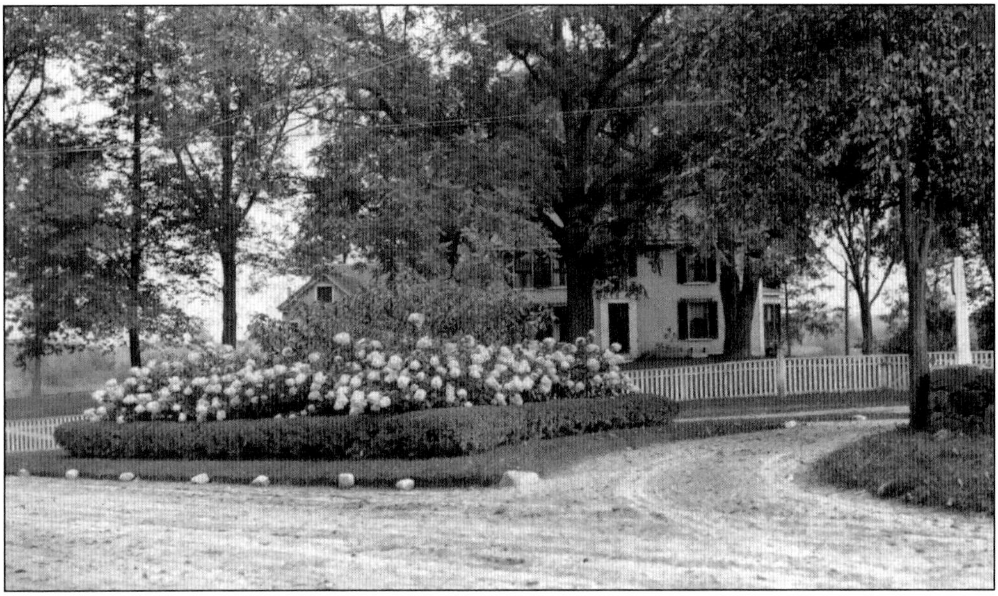

This is the intersection of Acton Road and Bartlett Street in September 1912, with 4 Bartlett Street in the background. In 1846, a portion of this house had been moved to 6 Boston Road (then called South Street) to become the home of Nathan P. Dadmun, owner of the blacksmith shop between that house and Beaver Brook. Both the original house and relocated portion still exist. (Linda Prescott.)

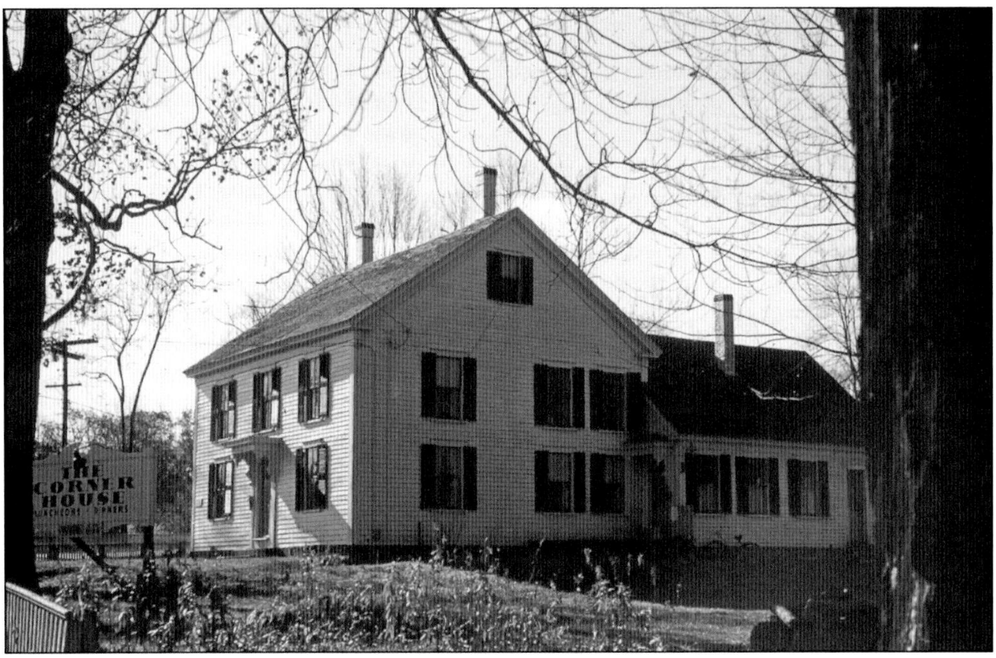

The Ark, seen here in 1954 as the Corner House Restaurant, was named for the numerous tenants who had lived there at the corner of Acton Road and Central Square. Dr. John C. Bartlett and his heirs owned much of the land on Acton Road in the late 1800s, including this house. The building was demolished in December 1961 to make way for a service station. (Chelmsford Historical Society Collection.)

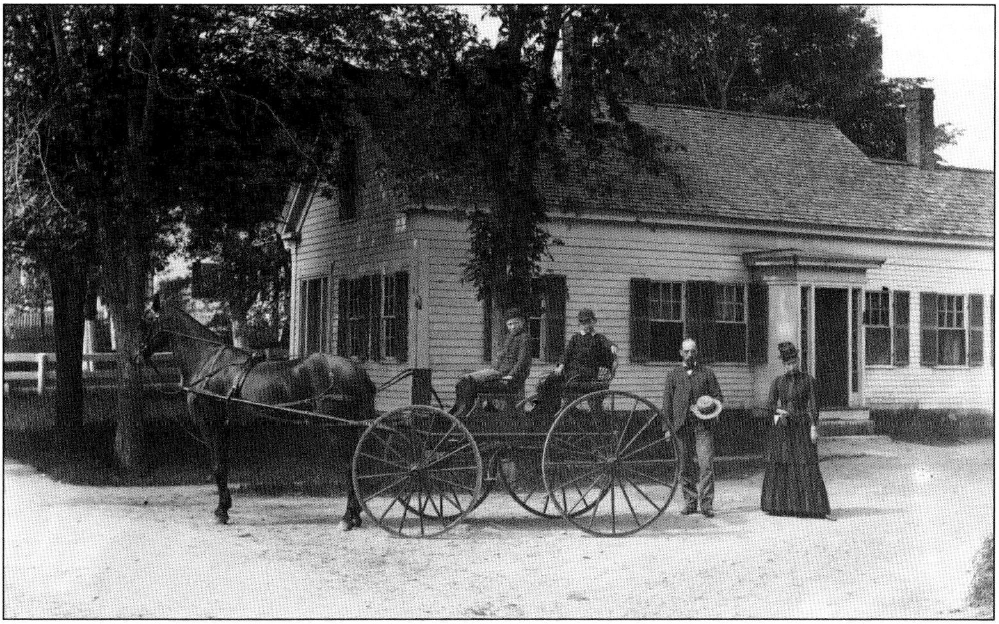

Mill owners Edwin E. and Lewis M. Dutton owned this house at 24 Central Square in the 1890s, and Flora E. Adams was a resident when this c. 1890 photograph was taken. Her brother Eben T. Adams, who opened a store in the Odd Fellows Building in 1896, is shown here with his family. Pictured, from left to right, are Ralph P., Arthur E., Eben T., and his wife, Lottie L. Adams. (Chelmsford Historical Society Collection.)

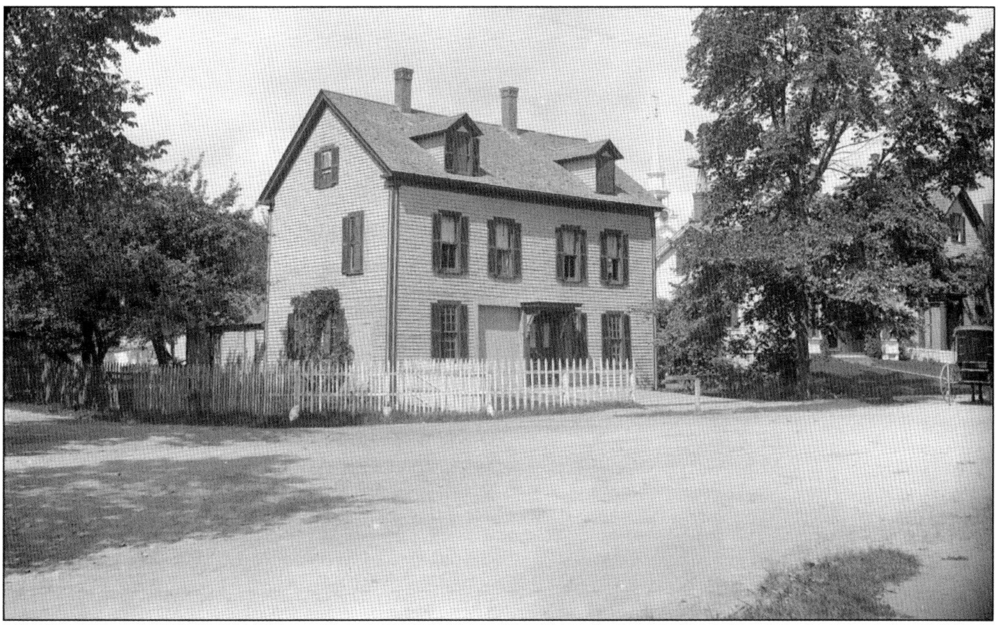

Cushing Place is on the left in this c. 1890 photograph, and the two-story building at center is the wheelwright shop constructed by Jonas Proctor in 1816. Beaver Brook runs directly underneath the shop before passing under Central Square and was used as a power source for wheel-making tools in the early days. This building still exists, sandwiched between two others at 19 Central Square. (Chelmsford Historical Society Collection.)

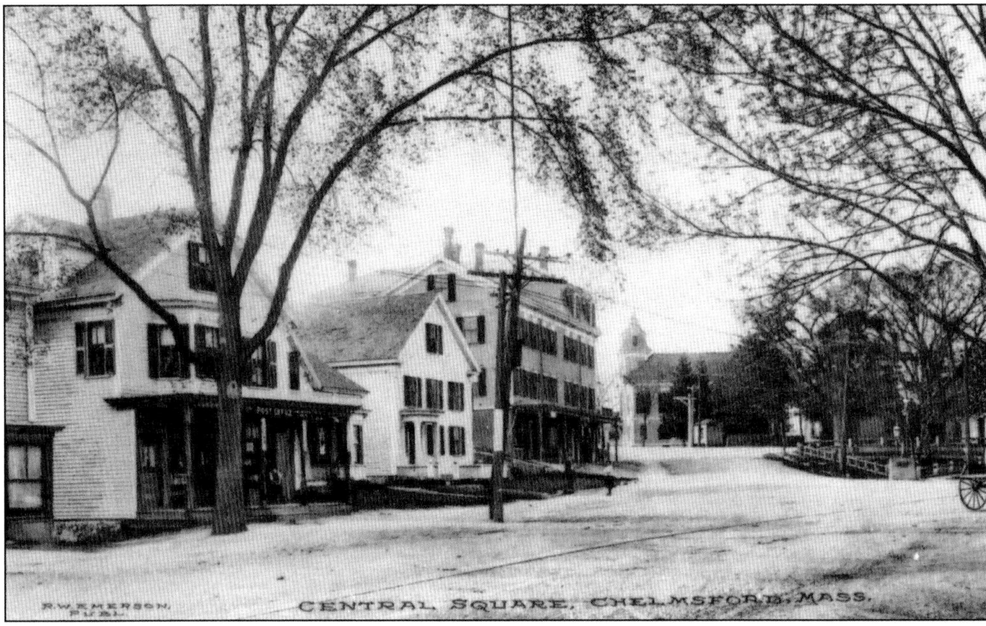

In 1898, James P. Emerson purchased the wheelwright shop at the extreme left in this c. 1900 R.W. Emerson postcard and constructed the post office building seen next door. His son Ralph W. Emerson was postmaster for 16 years and lived upstairs until 1908. In 1948, fire destroyed the first floor of the former post office, and the second floor was moved to 19 Perham Street. (Chelmsford Historical Society Collection.)

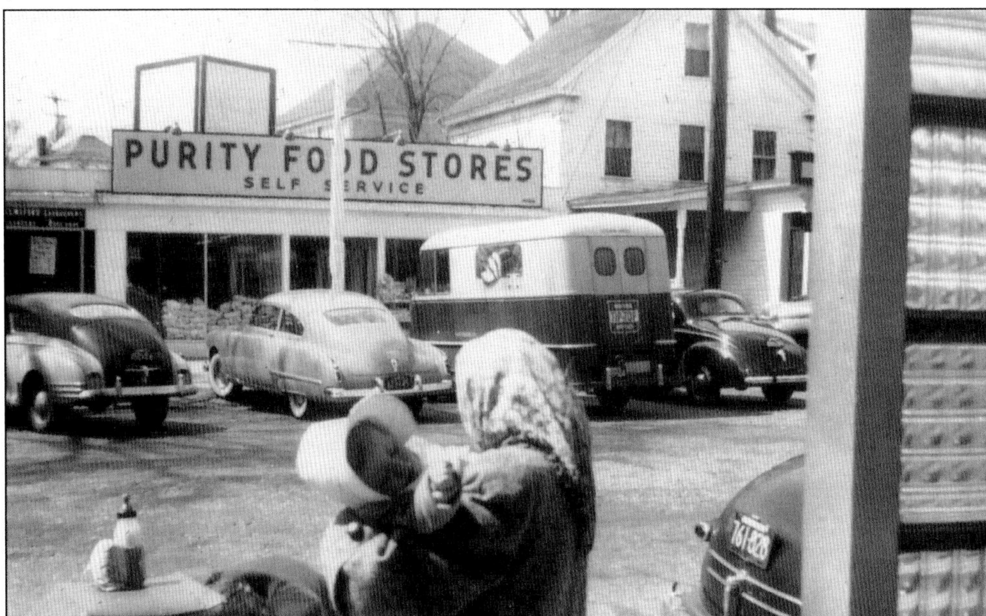

The house north of Ralph Emerson's post office was moved to 22 Fletcher Street in 1915, and a brick-and-concrete business block was built in its place. Originally occupied by auto dealerships, it was home to Leo Kahn's self-service Purity Food Store from 1947 to 1952. The building to the right of Purity was best known as Jack's Diner from 1950 to 1975. (Eric Johnson.)

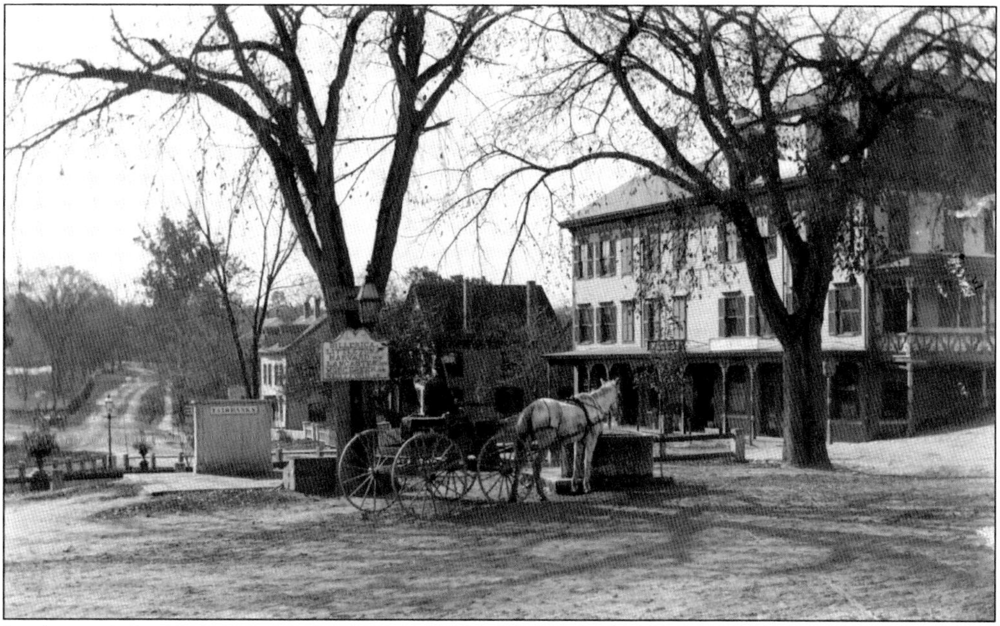

In this c. 1888 image, a traveler has stopped to water his horse at the watering trough next to the drive-on Fairbanks hay scale. George H. Wilson was the owner of the Central House and, until 1890, was the postmaster, with Ernest C. Nettel as his assistant. Nettel's wife, Flora, ran the store in the basement market space and, according to the sign, sold "groceries and fancy goods." (Chelmsford Historical Society Collection.)

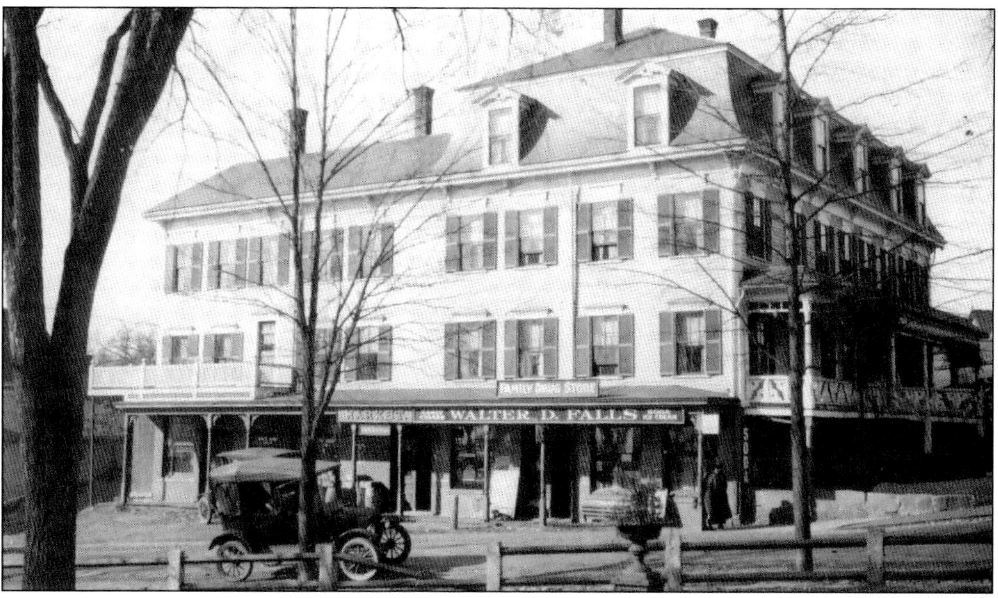

Central House is seen here around 1917 with the Walter D. Falls Family Drugstore in the lower right. The lower left storefront advertised White House Coffee and Tea and was operated by school lunch program pioneers Fannie Mitchell and Edith Hemenway as the Cookie Jar. George H. Wilson had retired and sold Central House to Edward J. Robbins and Herbert E. Ellis in 1916. (Linda Prescott.)

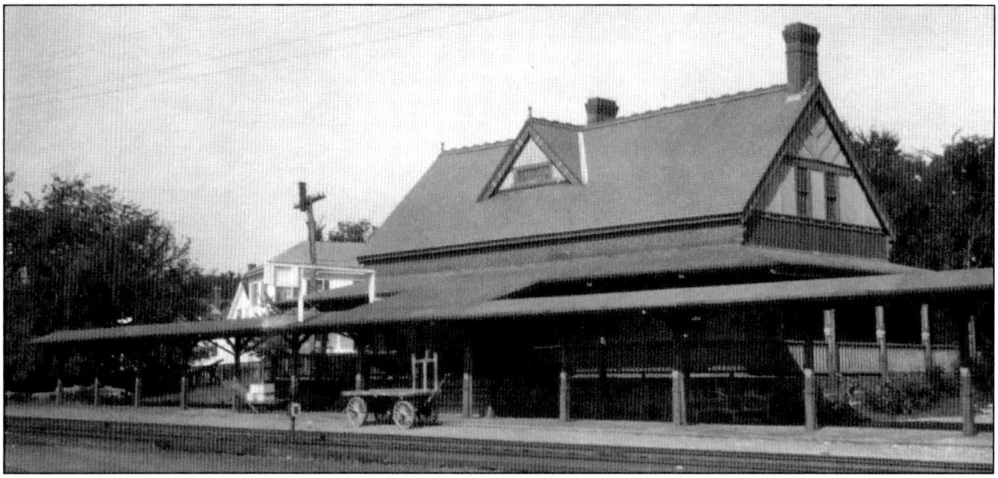

Chelmsford Center's second railroad station was opened on July 12, 1889, having replaced a smaller station that was moved to 37 Mill Road in September 1888. The gap between the platform and track in this c. 1900 photograph was intended for a second track that was never built. A hand truck sits in the gap, and the railroad house is to the left of the station. (Linda Prescott.)

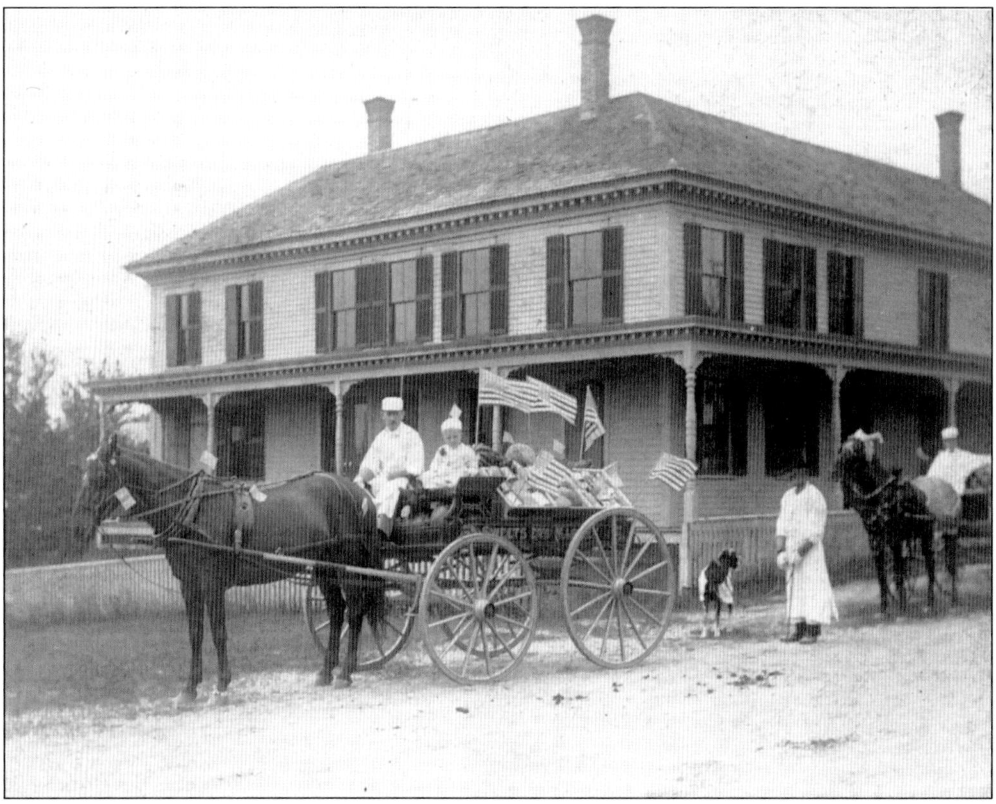

The railroad house is seen here during a Fourth of July parade around 1900, with the Sweetser's Market wagon passing by. The original portion of this building was constructed in 1677 with a room fortified with extra planks to provide protection for five assigned families in case of an Indian attack. In 1872, the house was moved to make room for railroad tracks, thus the name. (Linda Prescott.)

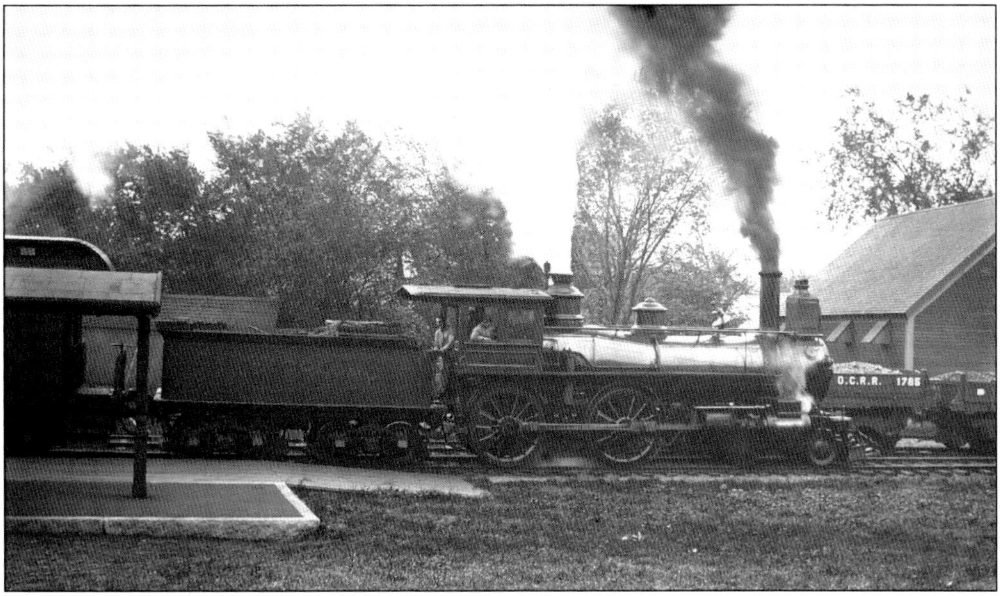

The west end of the Chelmsford Center train station platform is shown with Old Colony engine No. 154 on the track in this c. 1890 image. The fireman has shoveled extra coal into the firebox to blow steam through the safety valve, and the engineer has pulled the whistle to add more drama to the photograph. The freight house is seen on the right. (Chelmsford Historical Society Collection.)

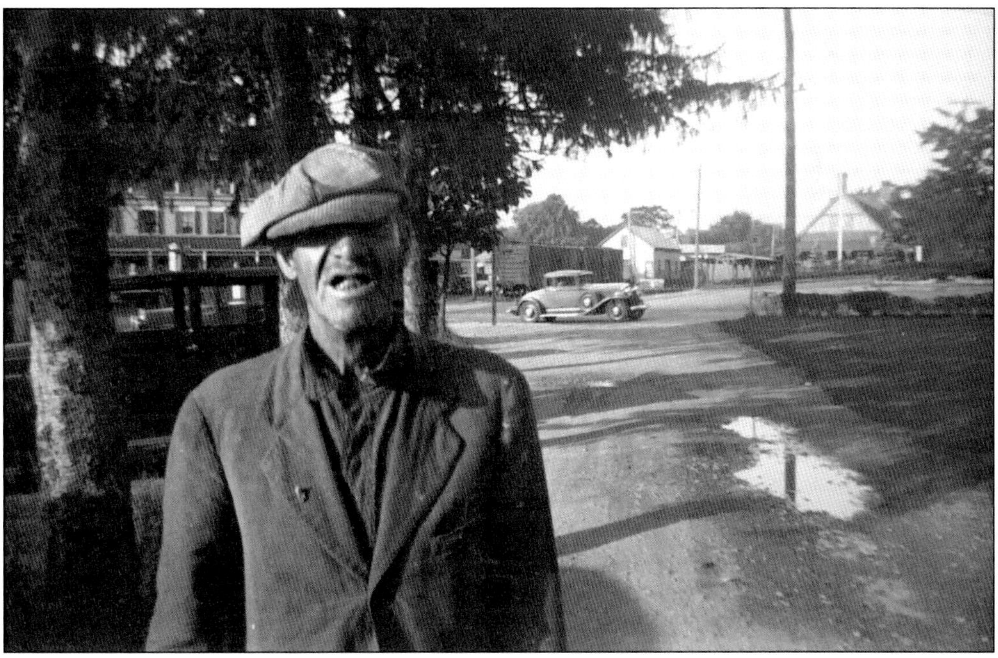

In this c. 1925 image, taken from the town hall driveway, the flagman's shack and Central House are on the left. The unidentified man with the railroad-style hat could be flagman Philip Donahoe. The freight house near the boxcar across the square is now Brickhouse Center Pizza, but the second railroad station at right was demolished by 1951 and replaced with a service station. (David Brow.)

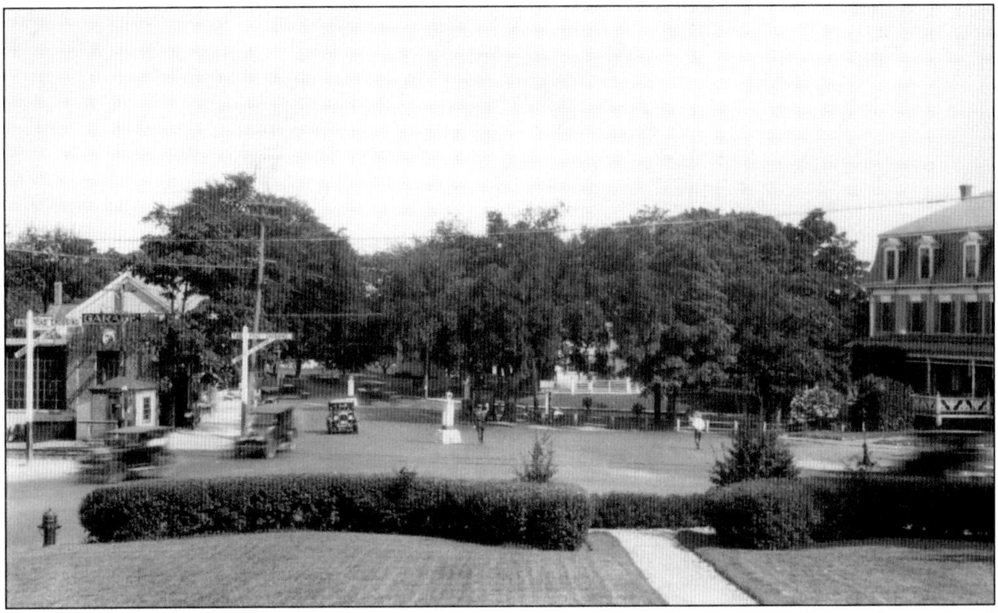

This photograph, taken around 1925 from the First Parish Church steps, shows the Central Square Garage, built in 1922; the railroad flagman's shack on the left; and Philip Donahoe, the flagman, sitting in a chair outside the garage. Officer Donald Adams is directing traffic next to the "silent policeman" signal, where Routes 4 and 110 intersect, and Central House is on the right. (Linda Prescott.)

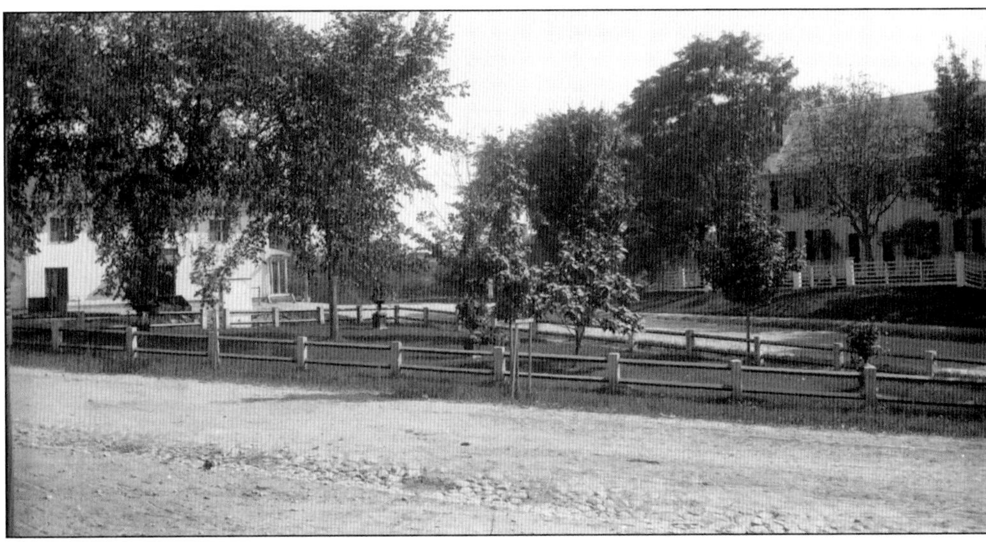

This c. 1890 photograph of the triangle at the top of Central Square was taken from the porch of the Central House. The back of the Fairbanks hay scale and S. Waldo Parkhurst's store and post office are on the left, but the Minuteman Boulder was not installed until 1899. The distinctive Fiske House fence, first built by John Minot Fiske in 1839, is on the right. (Chelmsford Historical Society Collection.)

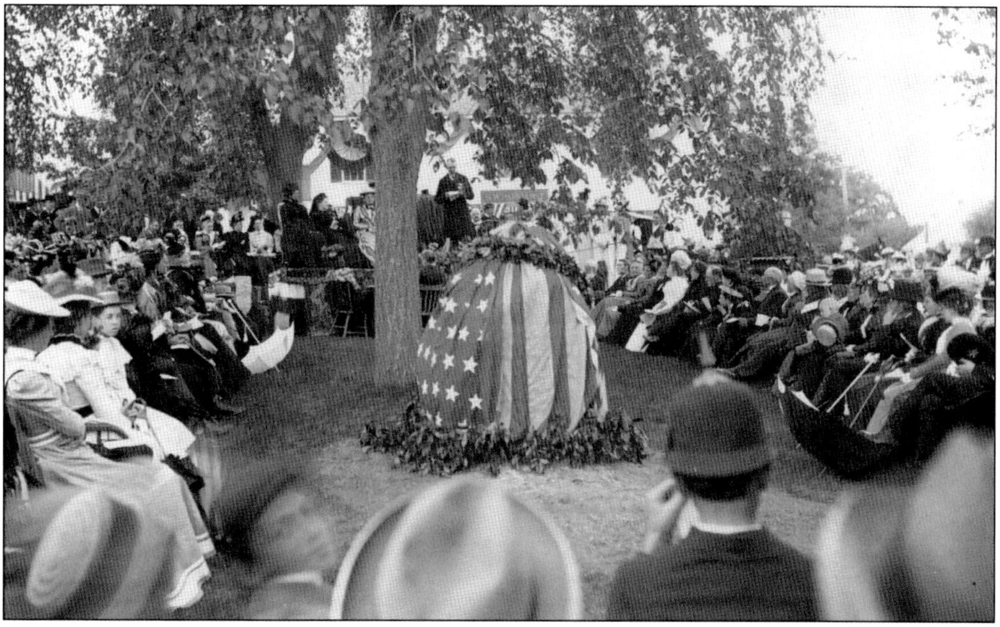

On June 17, 1899, the second monument commemorating the Revolutionary War (Minuteman Boulder) was dedicated. Gen. Francis H. Appleton is speaking here as president of the Sons of the American Revolution, and at the end of the ceremony, the rock was unveiled by eight-year-old Elizabeth Fiske Warren. The spiked hat on the lower right is worn by one of Chelmsford's seven constables in office that year. (Chelmsford Historical Society Collection.)

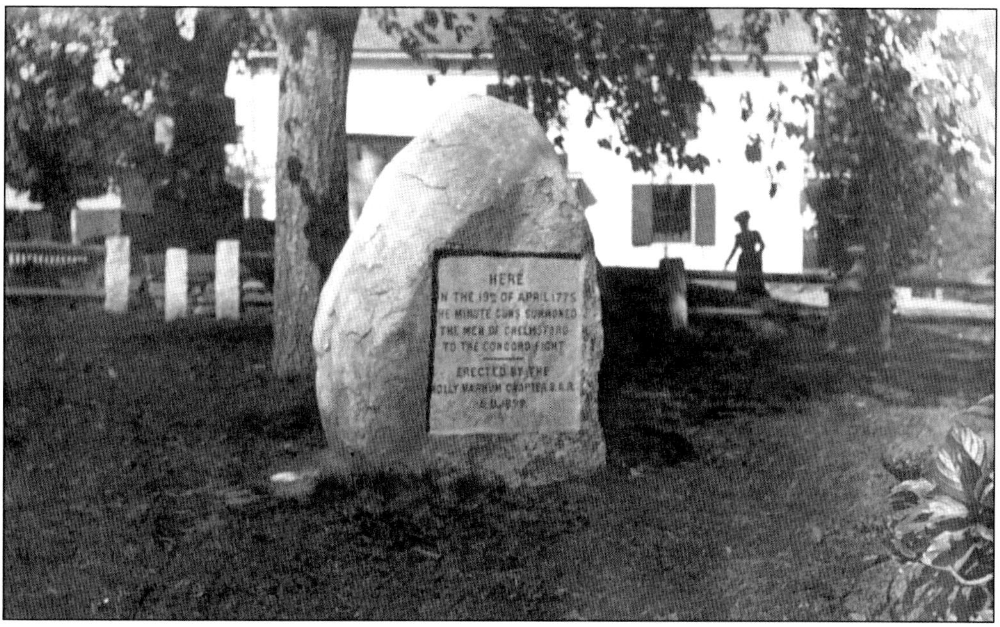

This boulder, seen here around 1900, commemorates the Chelmsford minutemen who responded when Joseph Warren fired off the alarm guns on April 19, 1775. There have been many changes to this triangle of land, which was given to the town by the Fiske family many years ago, but the rock still stands to remind people of a chain of events that led to this country's existence. (Chelmsford Historical Society Collection.)

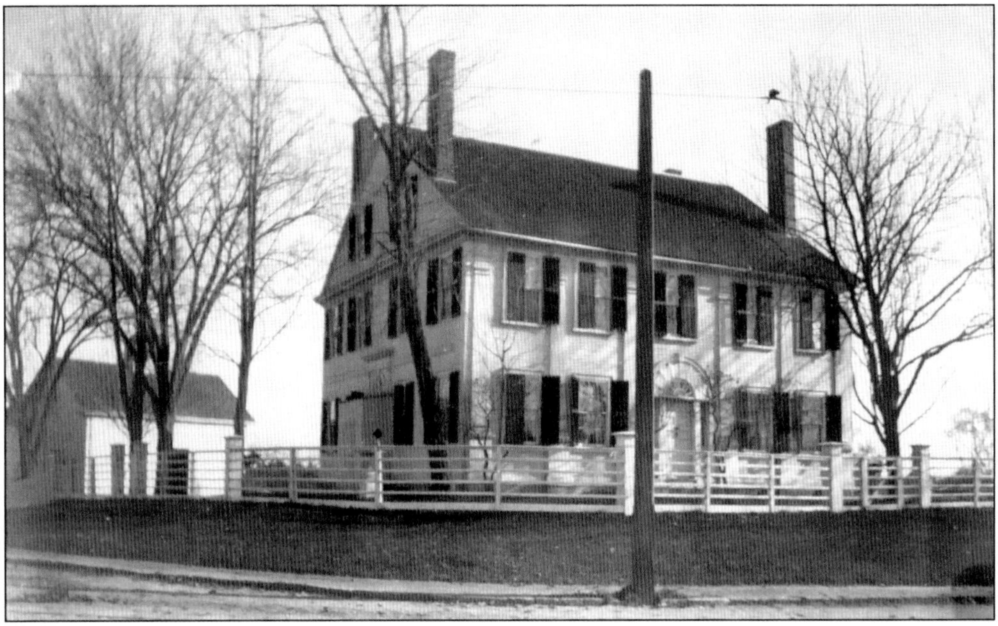

In 1798, Simeon Spaulding Jr., the son of one of Chelmsford's outstanding citizens during the Revolutionary War, built the Fiske House at 1 Billerica Road, seen here around 1900. John Minot Fiske purchased the property in 1839. The electric street railway tracks in the foreground went to Lowell (to the left) and as far as Warren Avenue (to the right). (Chelmsford Historical Society Collection.)

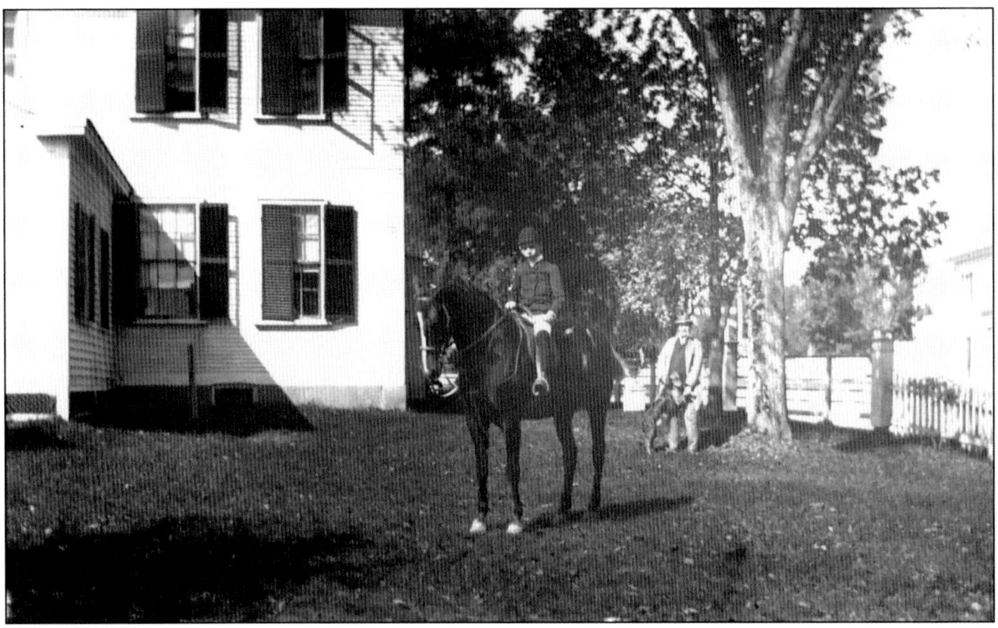

Benjamin M. Fiske is seen here around 1900 at his 1 Billerica Road home with his dog; the unidentified boy on the horse could be his grandson Warren or Howard from Passaic, New Jersey. His grandson Eustace B. Fiske, who owned the house until 1977, was only three years old when Benjamin died in 1901. Part of S. Waldo Parkhurst's store can be seen on the right. (Chelmsford Historical Society Collection.)

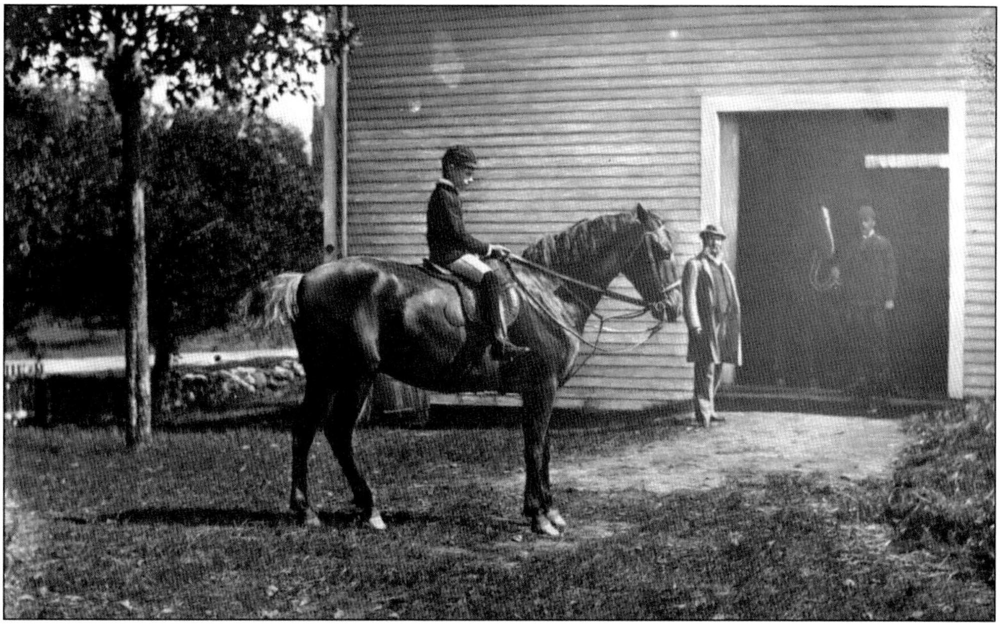

This image shows the barn at 1 Billerica Road with Benjamin M. Fiske standing just outside the door. In 2004, this barn was dismantled and shipped in a storage container to the "Old Chelmsford" Garrison House at 105 Garrison Road, where it was reconstructed for use as display space. A drive-through bank building now occupies the Billerica Road site at the approximate location of the old barn. (Chelmsford Historical Society Collection.)

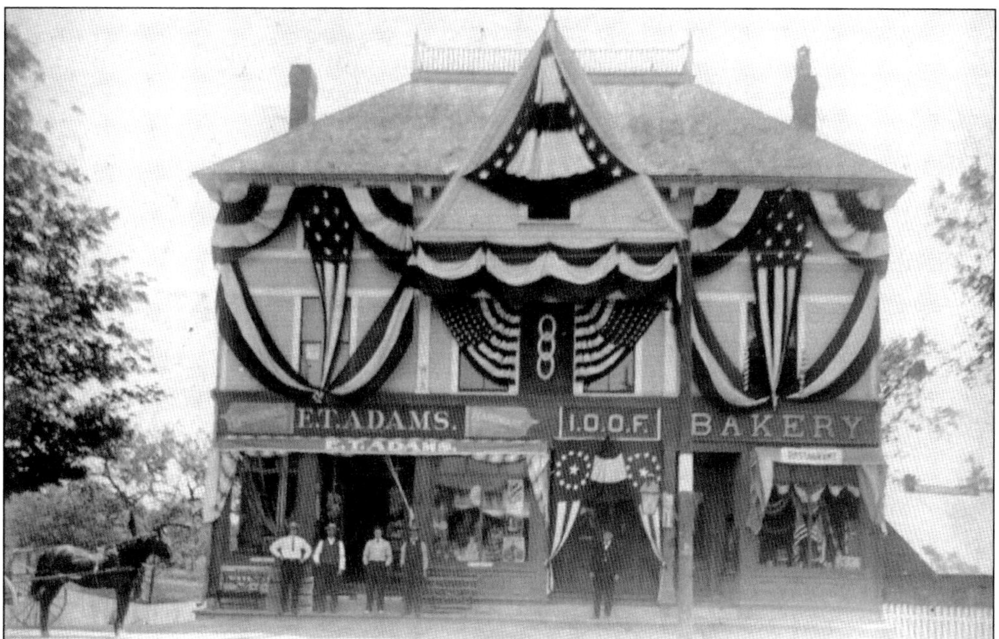

The Odd Fellows Building is decked out in bunting for Chelmsford's 250th anniversary in 1905. From left to right, son Ralph E., Eben T., and son Arthur E. Adams are standing in front of the store with Herbert Knowlton. John, the baker, is near the entrance to the Odd Fellows hall, and Girard P. Dadmun's blacksmith shop is on the right. (Chelmsford Historical Society Collection.)

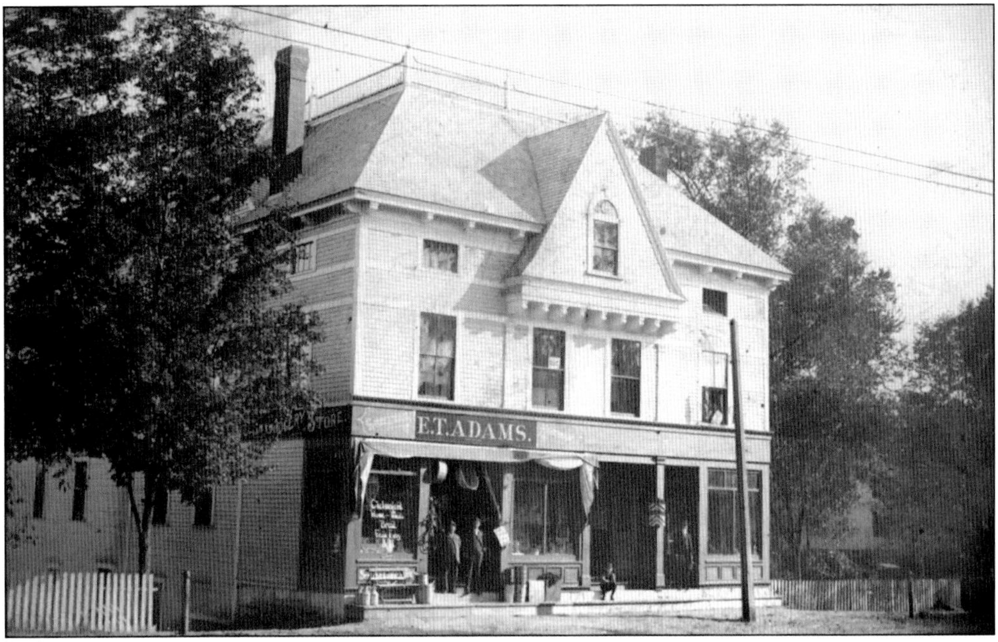

The Chelmsford Odd Fellows Lodge No. 218 abandoned this hall in 1908 after merging with the Oberlin Lodge No. 28 in Lowell. The mortgage was foreclosed in 1912, and the building was sold to private hands. Eben T. Adams operated his store until 1927, and Tony P. Mello, sitting by the window on the second floor, continued his barbershop until 1940. Girard P. Dadmun's house is on the right. (Chelmsford Historical Society Collection.)

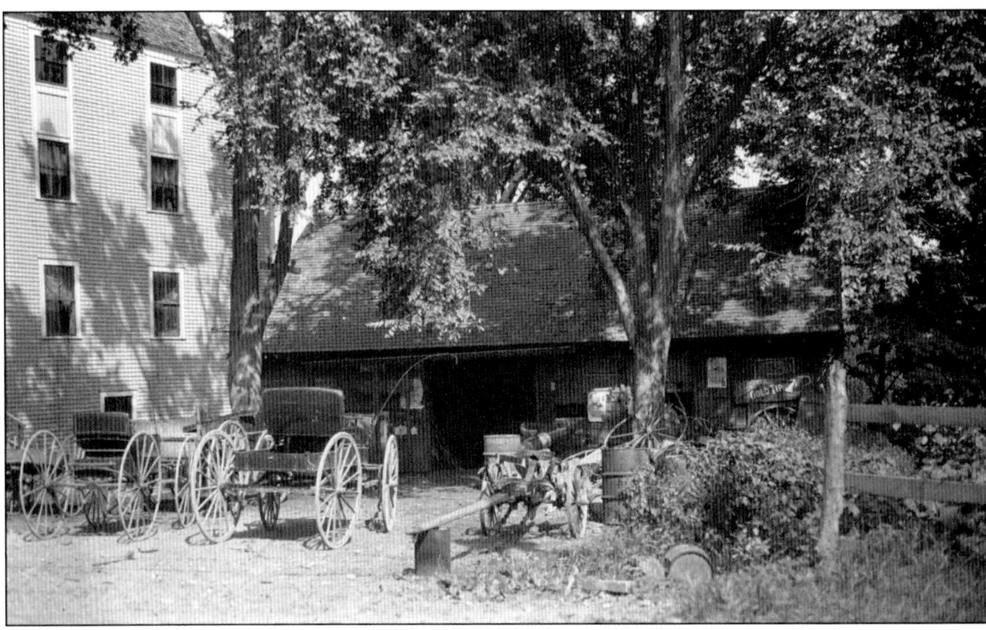

This former barn was moved from the rear of the First Parish Unitarian Church to Central Square in 1828. On a main route through town and across the street from Jonas Proctor's wheelwright shop, the location was ideal for a blacksmith shop. Nathan P. Dadmun and Eben H. Marshall purchased the blacksmith shop in 1842, and it functioned as a forge until 1923. (Linda Prescott.)

Three

Central Square Millpond

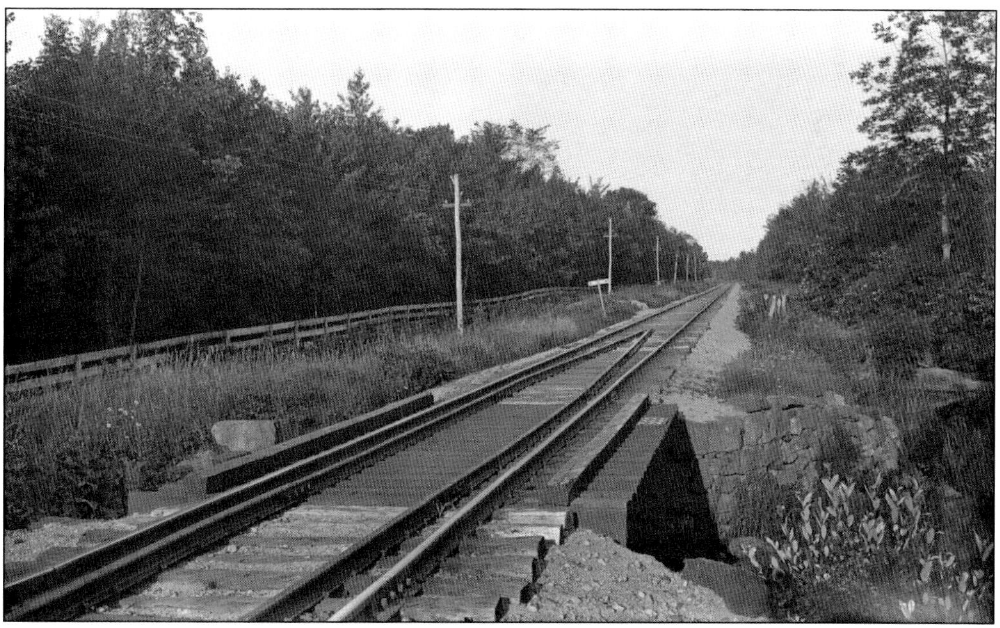

The Framingham & Lowell Railroad, which was opened on October 1, 1871, merged with the Old Colony Railroad in February 1886. It generally followed the course of Beaver Brook from High Street to Central Square. In this c. 1890 view of the Old Colony track, now the Bruce Freeman Rail Trail, Beaver Brook is flowing under the bridge from left to right on its way to Central Square. (Chelmsford Historical Society Collection.)

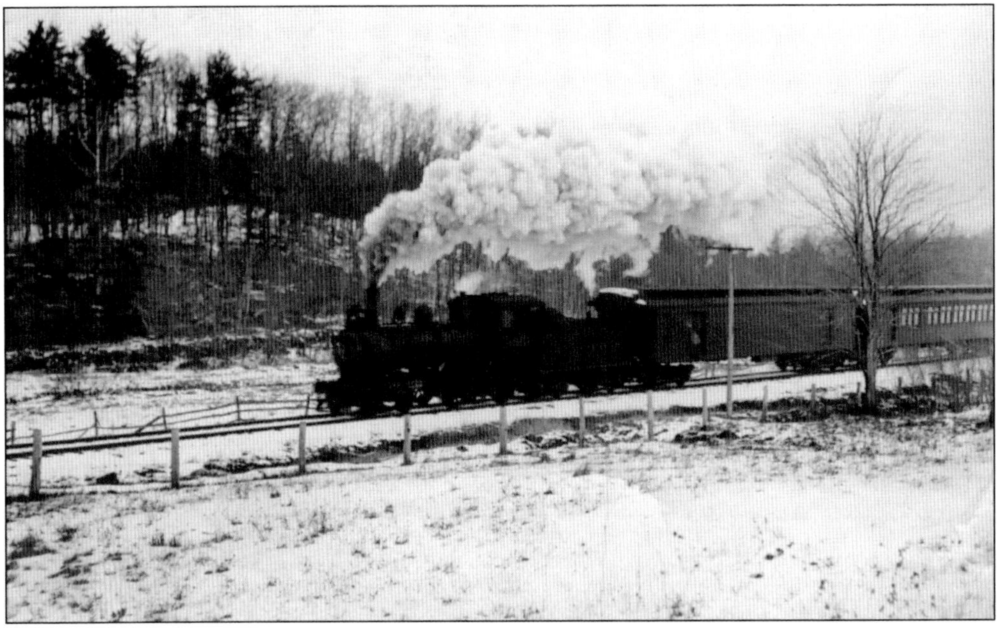

In 1893, the Old Colony Railroad became a part of the New York, New Haven & Hartford Railroad, which ran passenger service until about 1935. In this c. 1915 view, a New York, New Haven and Hartford passenger train is eastbound near Beaver Brook. Departing from the South Chelmsford station on Maple Road or from Chelmsford Center, one could travel nationwide using available rail and steamship connections. (John Crawford III.)

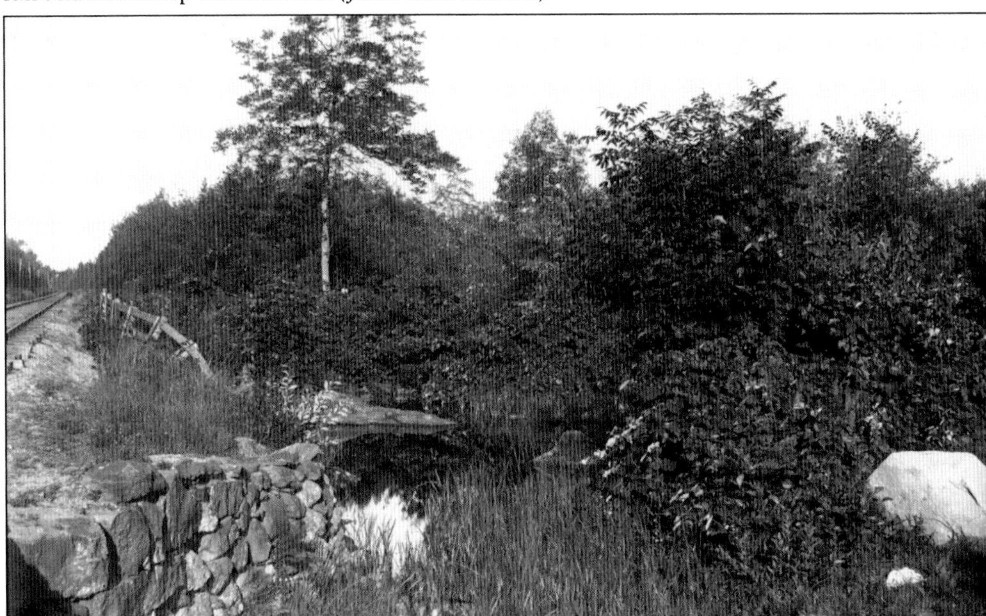

This 1888 image shows another view of Beaver Brook as it meanders eastward toward Chelmsford Center. As part of the conversion of the railroad into the Bruce Freeman Rail Trail, opened in August 2009, this bridge was reconstructed with concrete using some of the original granite foundation. The railroad bed, which was abandoned and overgrown since the 1980s, is now accessible for all to enjoy. (Chelmsford Historical Society Collection.)

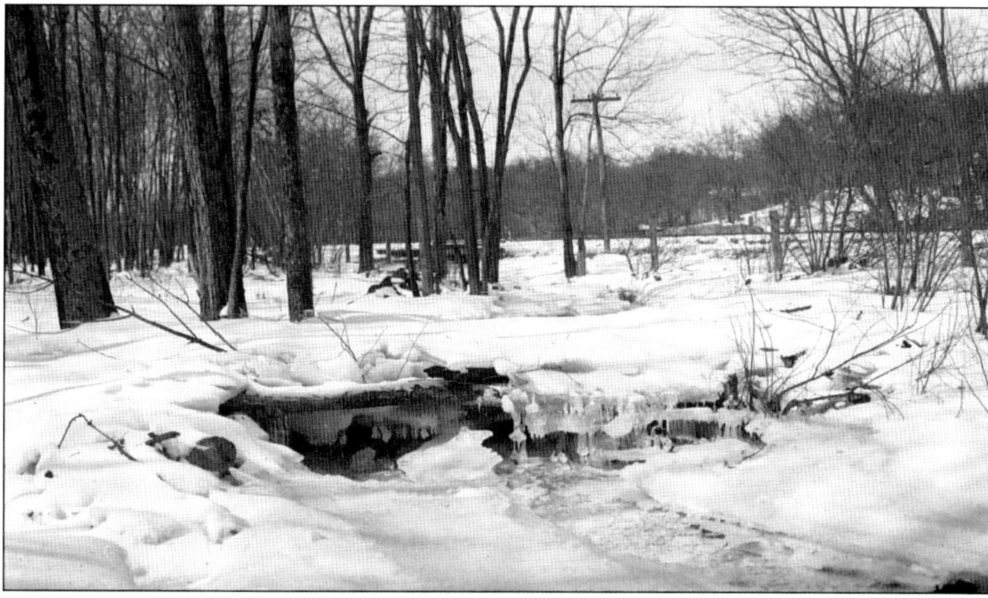

This view is looking back at the railroad bridge in winter around 1915. When water could not be used as a power source in winter, it was the season to harvest ice for use in homes. The Parker family constructed a dam and mill downstream in the 1600s, and in the early 1800s, the remaining mill on this site was moved to Central Square. (Chelmsford Historical Society Collection.)

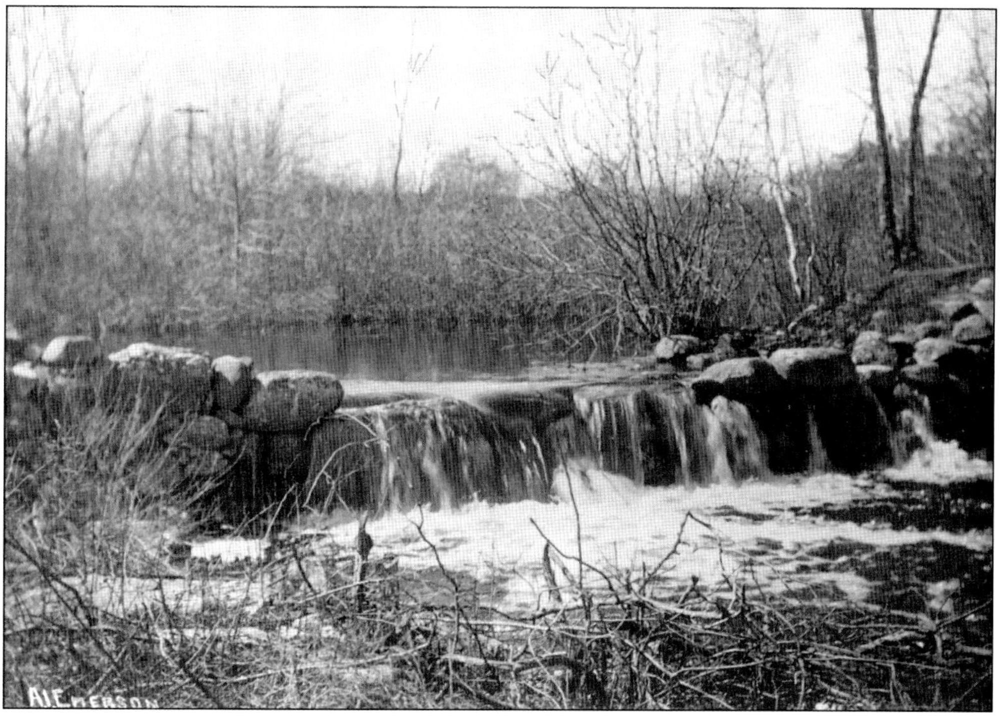

This is the spillway of the upper dam around 1890. Access to this dam was via Bridge Street since Littleton Road and the railroad had not yet been built when the mills were in use. Today, the spillway can still be seen by following a path leading from the Bruce Freeman Rail Trail across the top of the dam. (Chelmsford Historical Society Collection.)

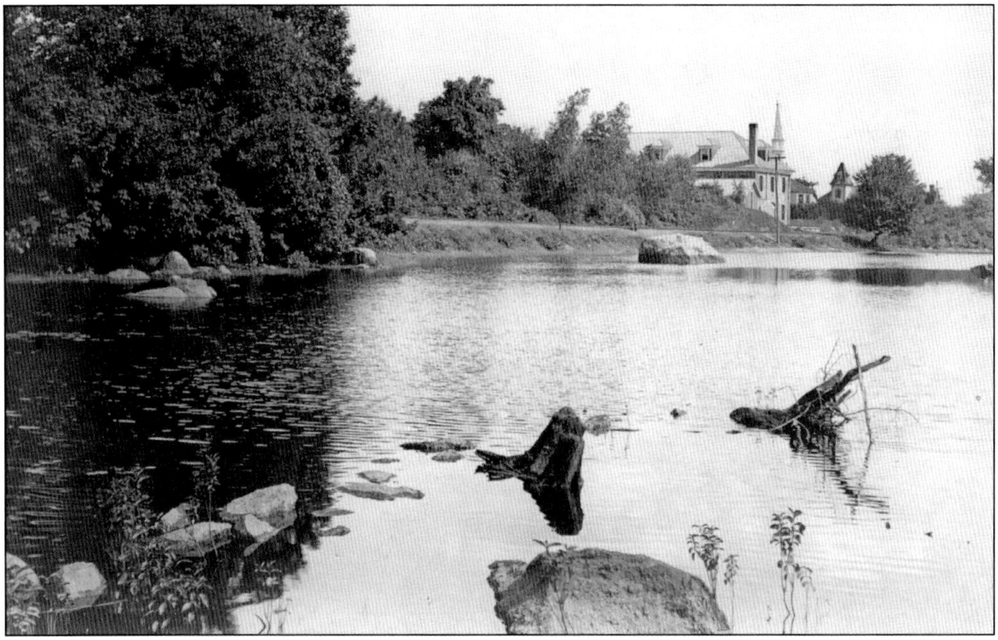

A short distance downstream from the upper dam, Beaver Brook widened out into another millpond. The Byfield Manufacturing Company, making knitting machinery and knit goods, can be seen in this c. 1890 image with the First Parish steeple and town hall in the background. The two-story brick building had a short life, being constructed in 1887 and burning to the ground in 1893. (Linda Prescott.)

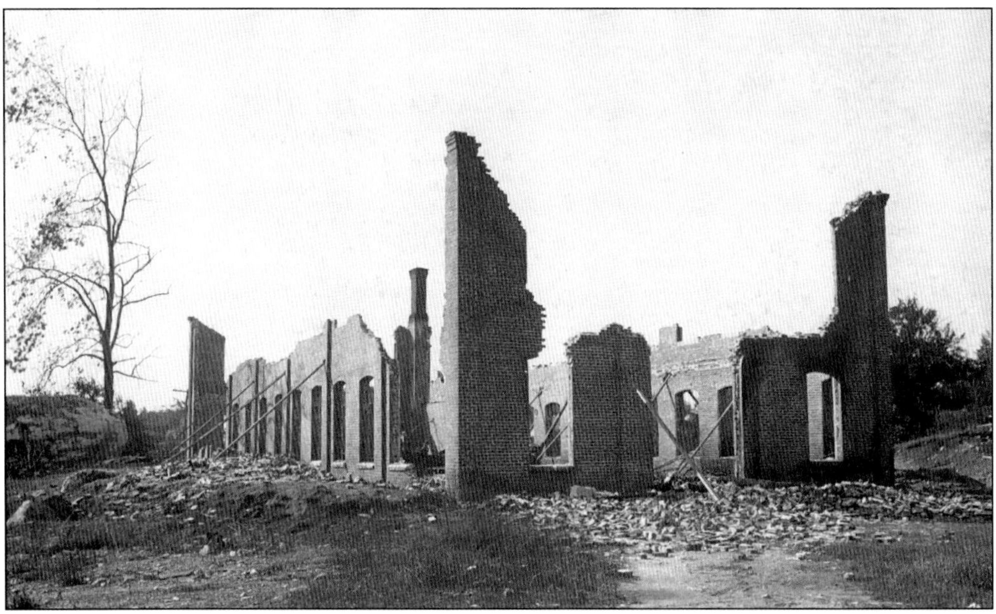

This is the burned-out shell of the Byfield Manufacturing Company, as it appeared around 1895. The Byfield machine shop, which manufactured knitting machinery, was housed on the first floor, and the Beaver Manufacturing Company, which produced knit goods such as hosiery, occupied the second floor. John Byfield, who previously owned a business on Market Street in Lowell, started both companies. (Chelmsford Historical Society Collection.)

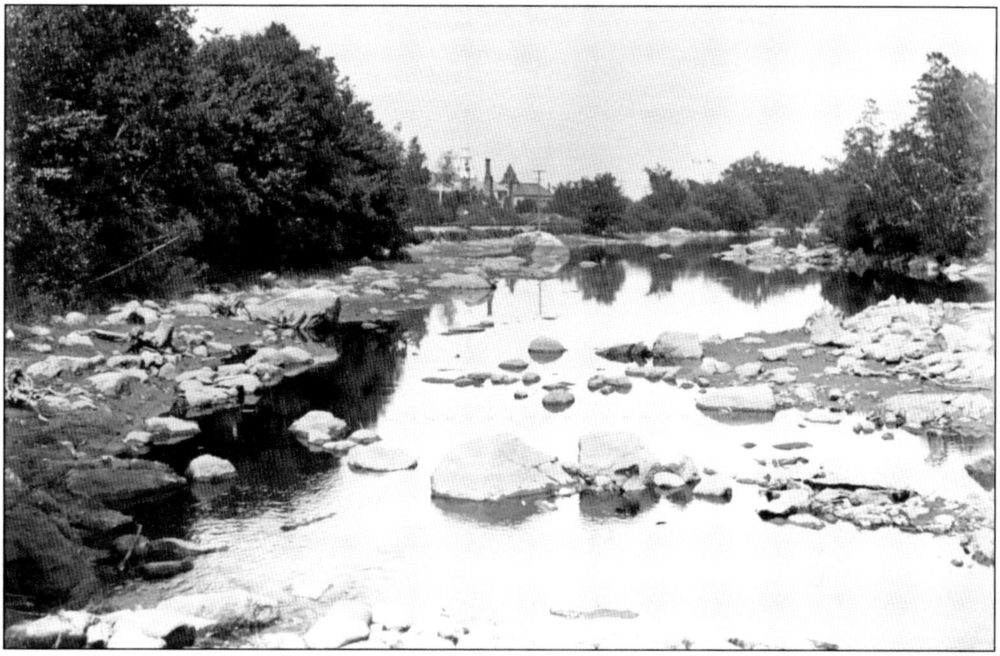

Taken from an upstream vantage point, this photograph is of the Byfield ruin, showing the chimney and a corner of the building. With the manufacturing building collapsed, the railroad house can be seen behind the ruin and in front of the First Parish Unitarian Church. C. George Armstrong purchased the Byfield property in 1901 and built the Chelmsford Spring Company, which later became Chelmsford Ginger Ale. (Chelmsford Historical Society Collection.)

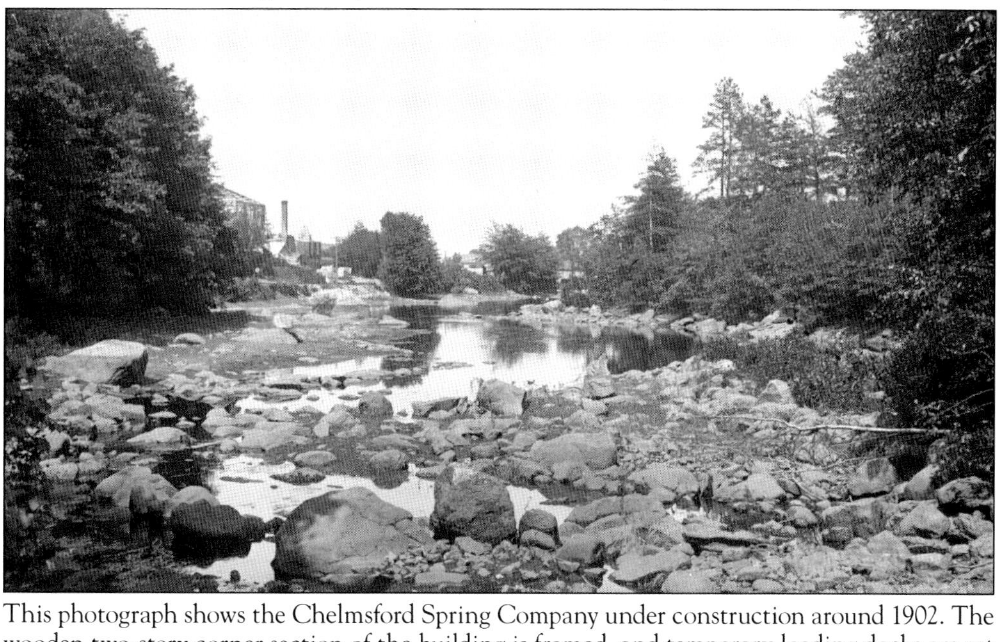

This photograph shows the Chelmsford Spring Company under construction around 1902. The wooden two-story corner section of the building is framed, and temporary loading docks are set up next to the railroad tracks. On November 12, 1912, most of these buildings burned—except for a section near the railroad tracks. By 1913, a new fireproof building had been constructed out of steel, cement, asbestos, and glass. (Chelmsford Historical Society Collection.)

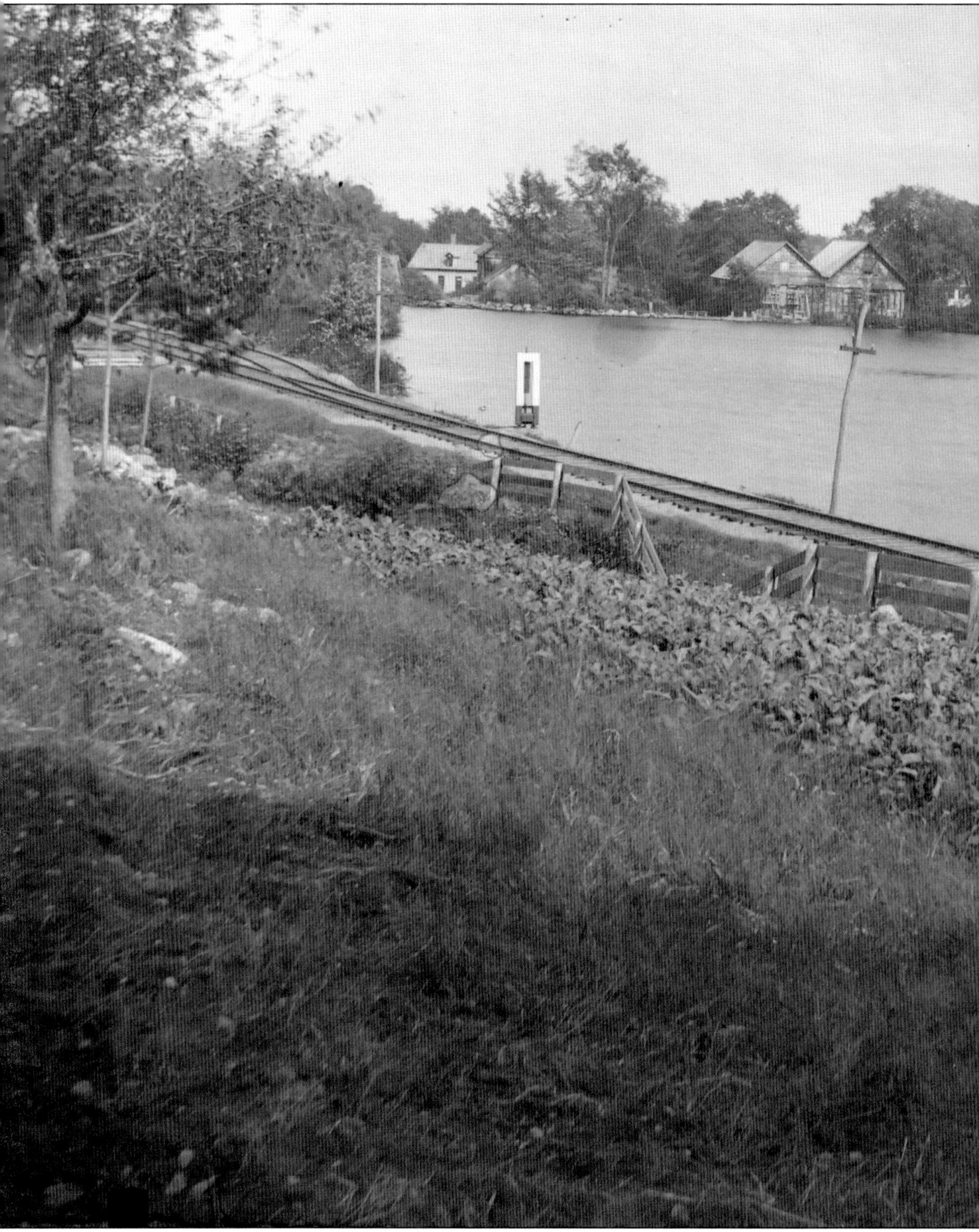

This c. 1890 view shows the Central Square Millpond filled with water and some of the buildings that utilized its output. From left to right, the clearly visible structures are the rear of the Proctor Wheelwright Shop, which fronts on Central Square; the Dutton Brothers Mill with its sluiceway just to the left; the Dutton Brothers' twin icehouses with adjustable ramps for loading during ice

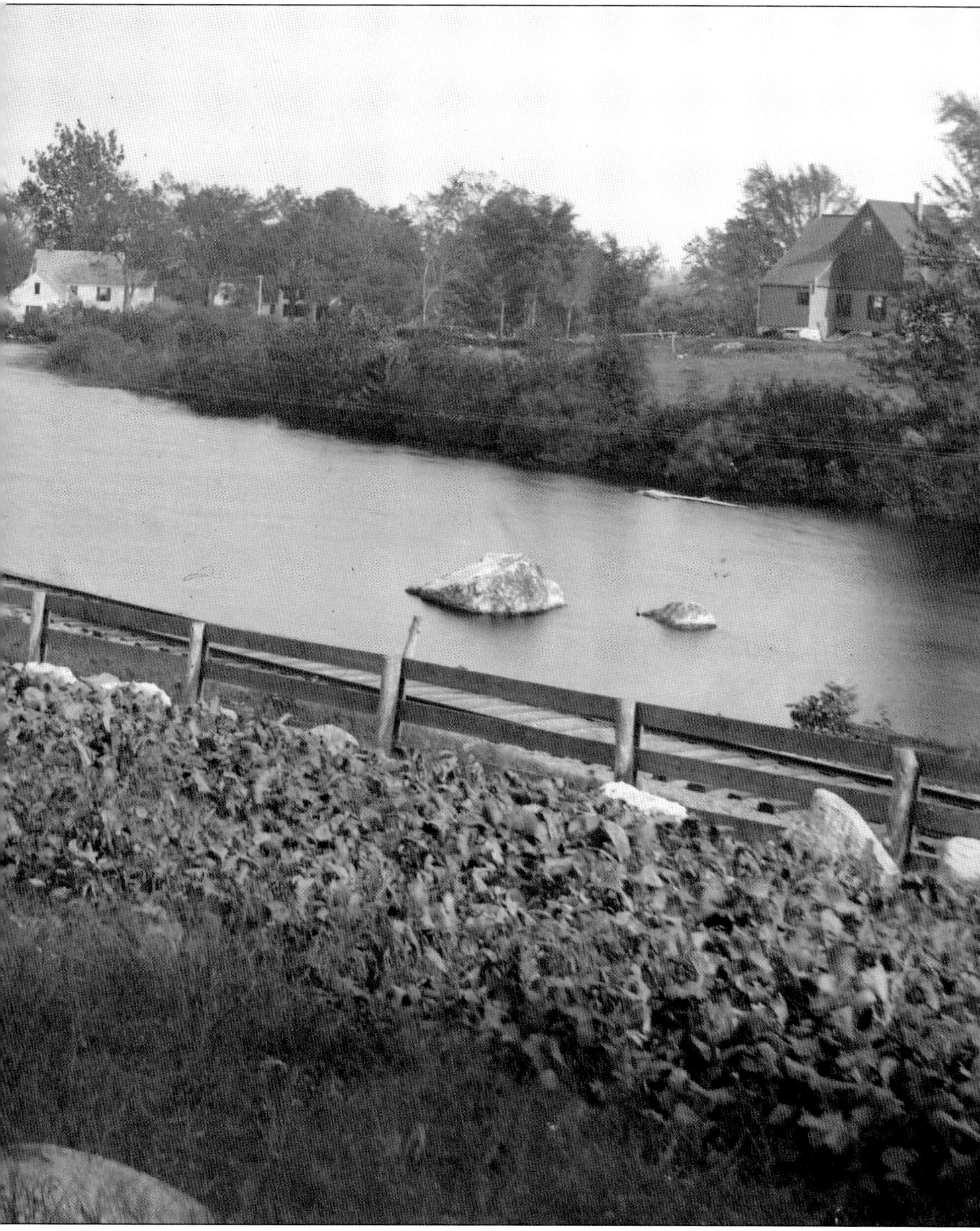

harvesting season; Girard P. Dadmun's house at 6 Boston Road; the Ark at the corner of Acton Road; J. Adams Bartlett's house at 4 Bartlett Street; and a Bartlett rental house at 19 Acton Road. The house at 15 Acton Road later occupied by Winthrop A. Parkhurst had not yet been built. The mill, the icehouses, and the Ark no longer exist. (Chelmsford Historical Society Collection.)

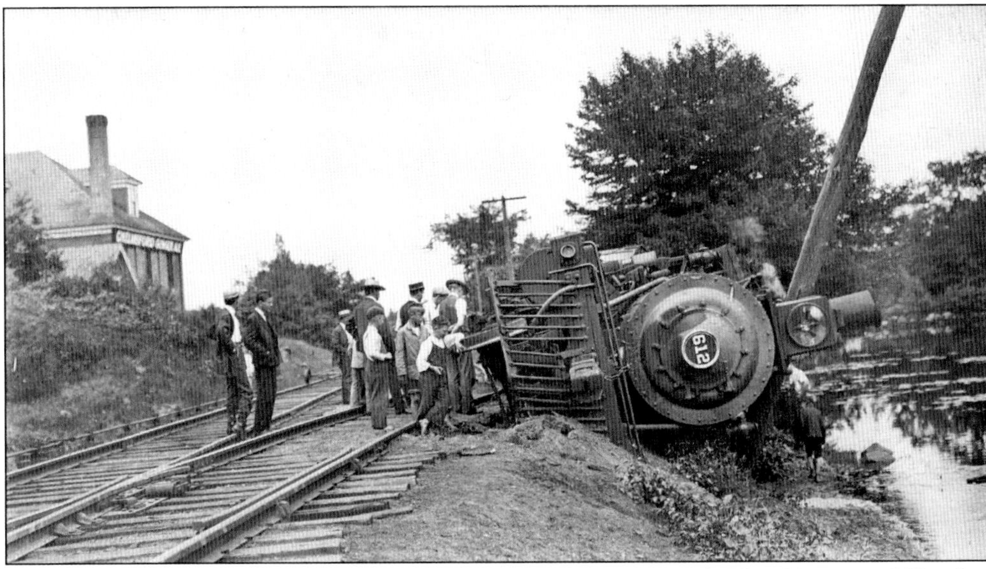

In the photograph above, curious onlookers are inspecting New York, New Haven and Hartford locomotive No. 612 that slipped off the railroad siding around 1910. Only a utility pole prevented it from rolling into the water. The original Chelmsford Ginger Ale plant is visible on the left, dating this incident to sometime after 1908, when Chelmsford Ginger Ale was incorporated, and before 1912, when it burned. The millpond dam is on the right. The photograph below shows a view of locomotive No. 612 from across the millpond, the rear of houses on Littleton Road, and the coal that dumped out of the tender into the pond. (Above, Chelmsford Historical Commission; below, Chelmsford Historical Society Collection.)

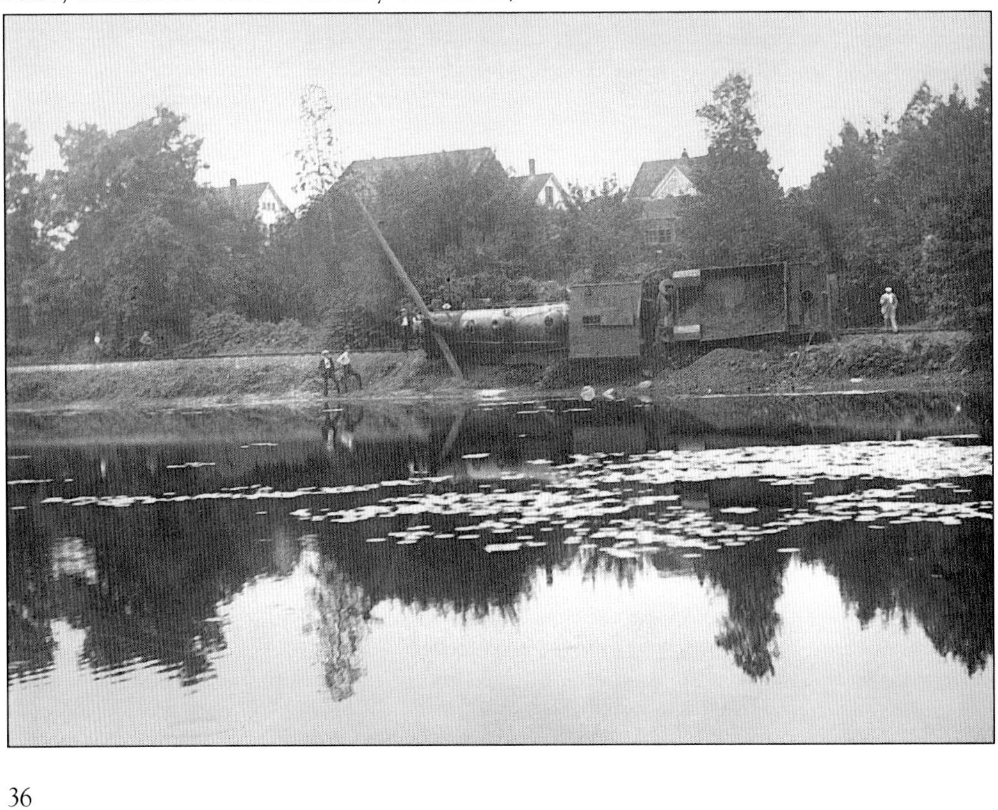

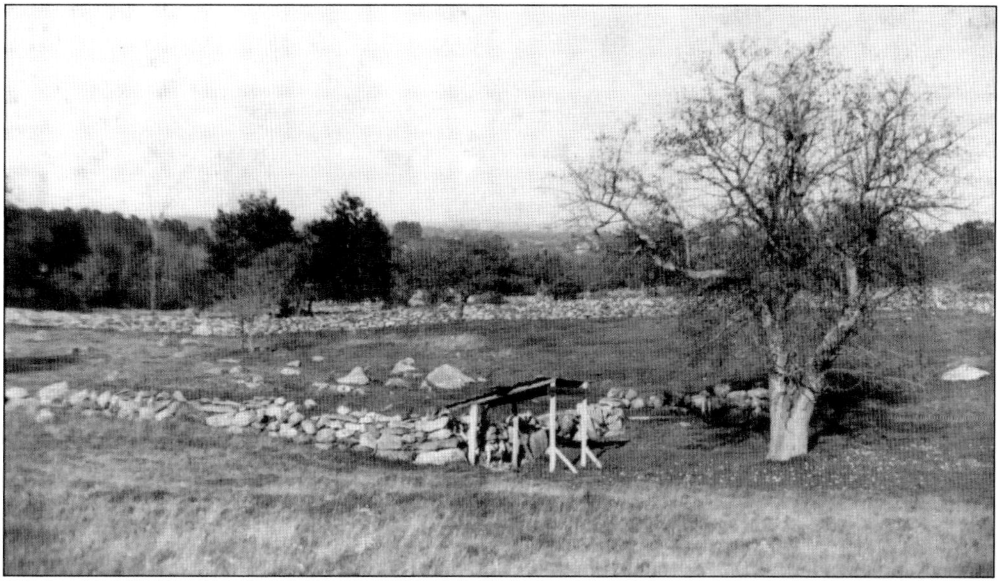

The Chelmsford Spring Company was supplied by water from a "never-failing" spring, located near the intersection of High Street and Robin Hill Road, shown here around 1902. Water was piped about seven-tenths of a mile along the railroad bed to the bottling plant. Although it was filled in prior to 1974, water still flows from the spring, now in the side yard of 101 High Street. (Chelmsford Historical Society Collection.)

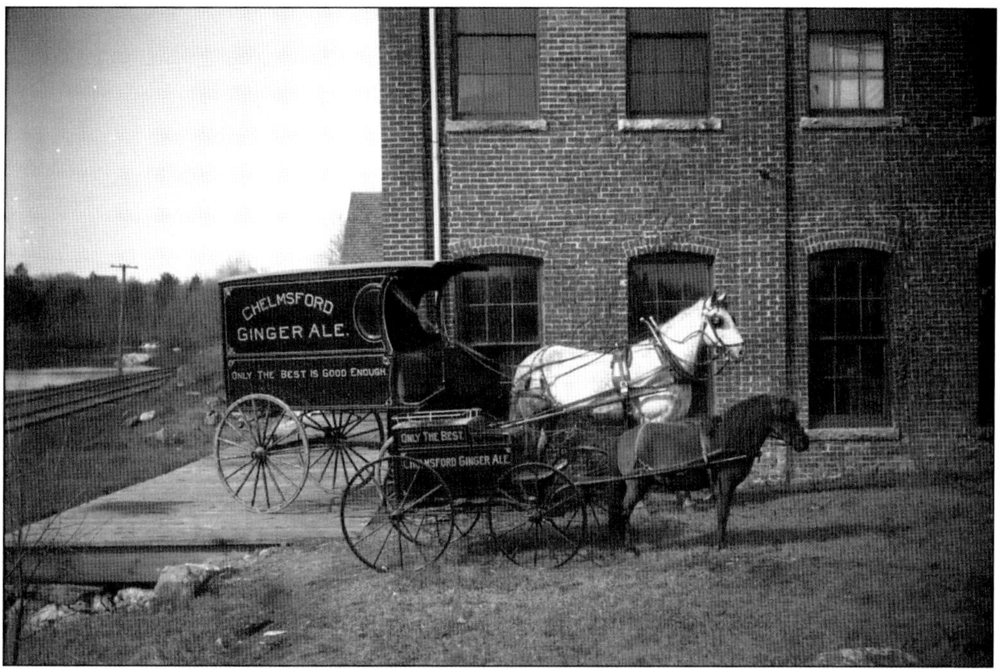

Horse-drawn vehicles distributed Chelmsford Ginger Ale products when the original plant was in use, as shown here around 1908. The pony cart, which appears to be too small to make regular deliveries, was likely used for publicity. The millpond with its distinctive boulder, the site of the locomotive rollover, and the turret at 55 High Street are seen on the left. (Chelmsford Historical Society Collection.)

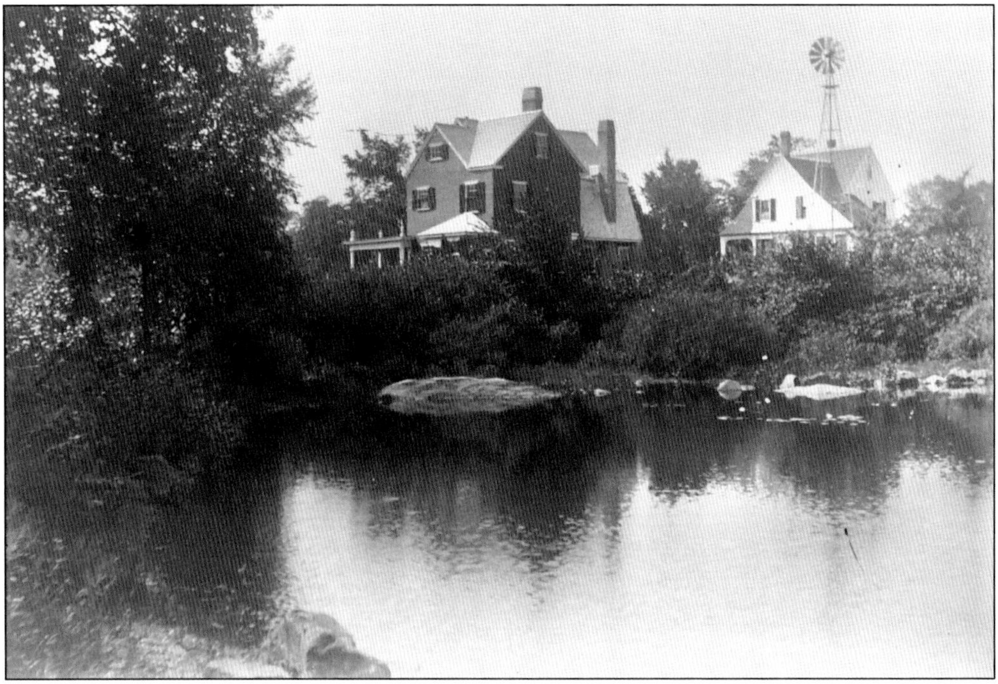

This view south from the milldam around 1902 shows the rear of homes at 15 and 19 Acton Road. Winthrop A. Parkhurst owned No. 15 on the left, and the Bartlett family owned and rented out the house at No. 19. The spillway located next to this camera position became the only outlet for Beaver Brook in the mid-1900s when the pond was filled in. (Chelmsford Historical Society Collection.)

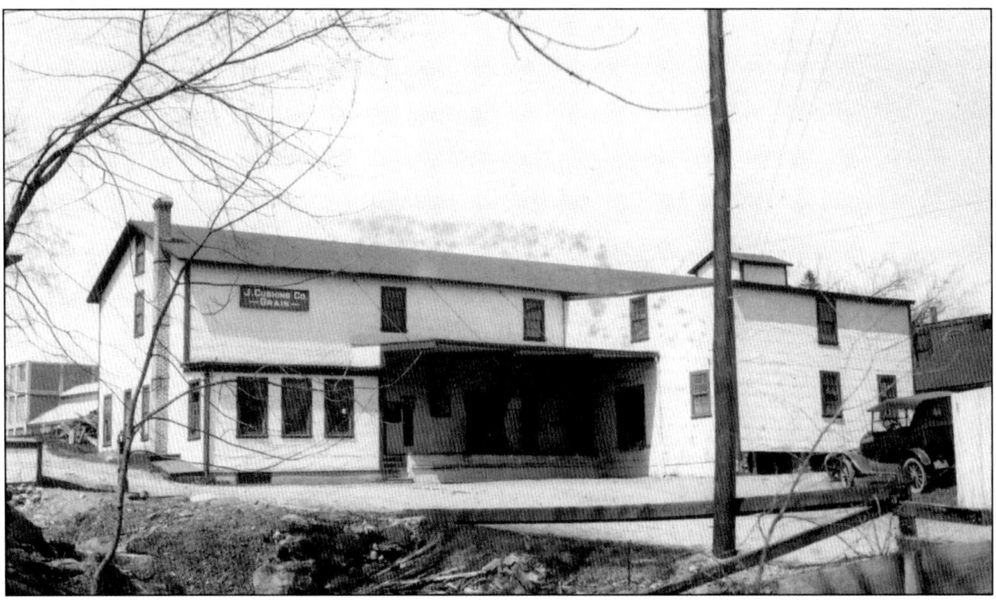

The J. Cushing Co. grain storehouse was constructed just below the milldam for Sweetser and Day in 1908. It was a storage and distribution center for grain products shipped in by railroad, with a capacity of 20 carloads and an elevator and conveyors to move grain between floors and to the older mill. The railroad freight house and a boxcar are at right. (Linda Prescott.)

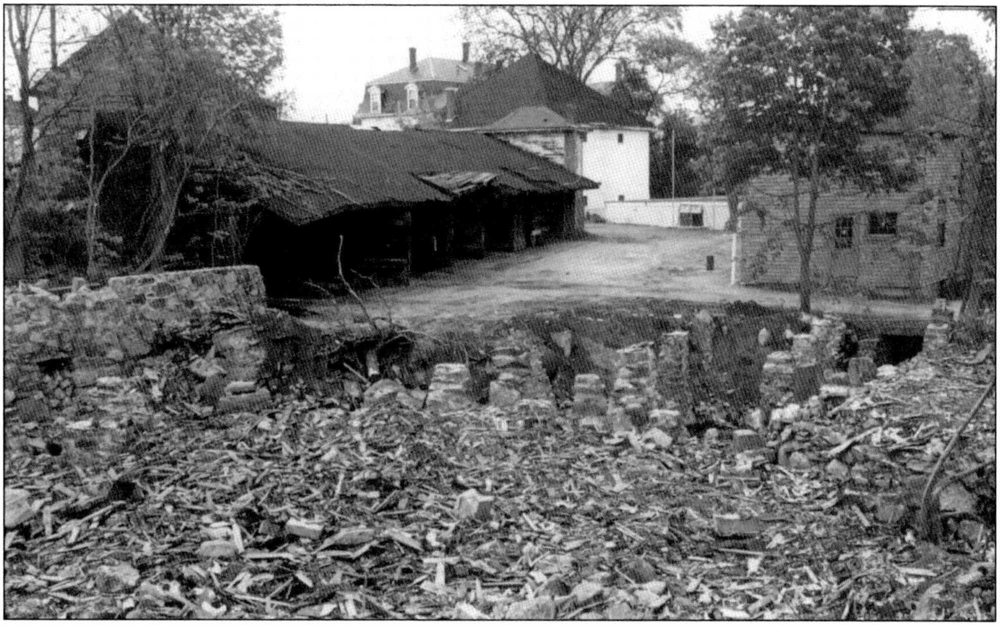

This view from atop the milldam shows the site of the J. Cushing Co. grain storehouse, later purchased by General Mills, soon after it was demolished. The buildings are, from left to right, railroad freight house, Harry L. Parkhurst's coal sheds, Central House, Central House stable, Godin's Store behind the gas pumps, and the J. Cushing Co. warehouse. All the buildings except the coal sheds still exist. (Linda Prescott.)

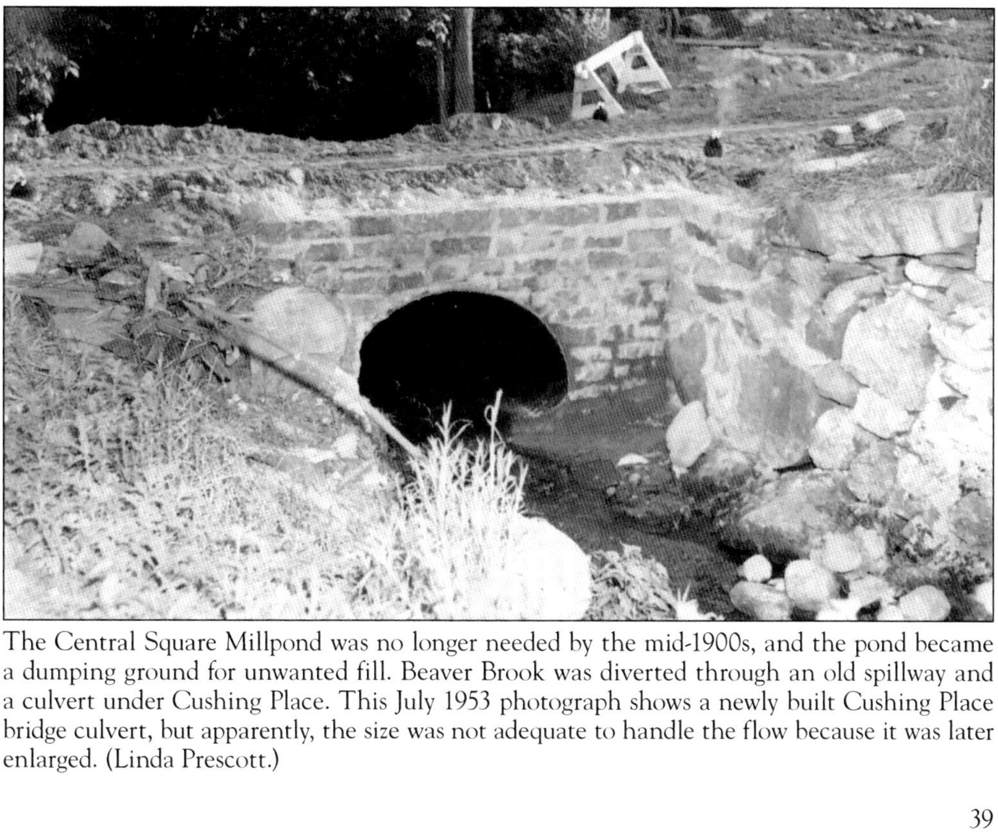

The Central Square Millpond was no longer needed by the mid-1900s, and the pond became a dumping ground for unwanted fill. Beaver Brook was diverted through an old spillway and a culvert under Cushing Place. This July 1953 photograph shows a newly built Cushing Place bridge culvert, but apparently, the size was not adequate to handle the flow because it was later enlarged. (Linda Prescott.)

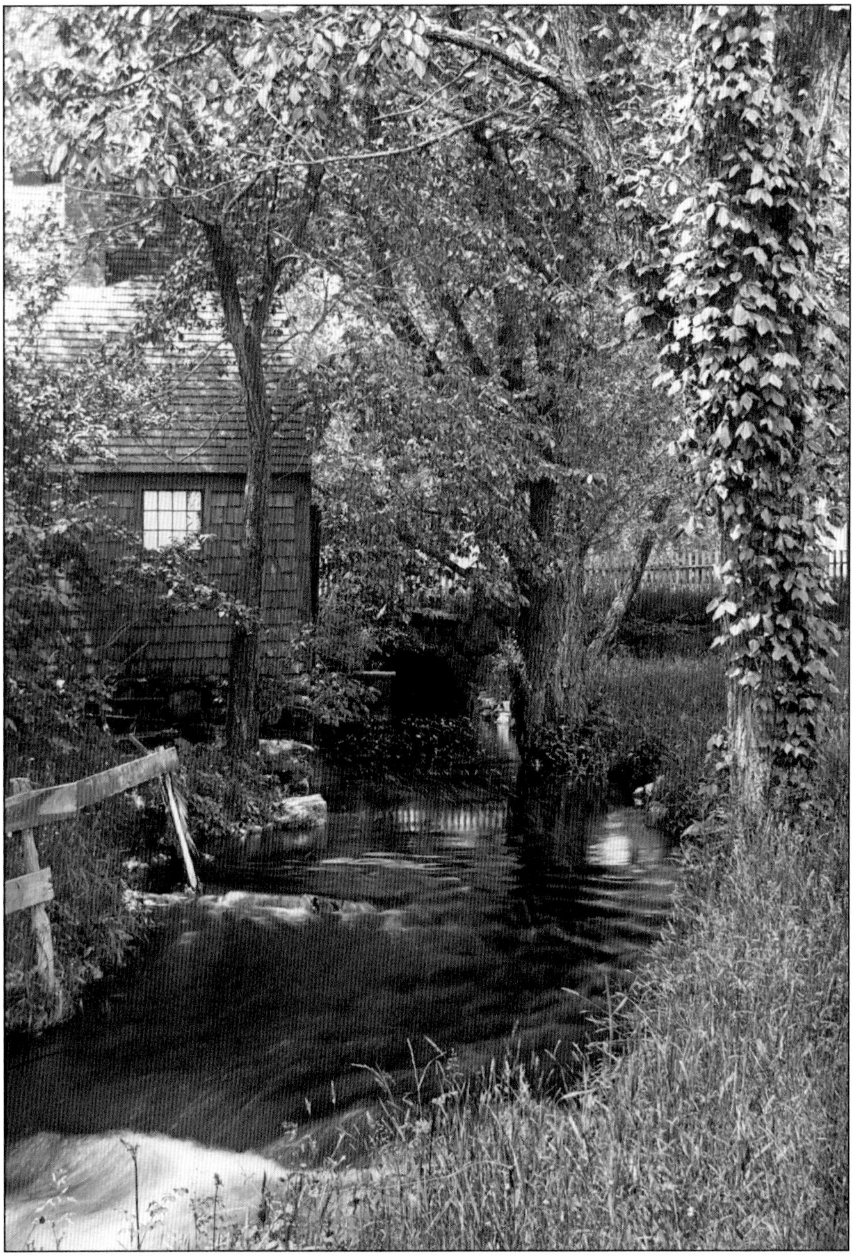

Two streams fed the Central Square Millpond. Beaver Brook arrived from the west, and a smaller stream, originating in the north behind Forefathers' Burying Ground, crossed under Littleton Road. The smaller stream now passes underground to an opening behind the Proctor Wheelwright Shop where it joins Beaver Brook. The combined stream flows directly under that building and then under Central Square. The round stone arch of the Central Square Bridge can be seen in the center of this c. 1890 view looking through to the other side of the road. The back side of Girard P. Dadmun's blacksmith shop is on the left, and water grass is waving in the current. By 1923, Beaver Brook was condemned due to pollution. Decades of cleanup and legal efforts by the town failed, and the pollution problem was not completely solved until the first phase of the town-wide sewer system was completed in 1998. (Chelmsford Historical Society Collection.)

Four

CENTER COMMON

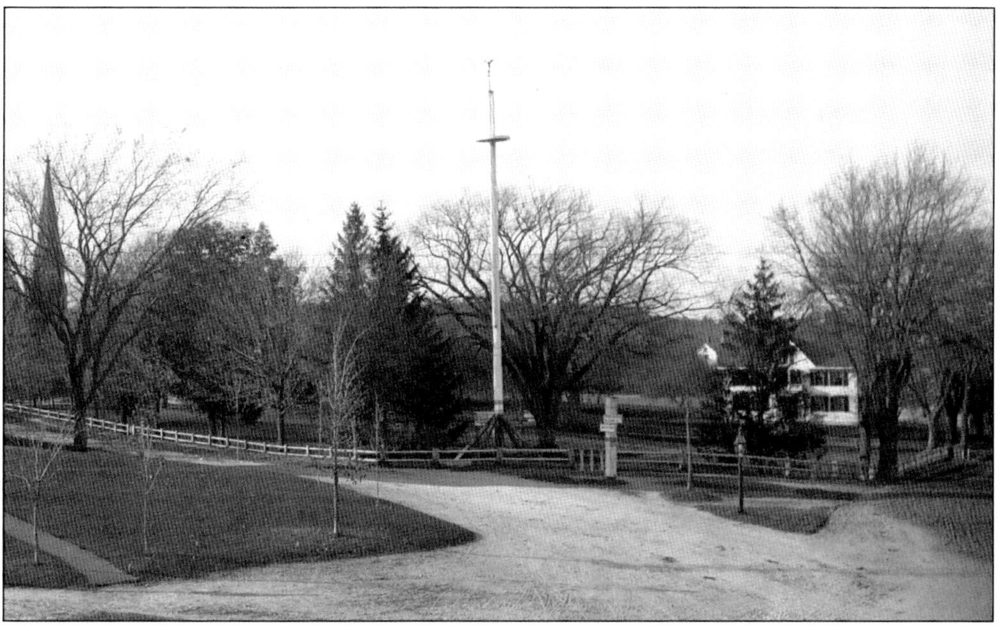

This c. 1904 view of Chelmsford Common shows the flagpole purchased by subscription as a liberty pole to commemorate Lincoln's second election to the presidency. Installed on November 7, 1864, it was about 100 feet tall with the topmast extended and had four wooden supports at the base. The flagpole served the town until 1905, when it was voted under Article 7 to purchase a new flagpole. (Chelmsford Historical Society Collection.)

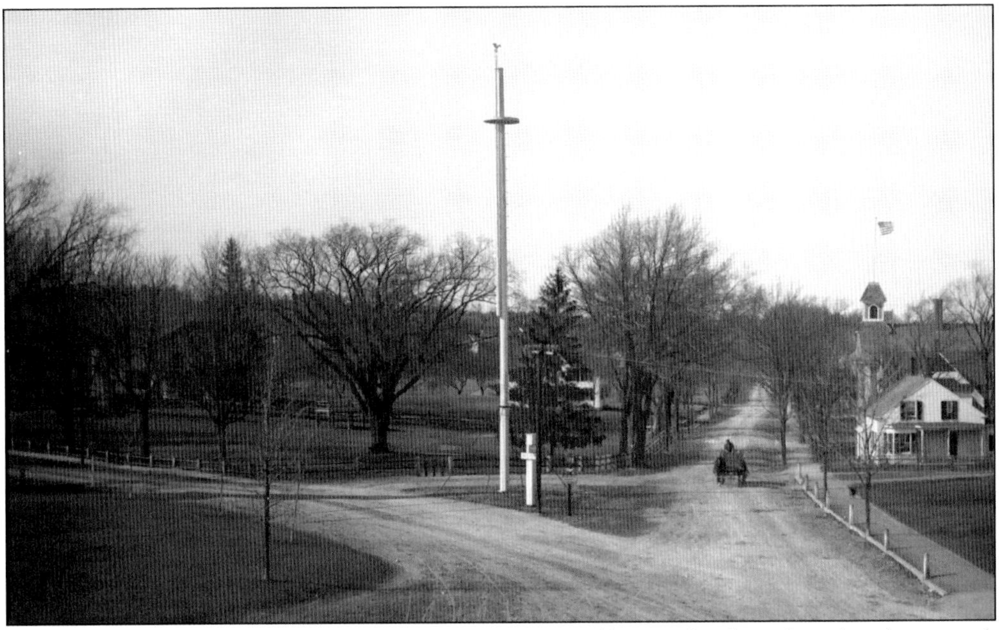

The new flagpole was about 108 feet tall and was supported by metal rods anchored in the ground. Its topmast was replaced in 1910, the crow's nest was replaced in 1928, and the pole was cut down and anchored in concrete in 1967. It was replaced with a hollow composite pole in September 2011, and the old wooden pole was reinstalled at the "Old Chelmsford" Garrison House in June 2013. (Chelmsford Historical Society Collection.)

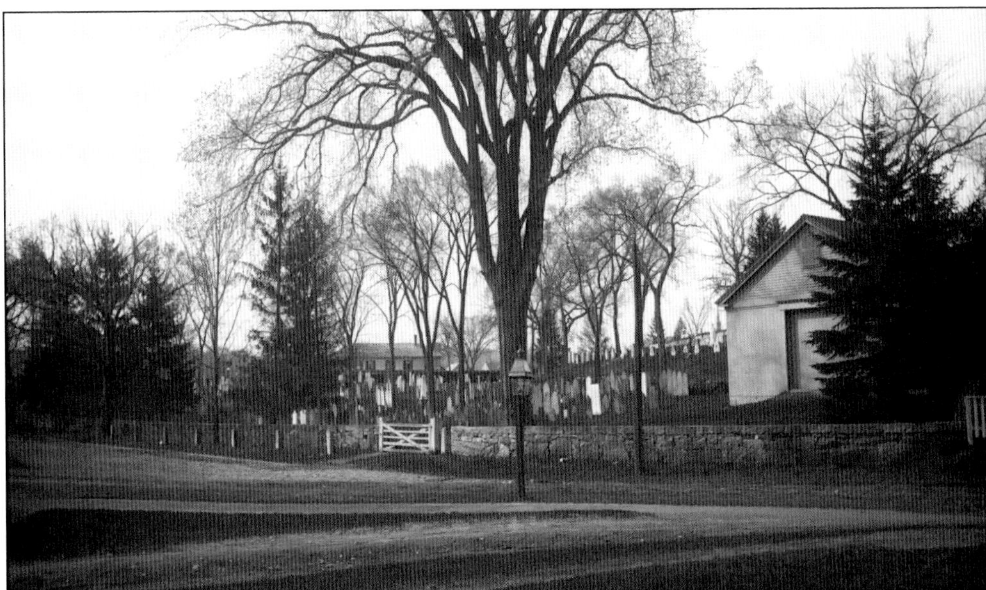

The c. 1890 view from the front of the Central Baptist Church shows the railroad house, Forefathers' Burying Ground, and the 1802 schoolhouse, which was used for storage of the town hearse at the time. Undertakers, such as Walter Perham, had their own covered wagons in the horse-drawn days but used the town's formal hearse, now in the care of the "Old Chelmsford" Garrison House, during funerals. (Chelmsford Historical Society Collection.)

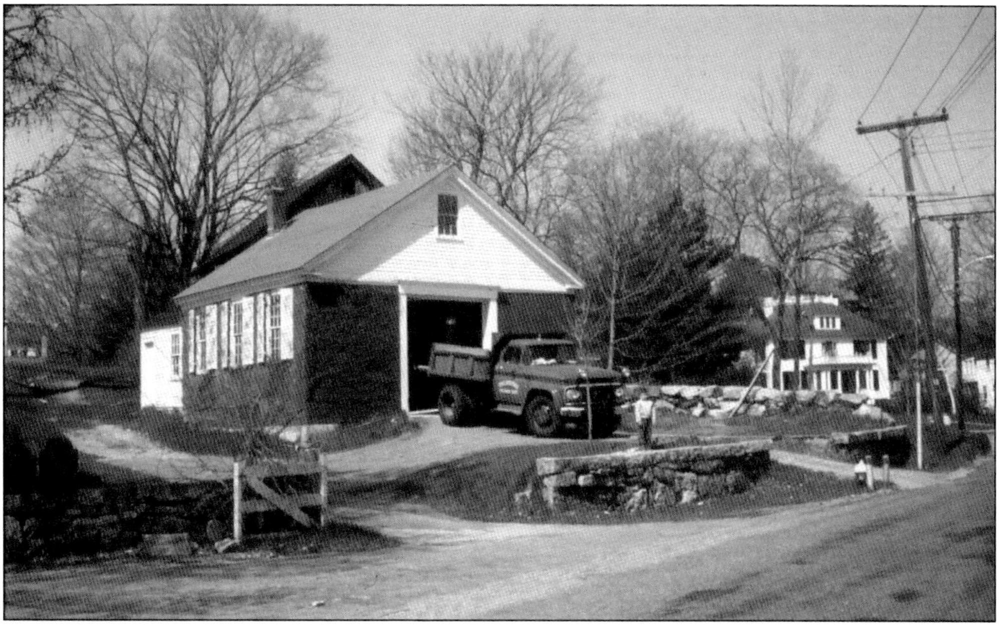

This c. 1973 slide shows a highway department truck pulled up to the 1802 schoolhouse, which had been transferred to the cemetery department in the early 1900s. The hearse remained in the building until after 1952. In November 1974, ownership of the schoolhouse was transferred to the Chelmsford Bicentennial Commission. The Middlesex Canal Tollhouse can be seen behind the school. (Chelmsford Historical Society Collection.)

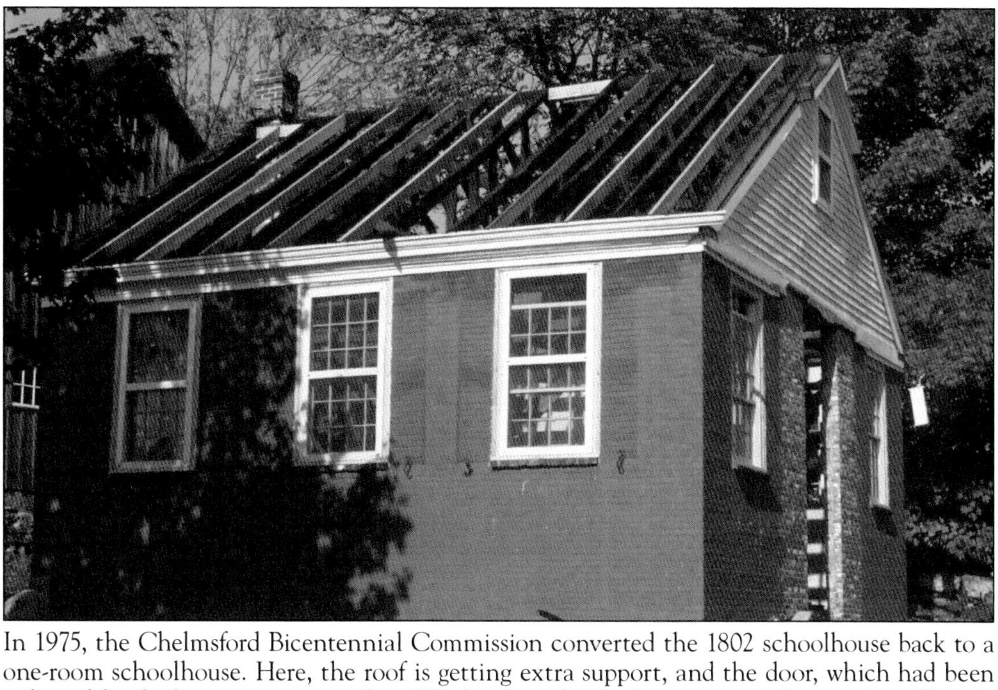

In 1975, the Chelmsford Bicentennial Commission converted the 1802 schoolhouse back to a one-room schoolhouse. Here, the roof is getting extra support, and the door, which had been enlarged for the hearse sometime after 1852, has been bricked in as a normal entry door. The old Chelmsford Academy school bell, moved to the Centre School tower in 1886, was installed in the 1802 schoolhouse in 1975. (Chelmsford Historical Society Collection.)

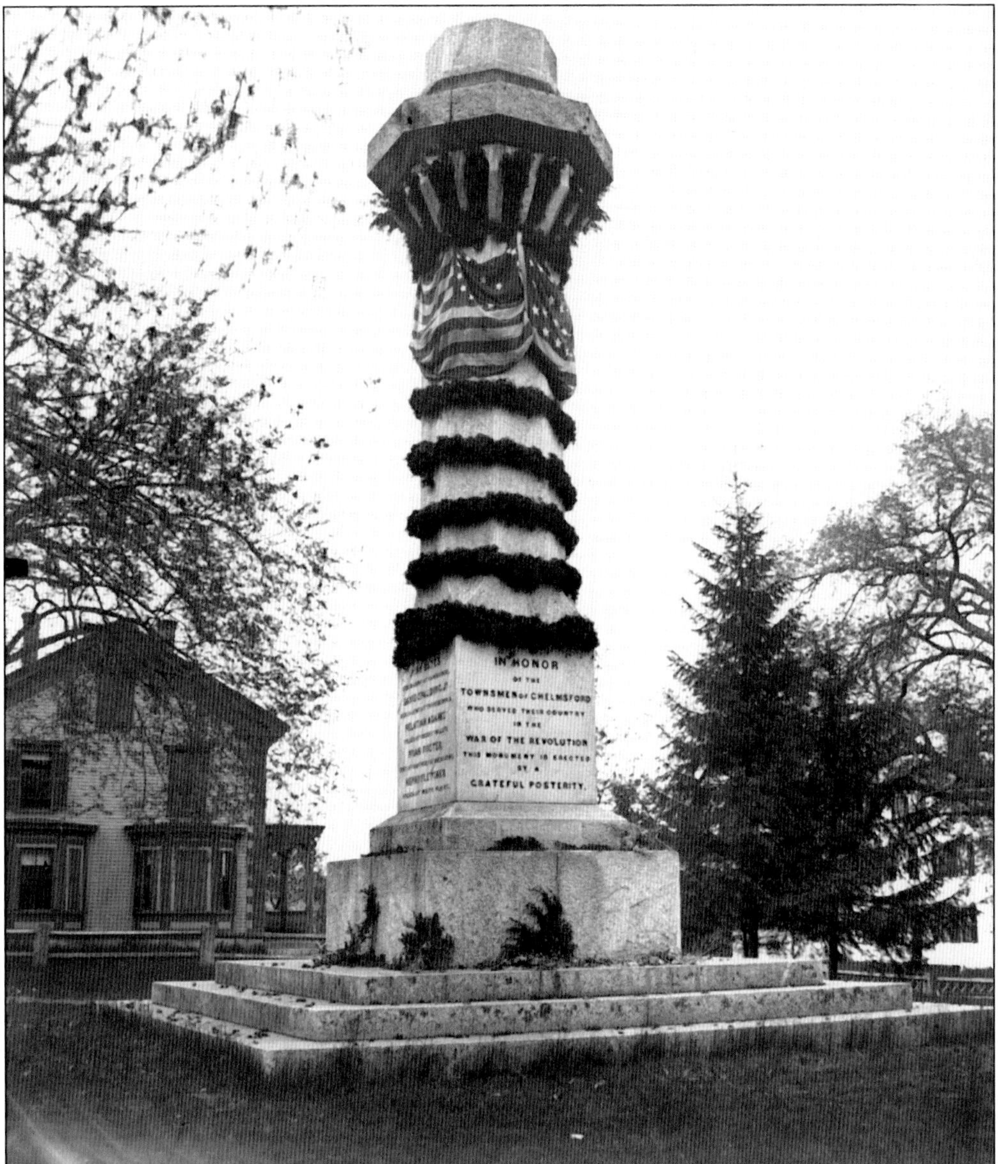

On March 25, 1859, a group of nine gentlemen met at the home of Deacon Otis Adams, seen here on the right, to discuss Charles A. Dalton's idea of building a monument to the Revolutionary patriots of Chelmsford. After a public hearing at town hall (the First Parish basement) on April 15, the Chelmsford Monument Association was formed, a prospectus was drafted, and contributions were received from 954 people, totaling $1,675. Loammi Chamberlain was the low bidder and received the contract. On September 22, 1859, the monument was dedicated with a parade and then music and speakers in the town hall. A dinner reception followed in a tent behind the First Parish Church. Decorating the Revolutionary War Monument became an annual town-sponsored Memorial Day tradition along with a parade, ceremonies in Forefathers' Burying Ground, activities in town hall, and a dinner. The 1825 Chelmsford Classical School, later the 1859 to 1862 Chelmsford Academy and then parsonage for the Central Baptist Church at 7 Academy Street, is on the left. (Chelmsford Historical Society Collection.)

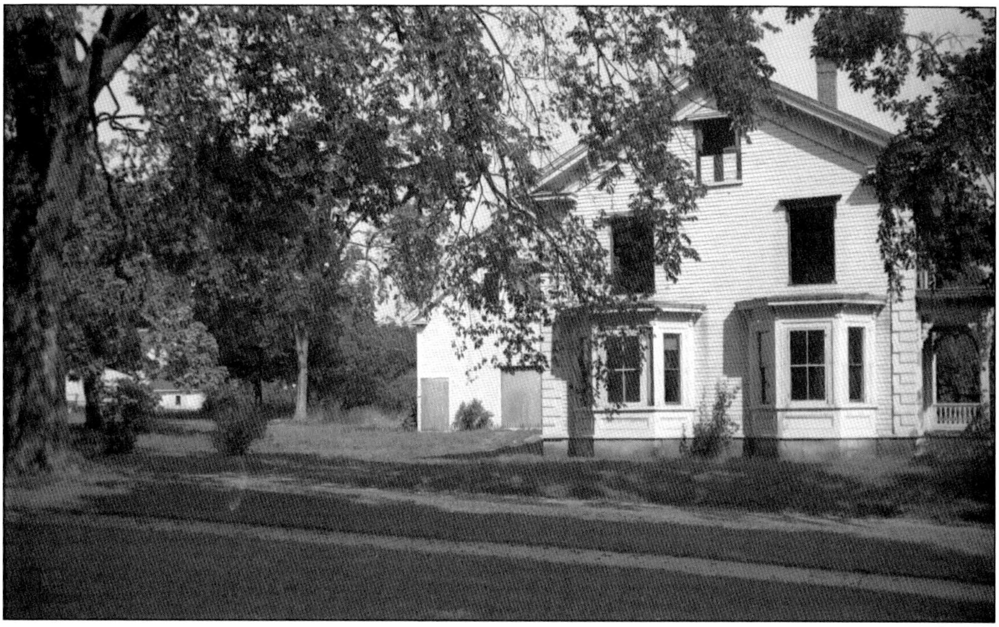

Ralph Waldo Emerson, the essayist and lecturer of the mid-1800s, was in charge of the Chelmsford Classical School when it opened in 1825. He was obliged to leave the school in December of his first year when his brother Edward became unable to care for his own school in Roxbury and did not return. Deacon David Perham, builder of the Central Baptist Church in 1868, was one of seven trustees of the Chelmsford Academy, which started in 1859. Several students joined the ranks of the Army to fight in the Civil War, known then as the War of the Rebellion, and as a result the school lost financial support and failed in 1862. While serving as the Central Baptist Church parsonage, the building was demolished in August 1955, as seen in these two progress photographs. (Both, Linda Prescott.)

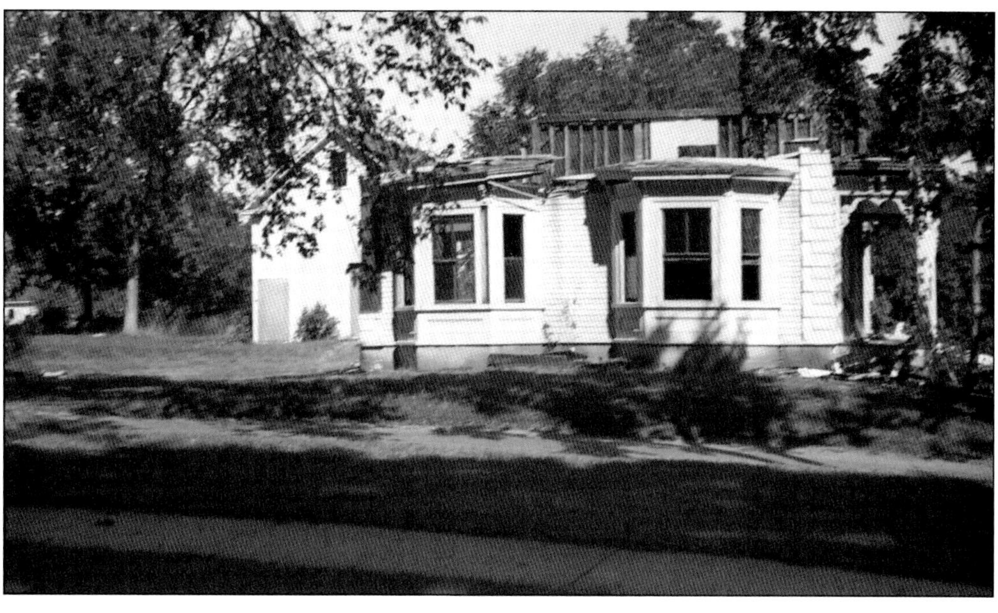

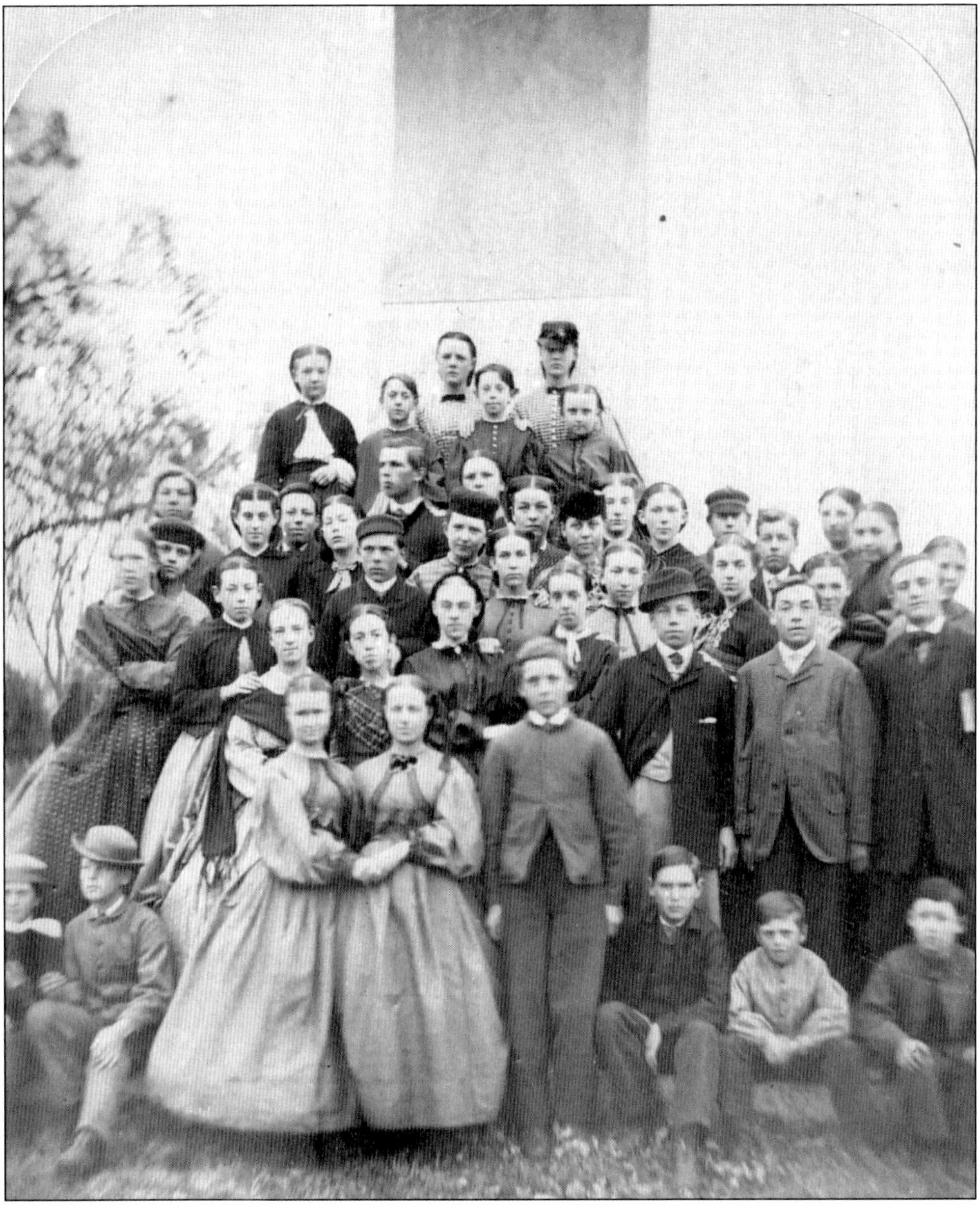

The Revolutionary War Monument was the location of this very early photograph identified as the 1862–1863 class at the District No. 2 schoolhouse at the intersection of Davis and Locke Roads. Frederic T. Greenhalge served as the teacher at this school in between attending Harvard University from 1859 to 1862 and a five-month stint in the Union army at New Bern, North Carolina. He was admitted to the bar in 1865, was mayor of Lowell in 1880–1881, and served as governor of Massachusetts from January 1894 until his death on March 5, 1896. While governor, he proclaimed the first Patriots' Day in 1894, ending a 200-year-old Fast Day tradition. New Hampshire was the last New England state to observe Fast Day when it converted to Civil Rights Day in 1991. In the 1860s, girls parted their hair in the middle following the fashion trend set by Queen Victoria. Eleven-year-old Juliette L. Wright is identified in this photograph as being just behind and between the two girls dressed alike. (Chelmsford Historical Society Collection.)

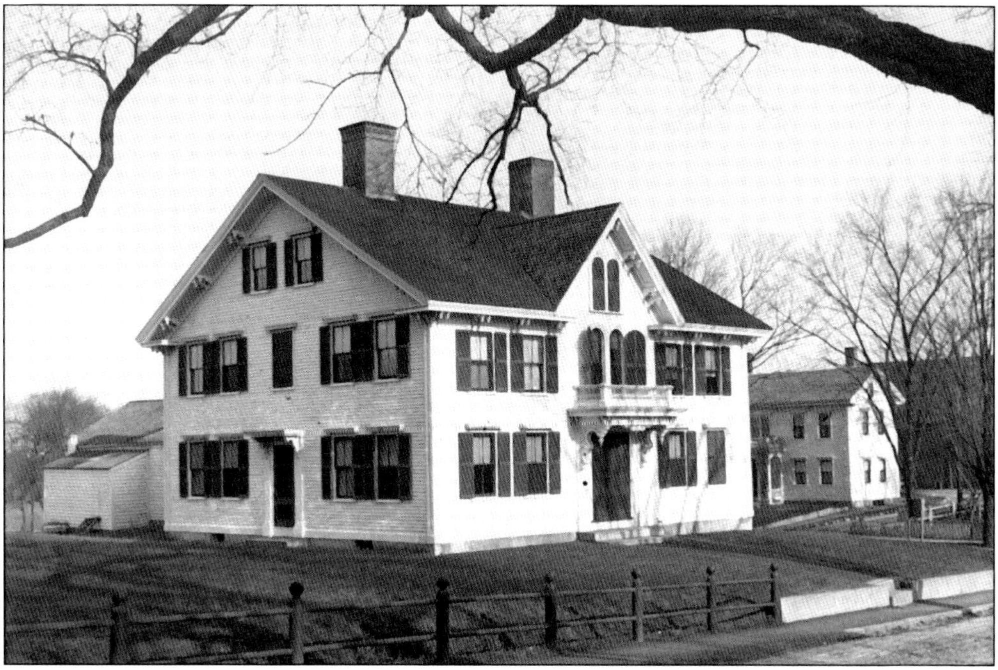

Deacon Otis Adams owned 6 North Road from 1849 to 1872 and is credited with the Revolutionary Monument inscription, which reads, "Let the children guard what the sires have won." Harriet B. Rogers started the Chelmsford School for the Deaf in one room in 1866. James P. Emerson, who purchased this house in 1908, owned the 11 North Road house and barn at right in this November 1907 photograph. (Chelmsford Historical Society Collection.)

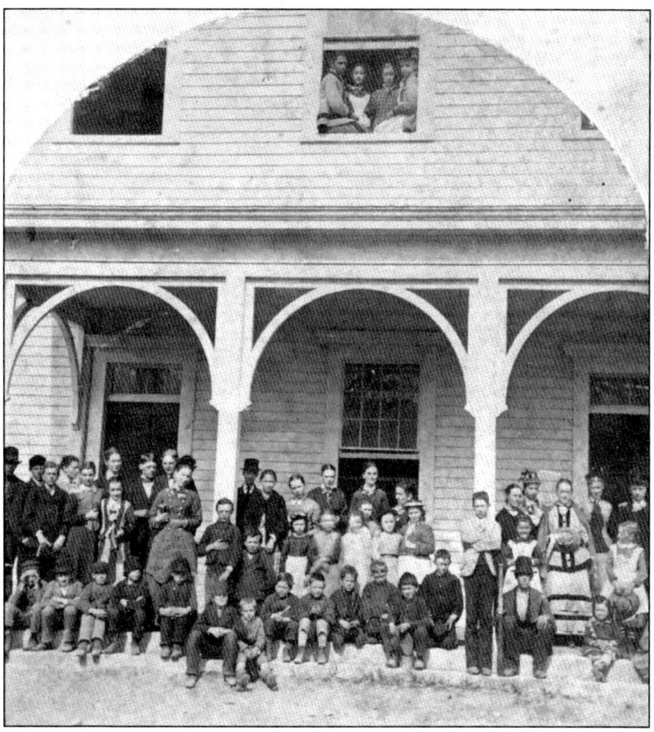

This is the right half of a stereopticon image of Centre School dated July 1875. There were separate doors for boys and girls and no bell tower in the front of the building at the time. Overcrowding of the school led to expansion in August 1886 when the main entrances were relocated to the sides of the building, the porch was removed, and the bell tower added. (Chelmsford Historical Society Collection.)

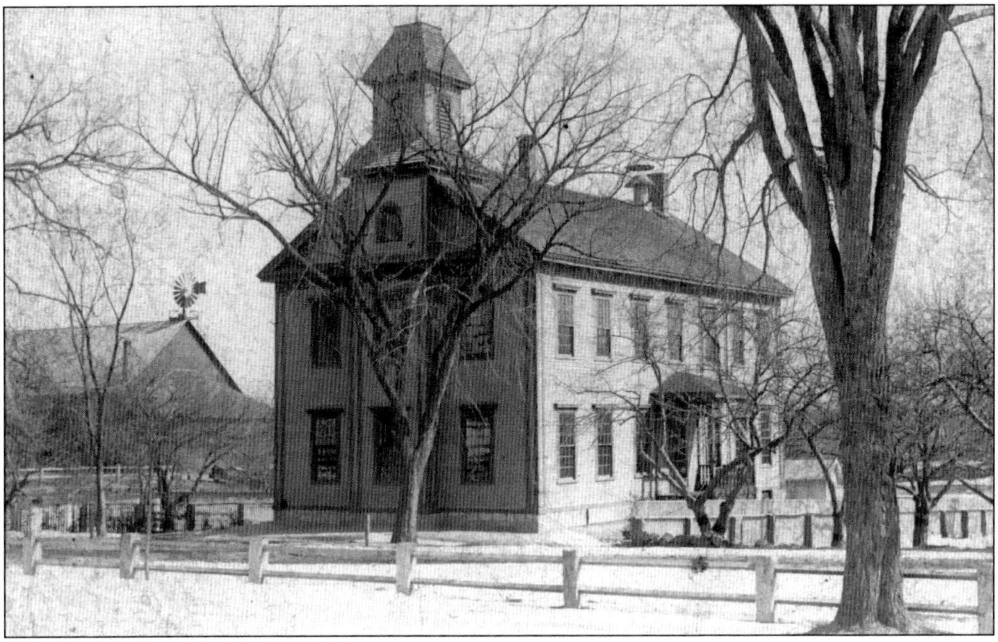

This photograph of Centre School above was taken from the common in March 1895 and shows the porch removed, the two front doors replaced with windows, and the new bell tower. James P. Emerson's barn and windmill are on the left. When James died in June 1926, his grandson Theodore "Ted" W. Emerson inherited the farm. On Sunday, September 9, 1951, a fire broke out in Ted Emerson's barn and tragically took with it a horse and 49 cows who were confined for the night in their stanchions. The fire had already peaked by 2:07 a.m. when neighbor Esther M. Woodward saw the flames and reported it by telephone; there was no time to rescue the animals. (Above, Chelmsford Historical Society Collection; below, Chelmsford Fire Department.)

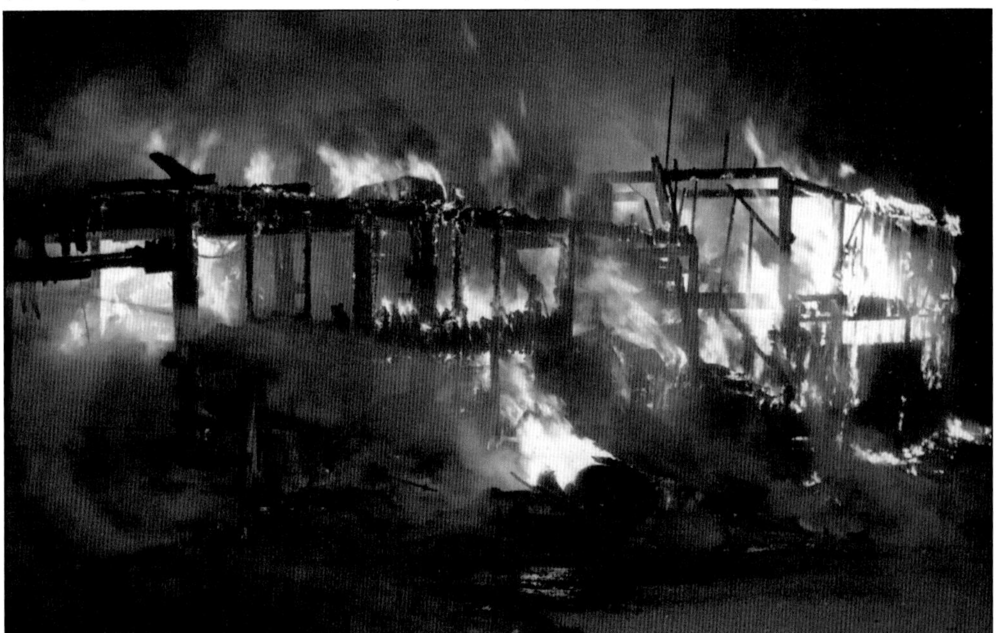

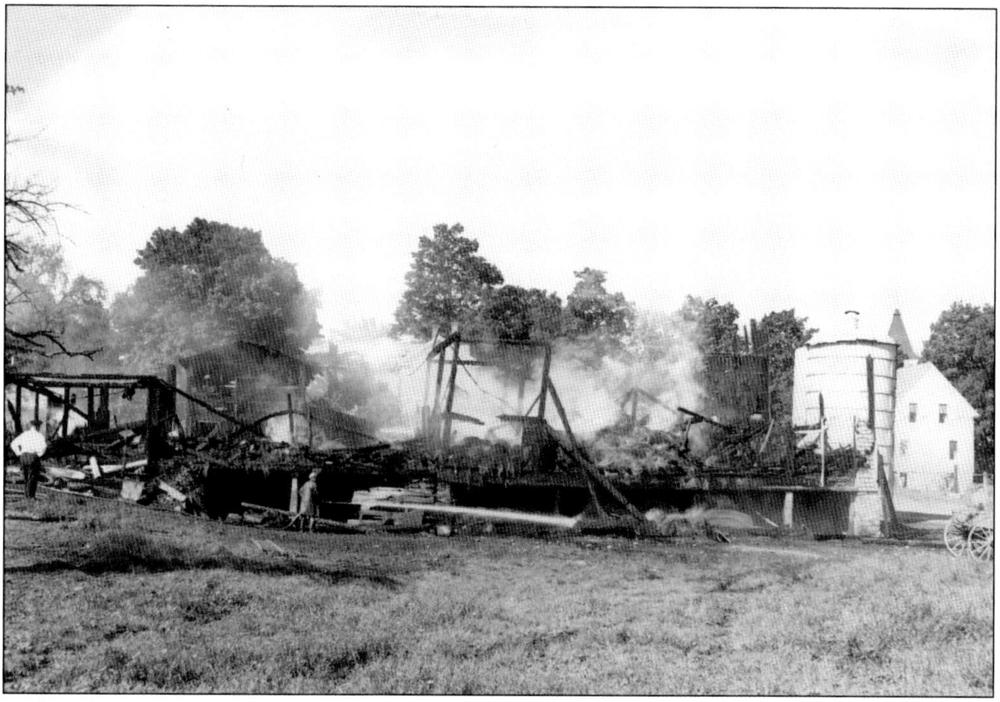

In this photograph, taken later on Sunday after the fire had been knocked down, the embers are being soaked with a fire hose. Firefighters from center, east, south, and north fire stations worked through the night to prevent the fire from spreading to the nearby house, town hall, and two churches. (Chelmsford Fire Department.)

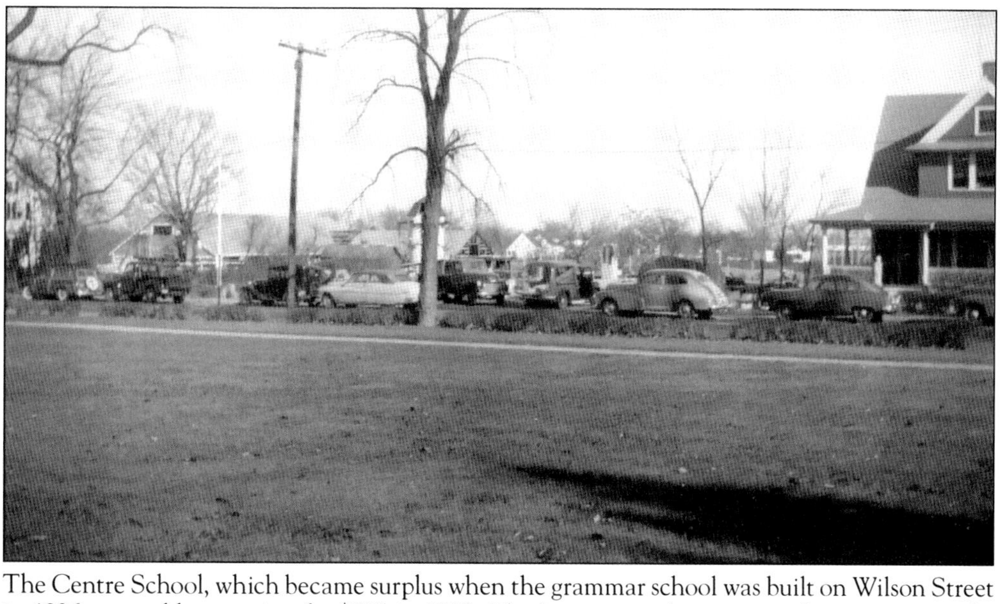

The Centre School, which became surplus when the grammar school was built on Wilson Street in 1926, was sold at auction for $595 in 1928. The lot remained vacant until construction of a new fire station began. This spring 1952 view from Center Common shows Ted Emerson's home and newly constructed barns on the left and the vacant school lot in the center. (Chelmsford Fire Department.)

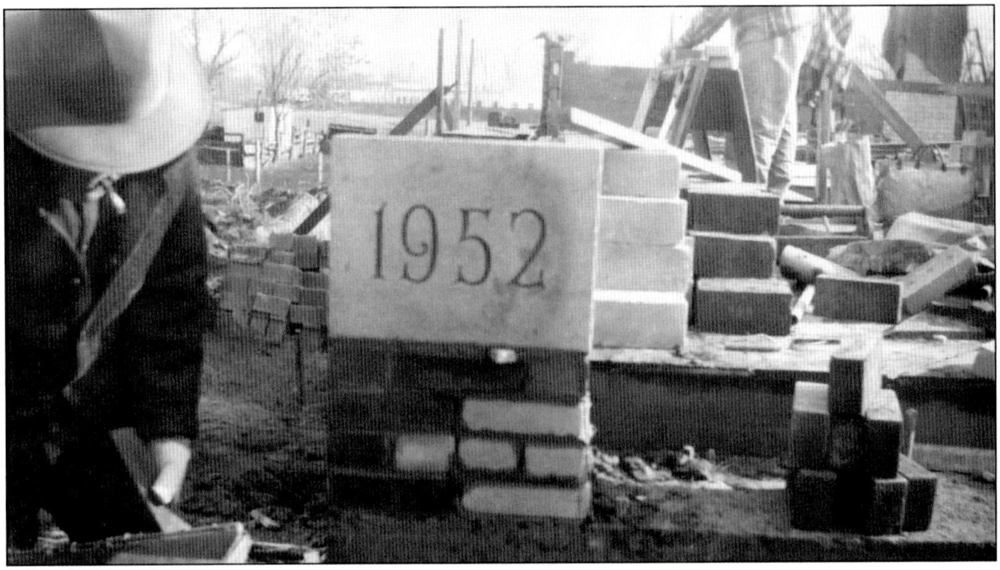

Attempts to get a fire station built on the town-owned Centre School property failed in 1926 and in 1944, but a study committee, appointed in 1950, succeeded in getting unanimous approval for construction in 1952. In this photograph with the Roger Boyd Chevrolet building in the background, the basement level has been constructed, and the cornerstone is being bricked into place. (Chelmsford Fire Department.)

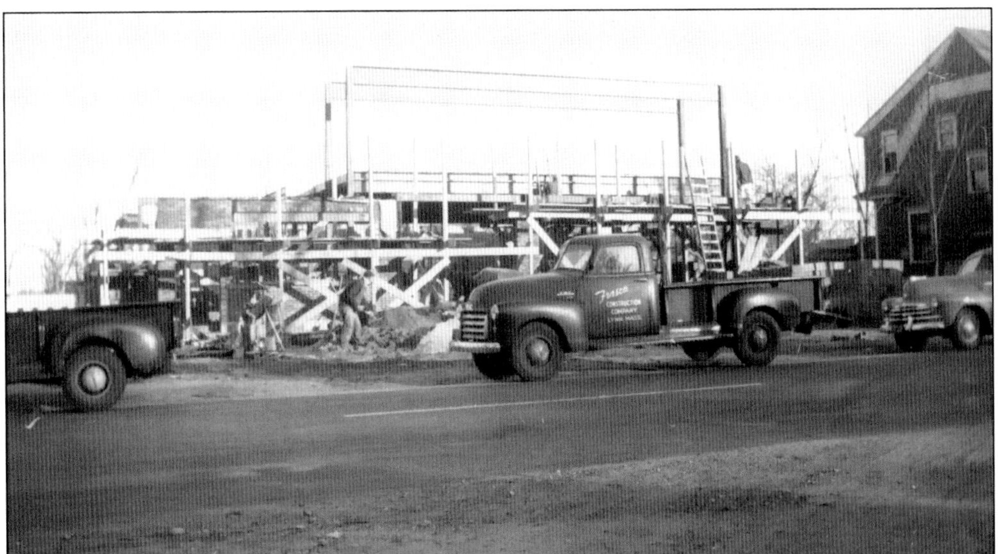

Here, the general contractor, Frasca Construction of Lynn, has installed the steel framework for the engine bays and front of the second floor, and the first-floor exterior masonry work is underway. At this time, most staging was constructed of boards attached with double-headed nails so that they could be pulled and repositioned as the masons worked their way up the walls. (Chelmsford Fire Department.)

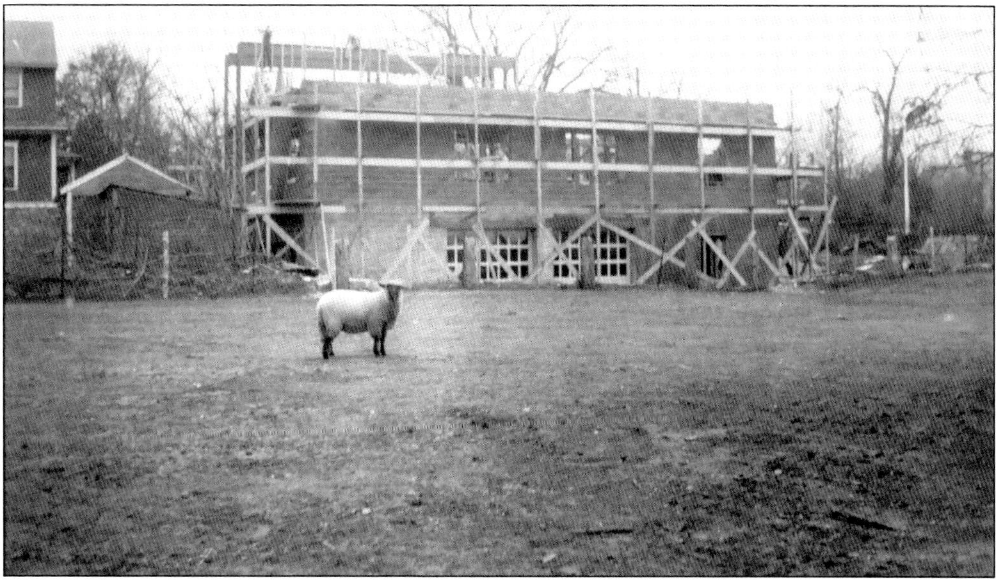

The view from the pasture behind the building shows a curious sheep, the first-floor exterior wall completed, the garage doors to the basement installed, and the framing of second-floor walls. The town purchased the Emerson farm in 1975, and a ramp was later built from the basement entry into the field. (Chelmsford Fire Department.)

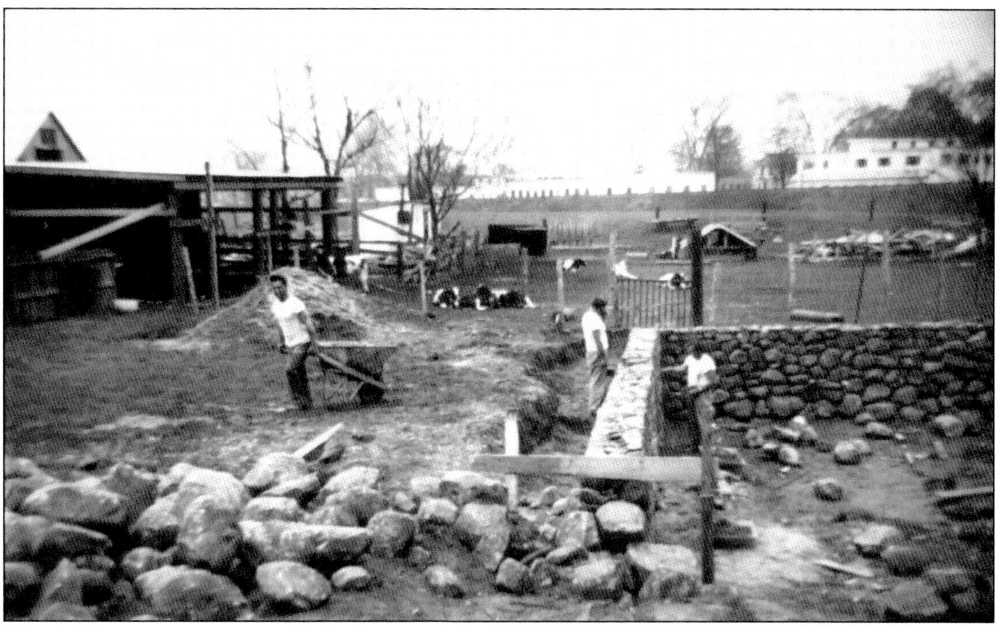

The fieldstone retaining walls for the north driveway are under construction, and Ted Emerson's cows are resting in the pasture behind the station. Several buildings on Chelmsford Street are seen just beyond the railroad track, which was still in use at the time. There is now a road to the left of the retaining wall that aligns with Academy Street at a stoplight. (Chelmsford Fire Department.)

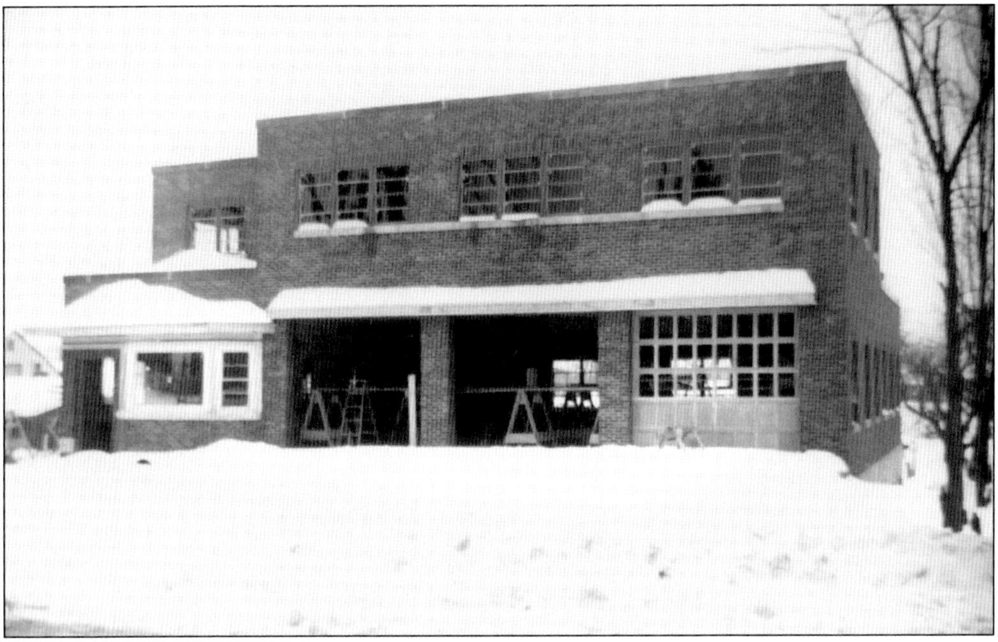

In the 1952 wintertime photograph above, the exterior walls and roof have been completed, and the masons have moved inside. In the photograph below, a team of masons is building the concrete block wall that separates the engine bays from the kitchen and shower room on the left rear of the station. By 2009, the concrete floor of the engine bays was starting to crumble, and 13 wooden pillars were installed below to prevent collapse. Efforts by the permanent building committee to get funding for a new station on Wilson Street failed in 2009 and 2011. In 2012, a scaled-down plan for a new Chelmsford Center Fire Station at 50 Billerica Road, using a portion of the town offices for office and classroom space, was approved. (Both, Chelmsford Fire Department.)

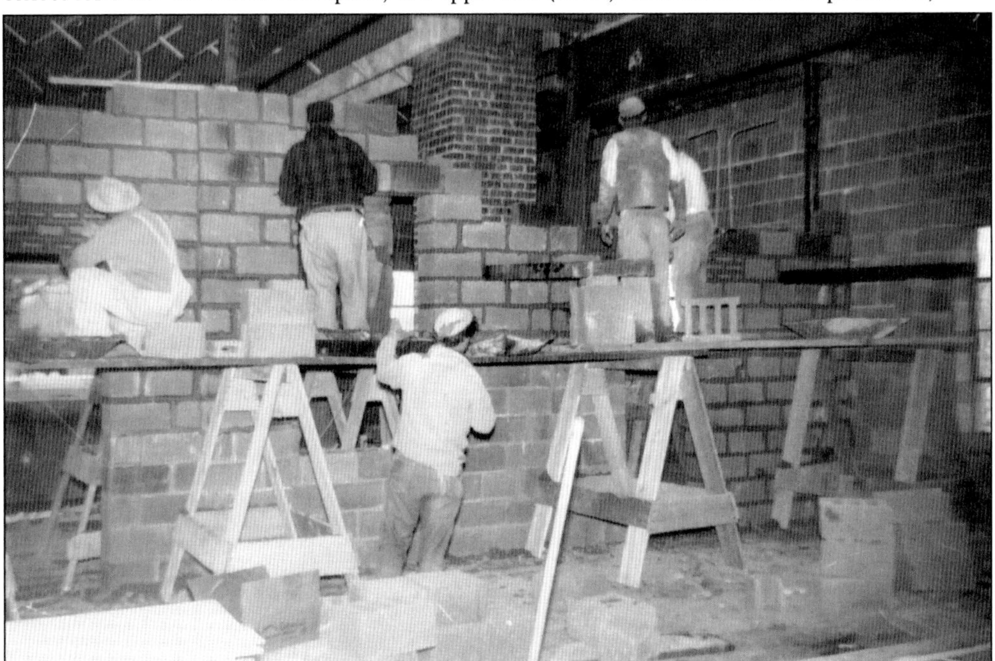

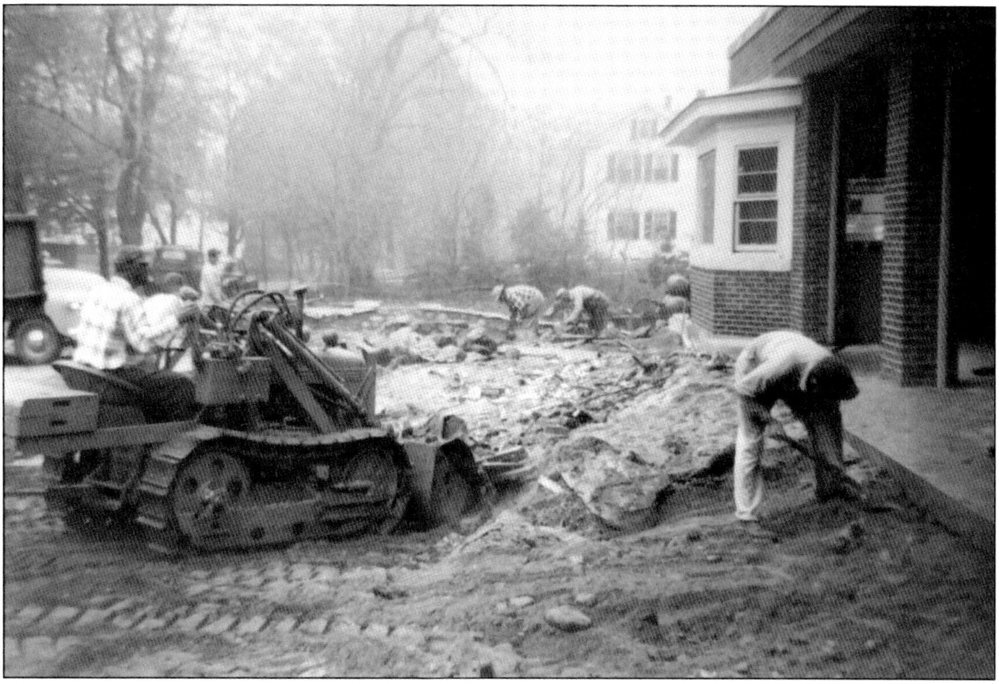

Grading of the apron in front of the dispatch room and engine bays is underway in the spring of 1953. The study committee of 1950 had become the Chelmsford Center Fire Station Building Committee, consisting of the following board members: William L. Colmer, Charles D. Harrington, Allan Kidder, Gilbert H. Perham, Leo A. Williams, Ulysses Lupien Sr., George W. Marinel, and Arnold C. Perham. (Chelmsford Fire Department.)

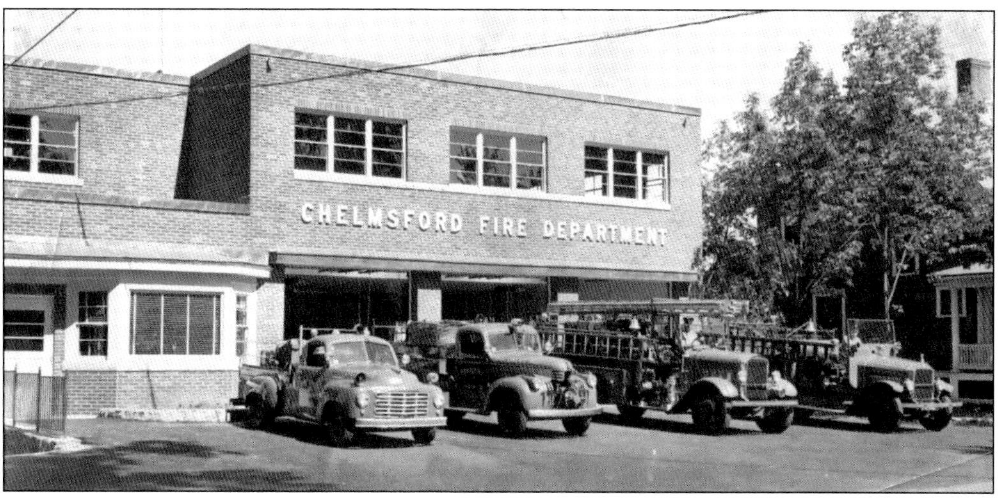

Fire apparatus was moved into the completed Chelmsford Center Fire Station on August 1, 1953. Shown, from left to right, are emergency truck No. 7 (1951 Studebaker), forestry engine No. 8 (1941 Chevrolet), engine No. 1 (1935 Maxim Pumper), and engine No. 6 (1926 Maxim Pumper). The upstairs section was left unfinished until 1958, when it was completed and painted by full-time firefighters during their regular tour of duty. (Chelmsford Fire Department.)

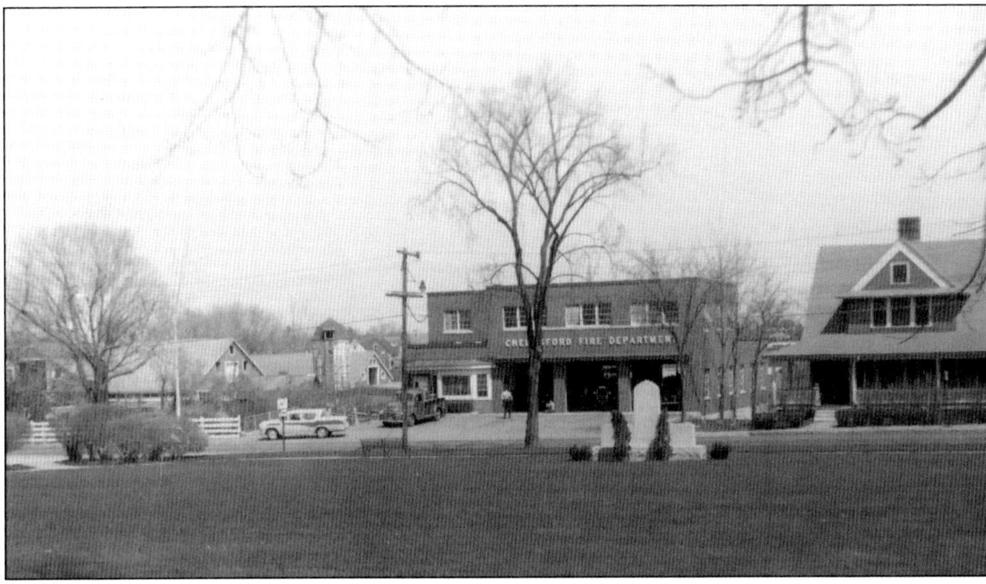

This c. 1957 photograph shows, from left to right, Ted Emerson's farm, the Chelmsford Center Fire Station, and the Leslie R. Davis house. The silo just above the 1957 Nash Rambler had been purchased from the Harvard Brewery in Lowell. The Chelmsford War Memorial on the common was dedicated with a ceremony on May 30, 1955, to Chelmsford men and women who had served in all wars. (Chelmsford Fire Department.)

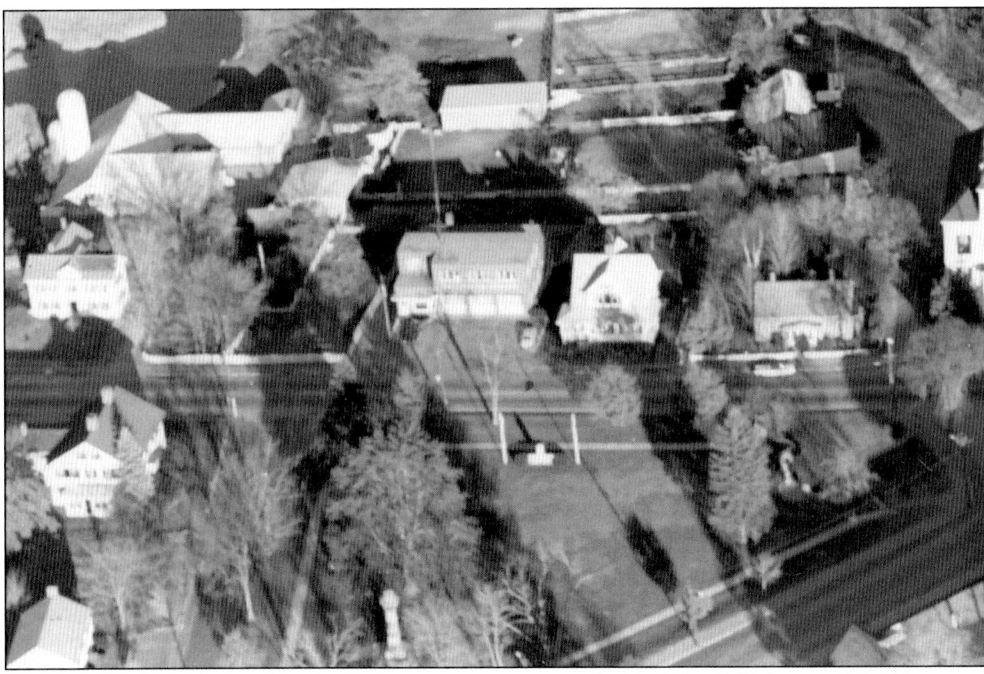

This aerial photograph shows the Center Common around 1958. The "U" shape of Ted Emerson's new barn can clearly be seen along with miscellaneous outbuildings and fenced in fields. The silo casting a long shadow had "Emerson Farm" written on it in big letters. The sheds in back of town hall housed highway department equipment and fire apparatus before the fire station was built. (Chelmsford Fire Department.)

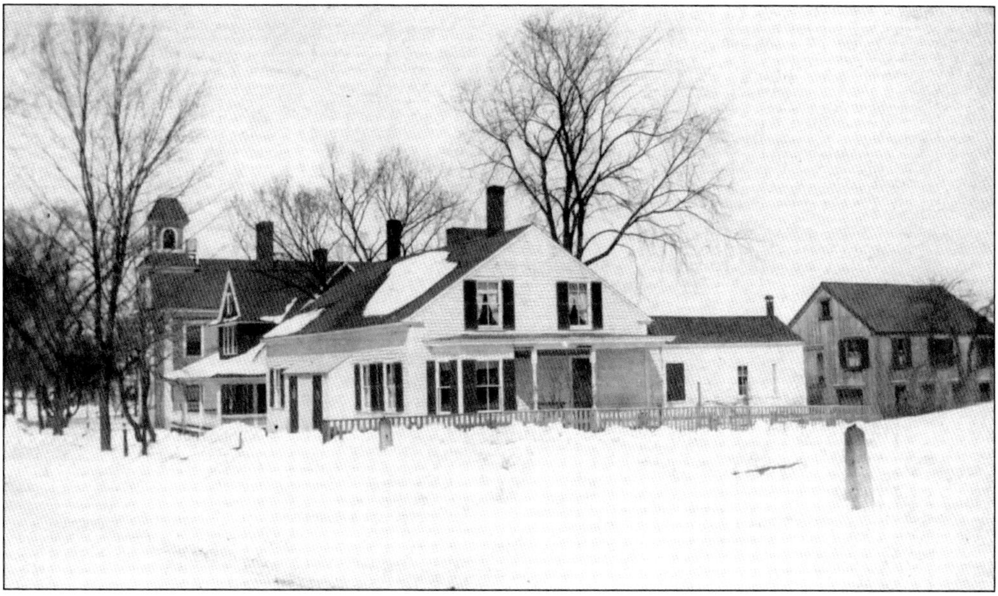

Mary E. Richardson owned the house at 1–3 North Road since 1867, and Albert H. Davis and his wife, Ellen (née Richardson) Davis, Mary's younger sister, came to live here in 1884. Albert built the two-story workshop behind the house, seen above. When Albert's father died in 1909, Albert moved to the family's Boulder Farm on Davis Road and sold the workshop to James P. Emerson, who combined it with a barbershop from Chelmsford Street to make a house at 20 Fletcher Street. Albert returned to North Road with his family in 1921 and built another workshop similar to the original, as seen below under construction in 1923. Albert's son Leslie R. Davis built the house on the left at 5 North Road in 1904 on land purchased from his aunt Mary. (Above, Chelmsford Historical Society Collection; below, David Brow.)

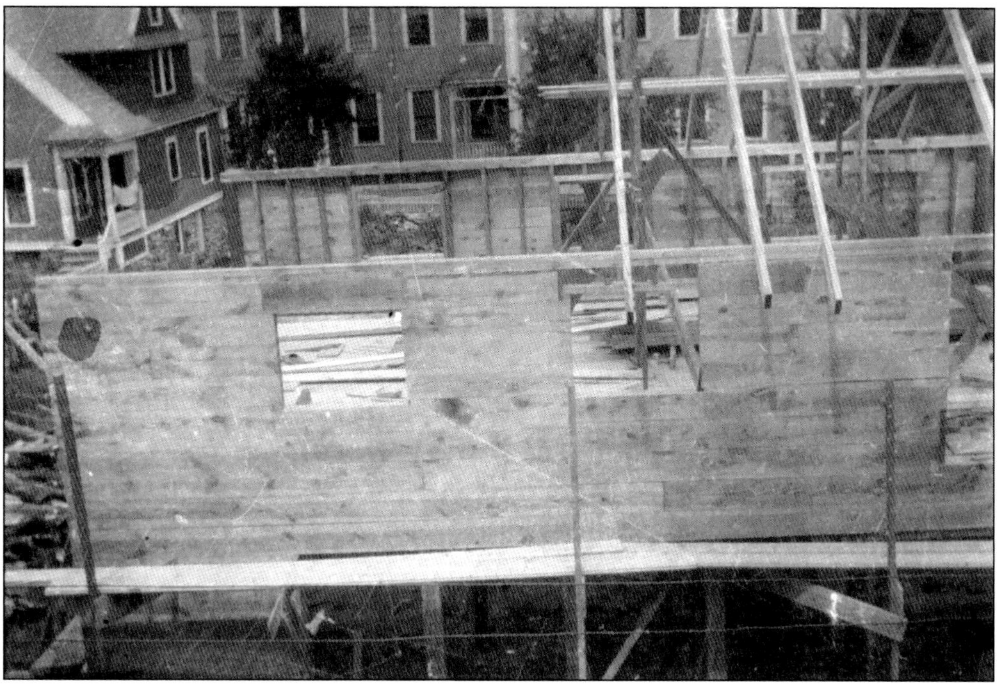

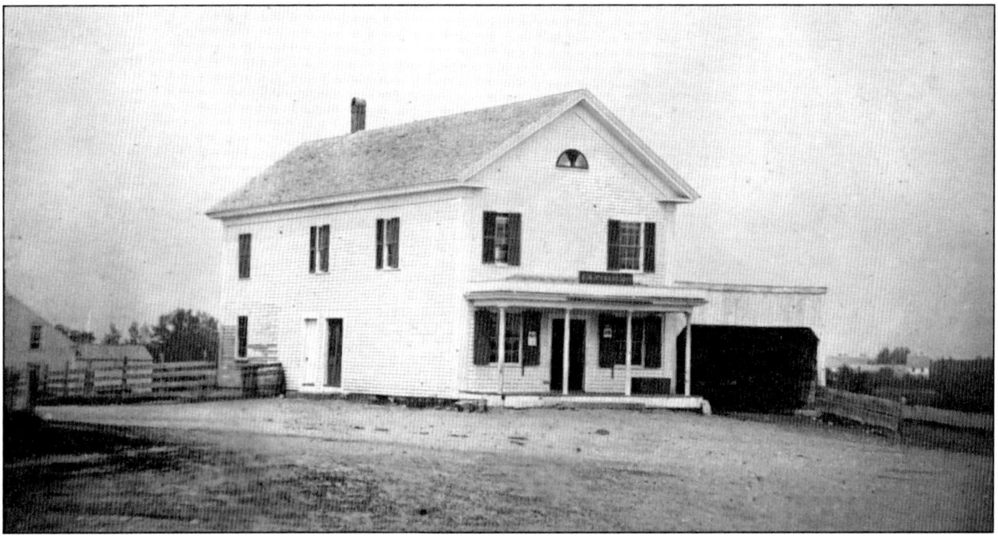

This c. 1870 image shows, from left to right, the Richardson-Davis house, the 1861 Edwin K. Parkhurst store, and the Amos B. Adams farm. An upstairs room in the store called Central Hall was used by the Soldiers' Aid Society for charitable activities during the Civil War. The store was moved to 2 Chelmsford Street in 1871 to make room for the Framingham & Lowell Railroad. (Chelmsford Historical Society Collection.)

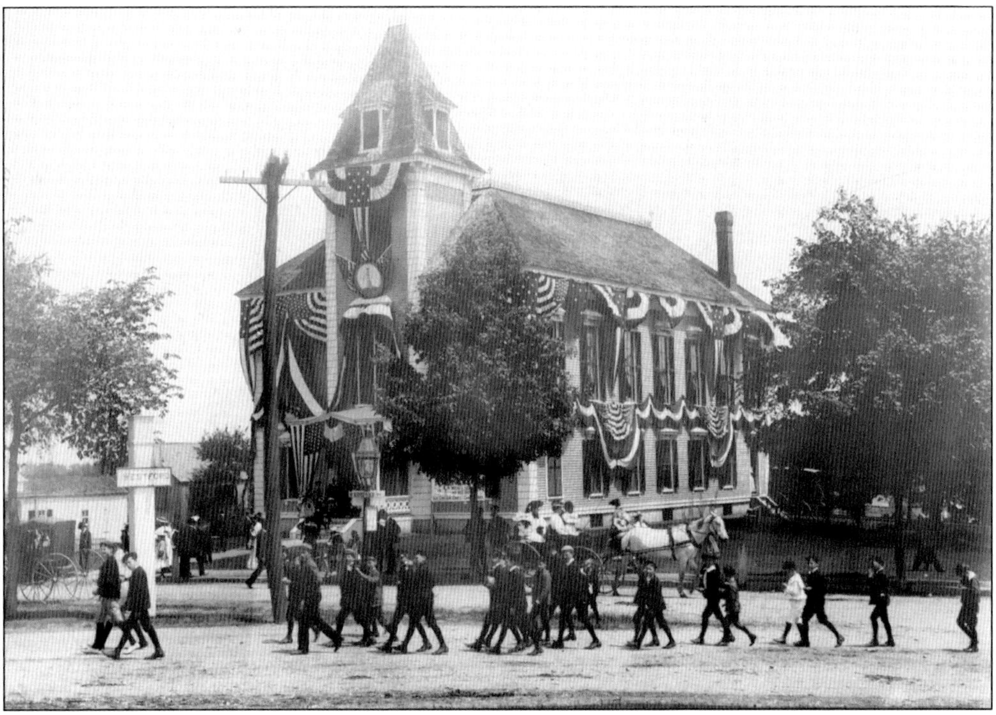

Chelmsford's 250th anniversary celebration took place from May 28 to May 31, 1905. May 30 (Tuesday) started with a Memorial Day address and music by the Chelmsford Centre Band. In this photograph, Simon Towle likely captured the children headed to one of the afternoon children's events. Prof. F.O. Harrell, a magician and entertainer, followed by sports, games, and more music by the band provided entertainment. (Chelmsford Historical Society Collection.)

Five

SAWMILLS

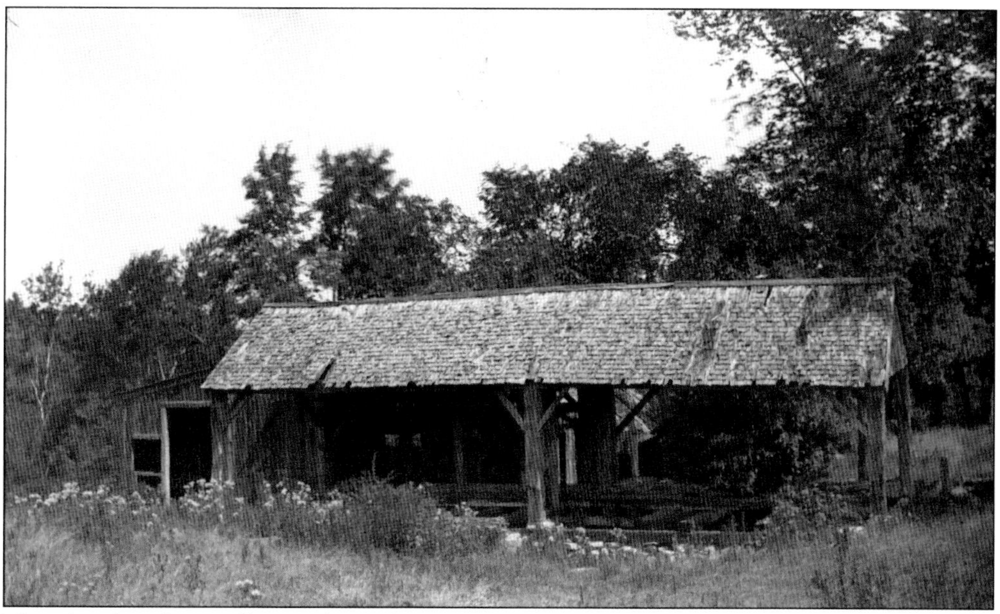

This abandoned sawmill around 1888 has an up-and-down blade at its center. A pitman pulled the blade down to make the cut, and a top man above pulled the blade up. When a source of running water was available, the rotating shaft from a waterwheel was converted to the up-and-down motion of the saw blade by means of a pitman arm. (Chelmsford Historical Society Collection.)

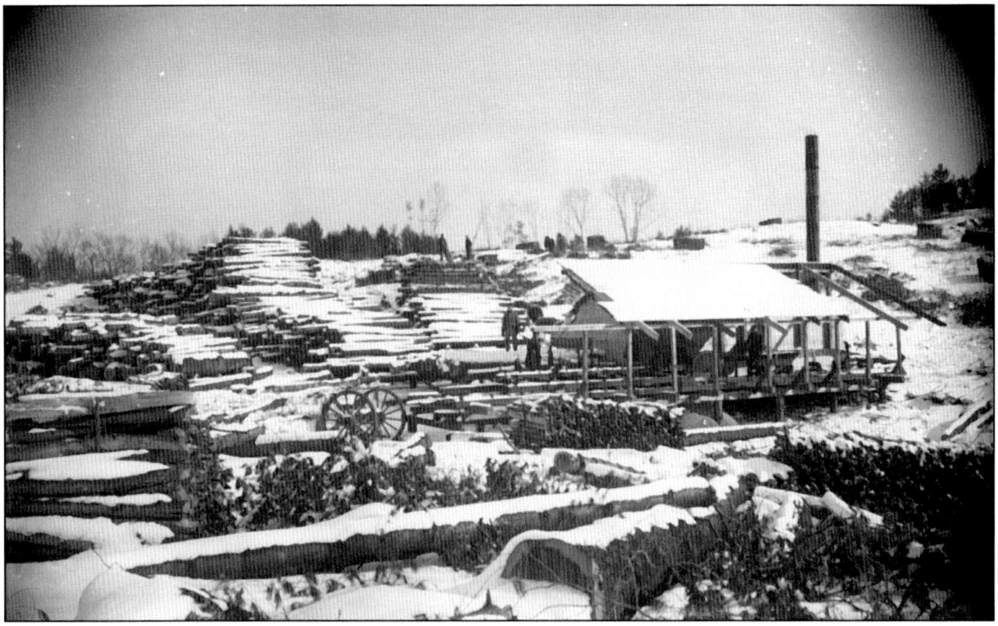

Steam power was a portable and reliable source of power for milling lumber in the late 1800s and could be purchased as a kit and set up near the source of timber. A temporary shelter was built over a carefully aligned log carriage, tracks, circular saw arbor, and feed works coupled to an engine by belts, shafts, and pulleys. The mill owner provided the steam engine and boiler. (Chelmsford Historical Society Collection.)

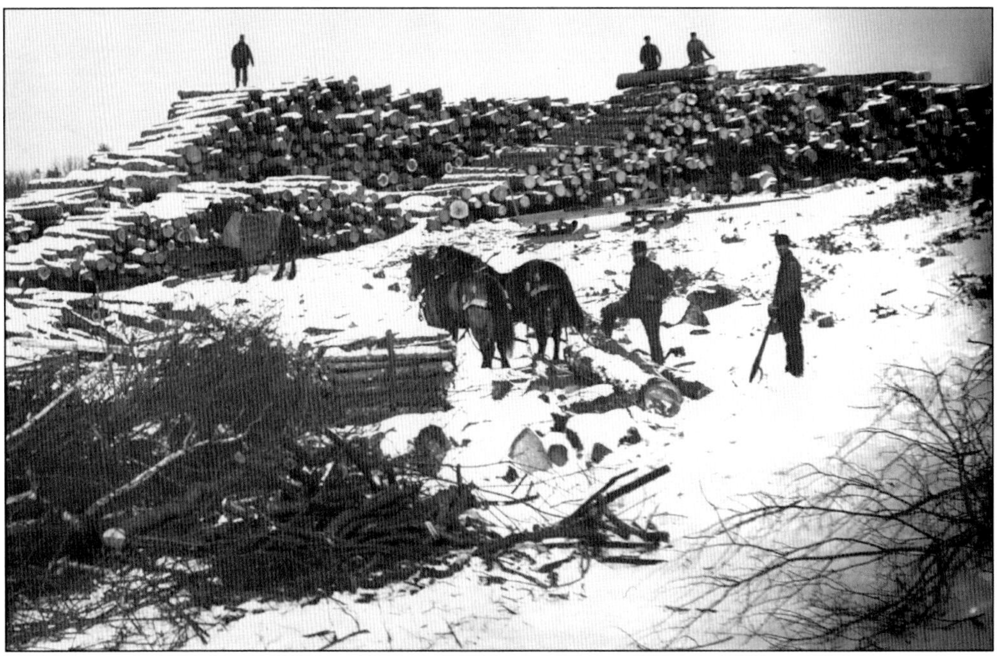

A sled for carrying smaller bundles of wood and supplies, a heavy sledge for carrying logs, and a sleigh for moving people can all be seen in this photograph. In the foreground, a team of horses is hitched up to a log for dragging through rough terrain. The two men on top of the pile with peaveys can roll large logs around the yard. (Chelmsford Historical Society Collection.)

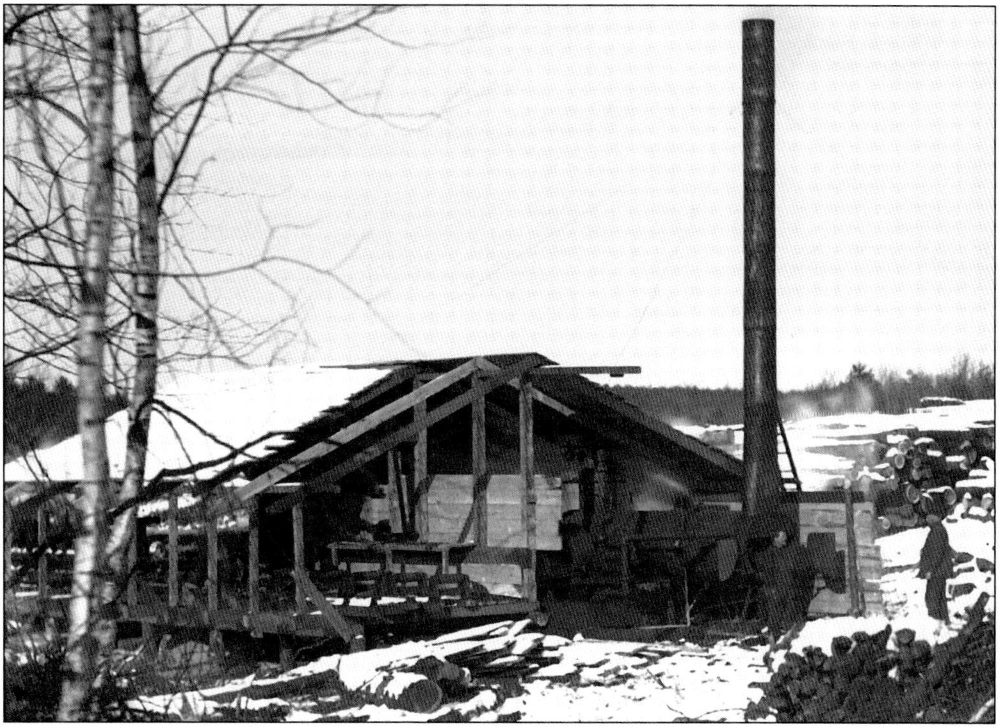

Steam pressure is up and ready to power the horizontal engine on the left side of the boiler in this photograph. The operator standing next to the open fire doors has a seemingly endless supply of wood to burn and a warm place to work. There is a small circular saw on a bench to the left of the engine for end cuts. (Chelmsford Historical Society Collection.)

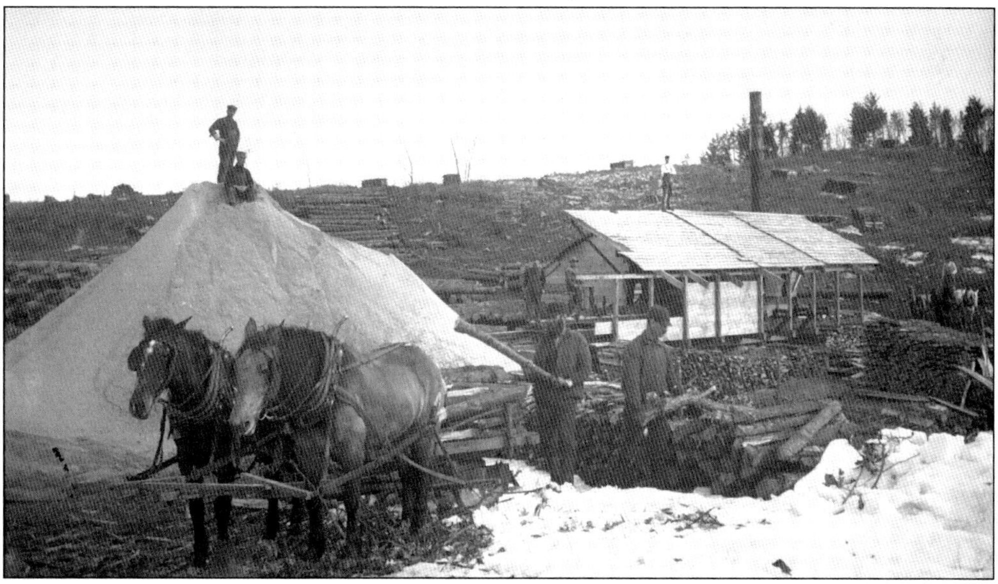

In this view of the same mill at a different time, much of the log pile has been milled into lumber, cordwood, and slabs. The lumber has been delivered to customers, but stacks of cordwood are spread across the field for seasoning. The sawdust likely found its way to the many dairy farms in the area as biodegradable bedding for the cows. (Chelmsford Historical Society Collection.)

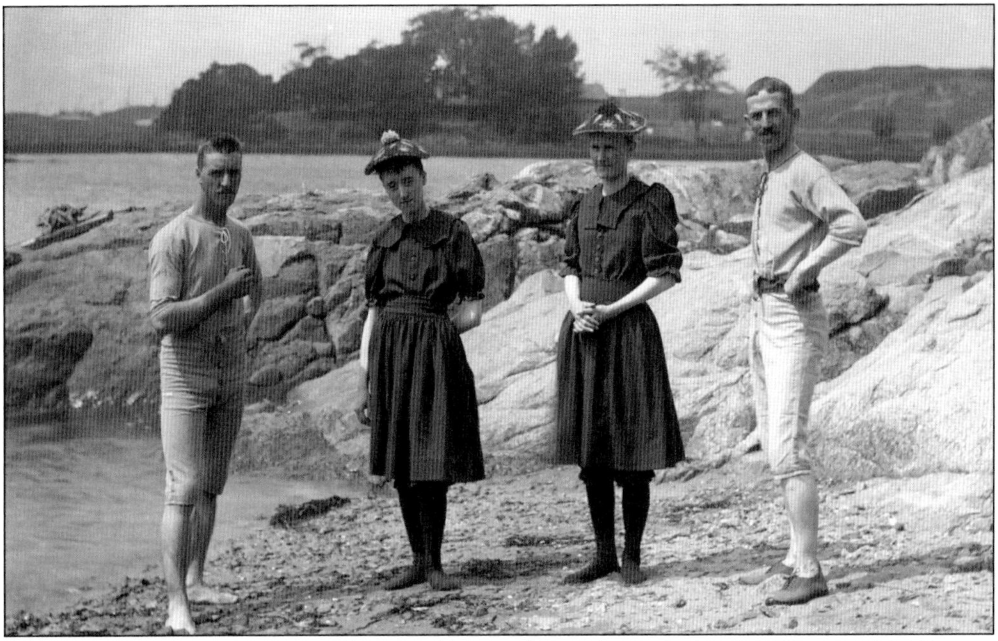

The owner of at least one portable sawmill on Mill Road was Arthur M. Warren of 86 Boston Road. Pictured at this c. 1895 beach outing are, from left to right, Arthur M. Warren; his wife, Mabel E. Warren; Emma L. Parkhurst; and Arthur I. Emerson. Mabel was an Emerson cousin and was the first in the area to wear a white wedding gown instead of a traditional dark color. (Chelmsford Historical Society Collection.)

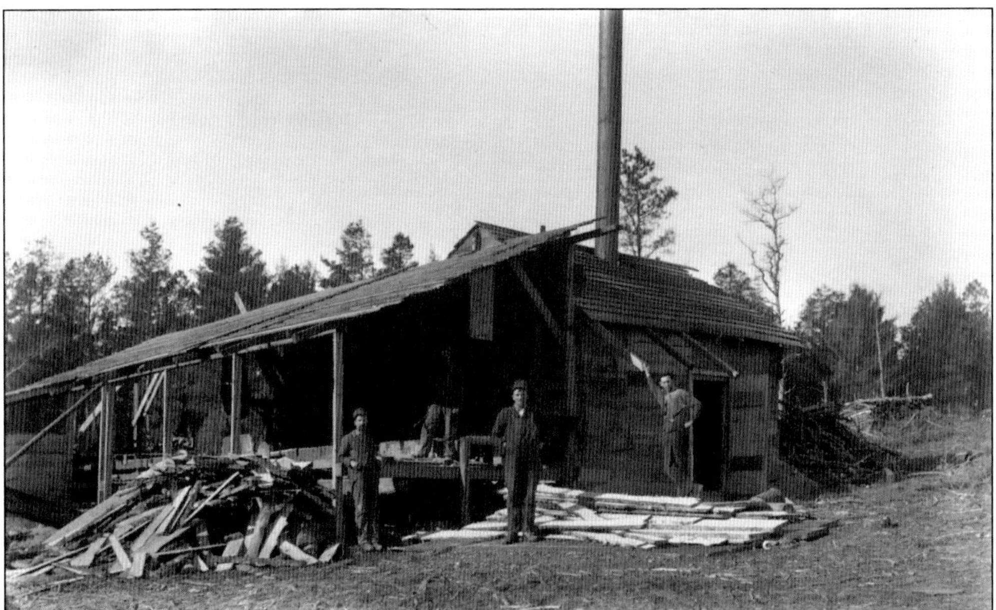

Arthur I. Emerson is dressed for work and holding onto a roof rafter while someone else takes this photograph with his camera. The teeth on the main blade in this mill are surprisingly large, and there is a smaller overhead blade staggered ahead of the main blade for cutting oversized logs. The crew has taken a break to pose for the photograph. (Chelmsford Historical Society Collection.)

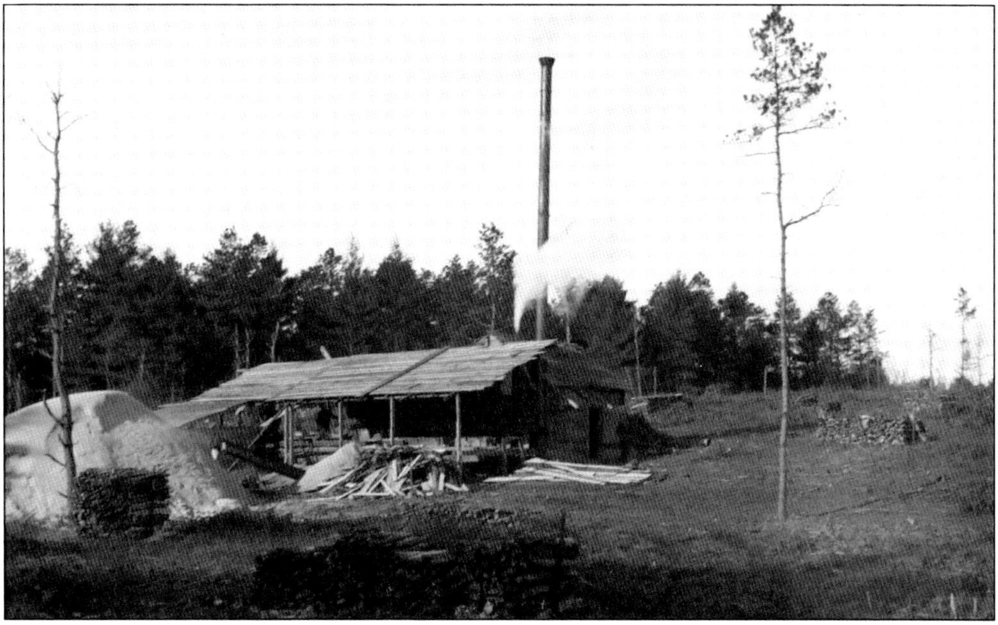

In the photograph above, the crew is running a log through the saw. The mill is operating under a full head of steam, and a blower is forcing sawdust onto the pile through a wooden chute. Two men are at the controls by the log carriage, and Arthur I. Emerson is leaning on the door of the enclosed engine house. After a snowstorm, in the photograph below, there are a few logs ready to roll onto the carriage, but the mill is idle. The heavy-duty axle seen on the right would be used to move logs when there was not enough snow for dragging or sledging. (Both, Chelmsford Historical Society Collection.)

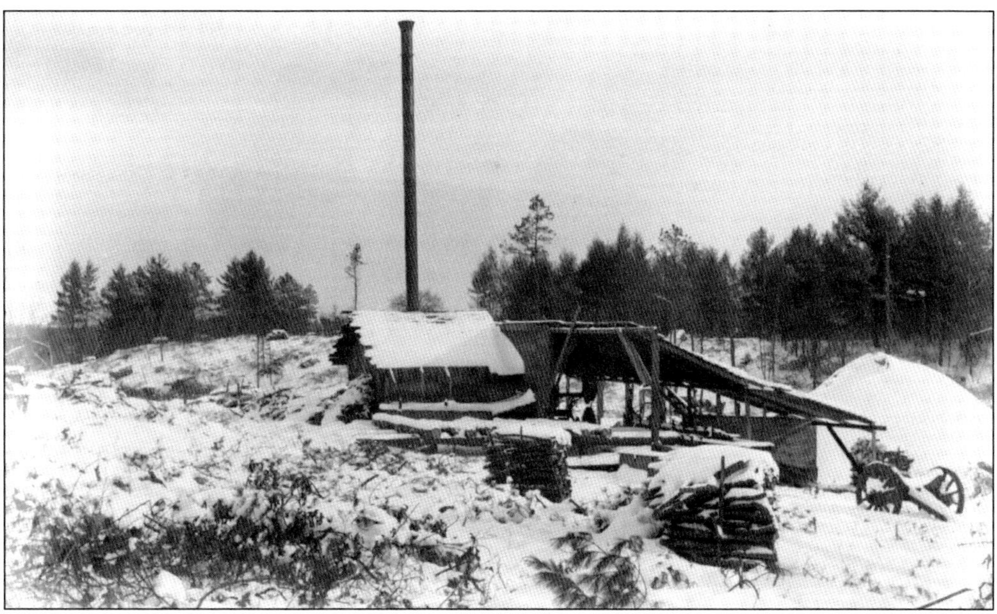

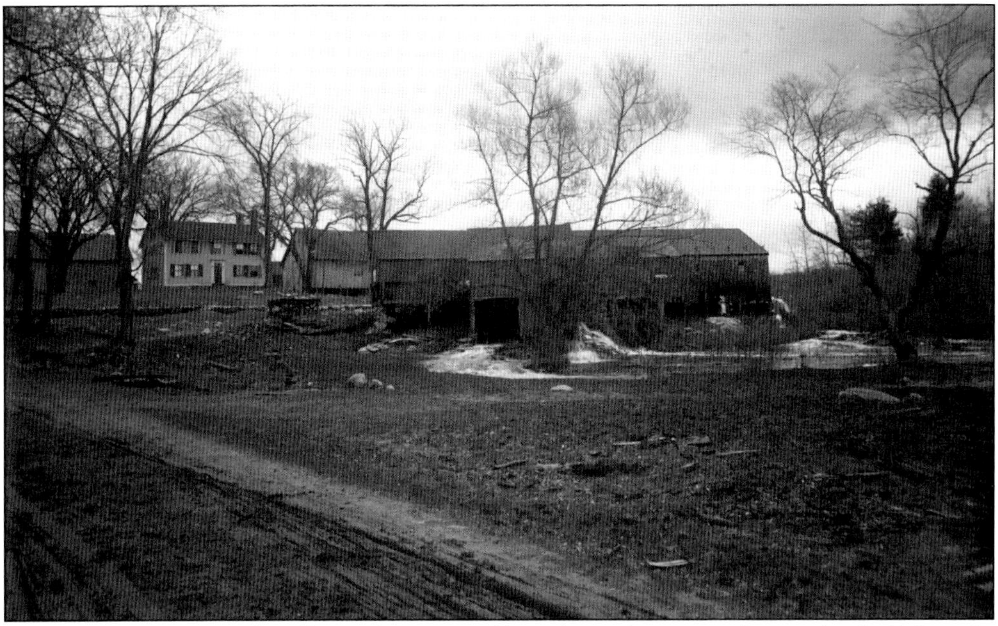

This is the Adams-Russell Mill complex at 99 Mill Road in its last years of ownership by E. Lincoln Russell around 1895. Pictured, from left to right, are the barn, house, icehouse, and sawmill. Lumber was not being produced at this time, but the millpond water appears to be overflowing the spillways and passing through the sawmill building after some heavy rain. (Chelmsford Historical Society Collection.)

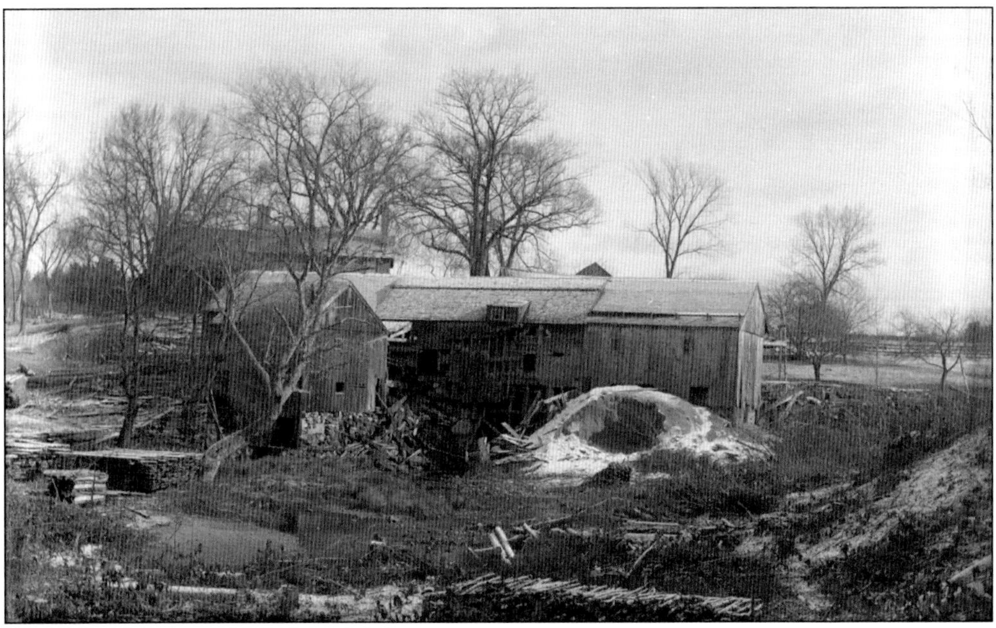

This c. 1905 image by Fred W. Park shows that the sawmill is in shabby condition but is producing lumber again. Arthur M. Warren, who had previously harvested much of the forestland on Mill Road using portable sawmills, purchased the Adams-Russell Mill property in September 1904 and sold it in December 1905. He also ran the icehouse operation on the pond for several years. (Chelmsford Historical Society Collection.)

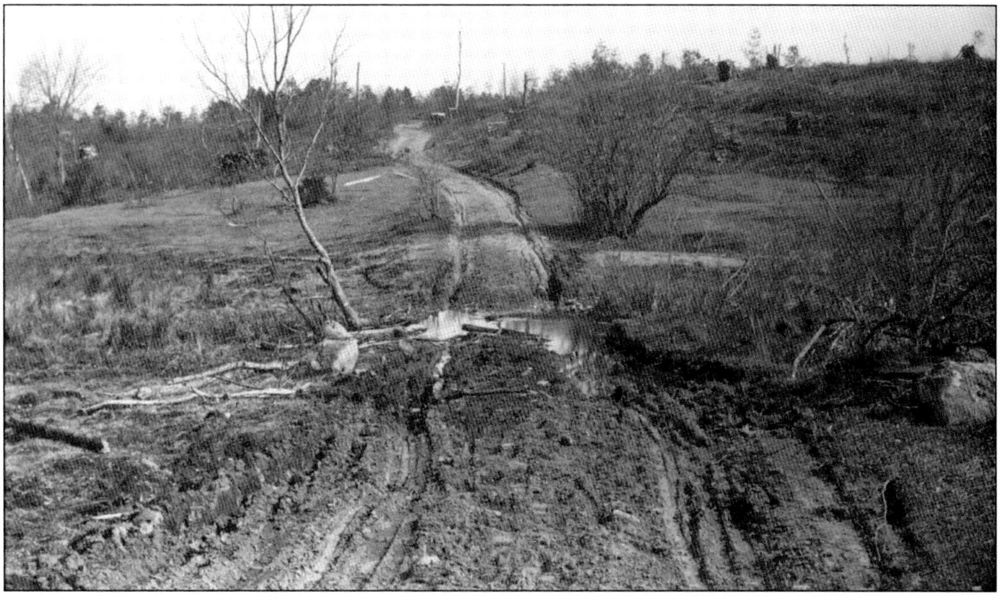

On June 9, 1901, a headless body was discovered behind a woodpile in this woodlot off Mill Road, and the next day, a head was found in River Meadow Brook under the Mill Road Bridge seen below. On January 17, 1904, J. Wilfrid Blondin of Boston confessed to the murder of his wife of three months, Margaret C. Blondin, back in April 27, 1901. Blondin eluded police until February 1902, when he was captured in New York City, but the truth of what happened was not known until the trial in Lowell in 1904. They were having financial trouble, and he took her to a bank in Lowell believing she had money in an account there, and on discovering she did not, he took her to Chelmsford under the pretext of visiting a rich uncle and strangled her. (Both, Chelmsford Historical Society Collection.)

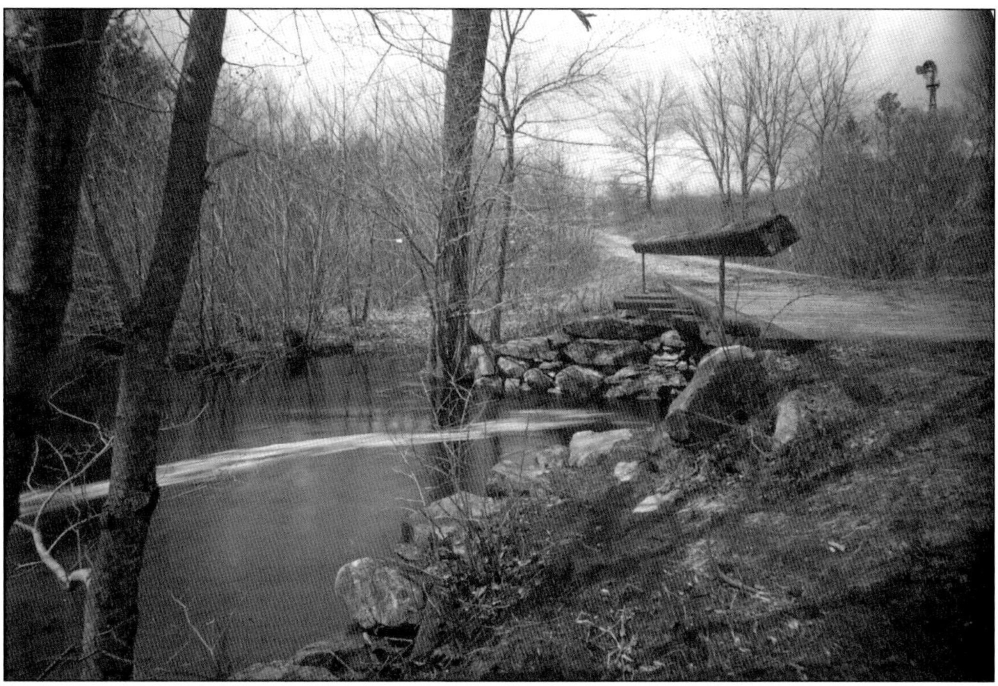

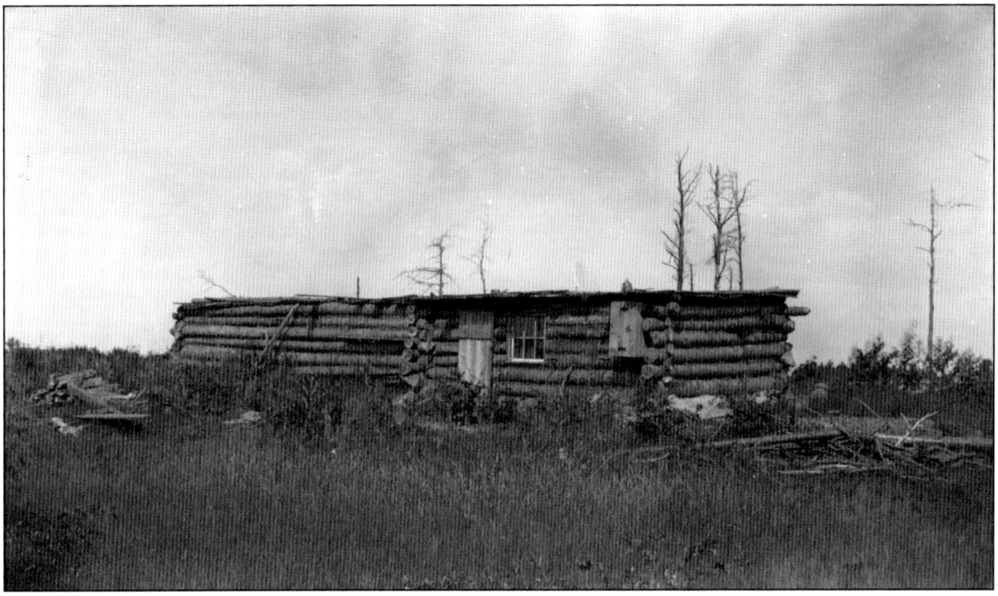

The temporary shack above was described as "a woodchopper's log house 1888." The c. 1895 view below from one of Arthur M. Warren's woodlots shows the intersection of Mill Road and Boston Road with both South Row Schools to the right of center. The smaller first school was built of brick in 1801, discontinued in 1870, and became a residence until torn down around 1958. The second school, built in 1871 with a recessed entrance, served as a school until 1935. The South Row Improvement Association used the building from 1947 to 1955; the Veterans of Foreign Wars, until 1974; and, finally, the town, as its Senior Drop-in Center, from 1977 to 1989. The James H. Hazen farm at 203 Boston Road, now the site of the Chelmsford Lumber Company, is to the left of the second school. (Both, Chelmsford Historical Society Collection.)

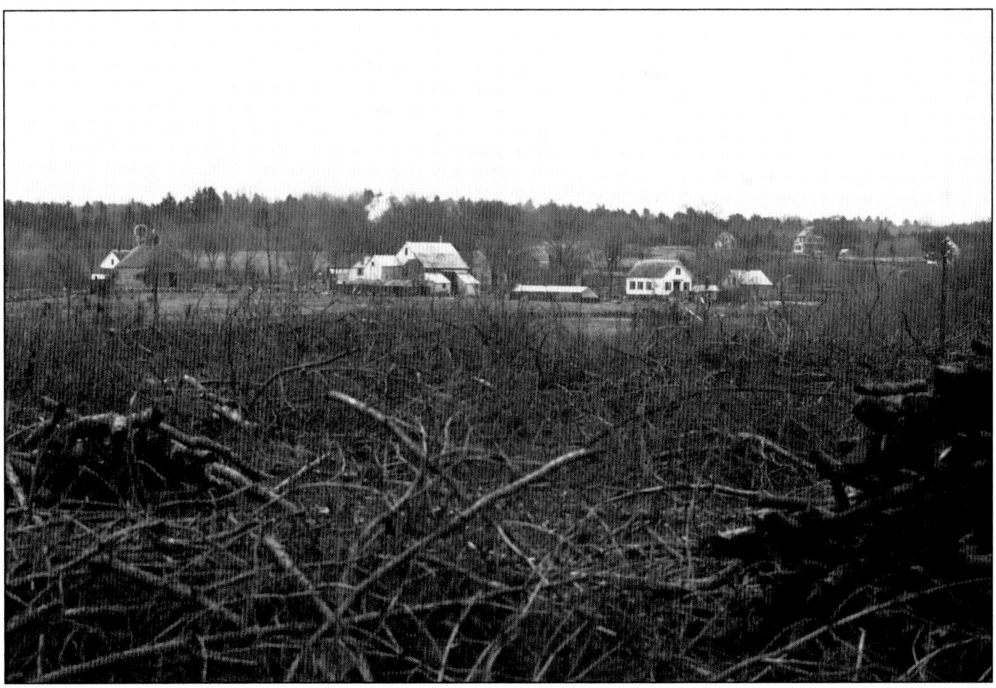

Six

Acton Road and High Street

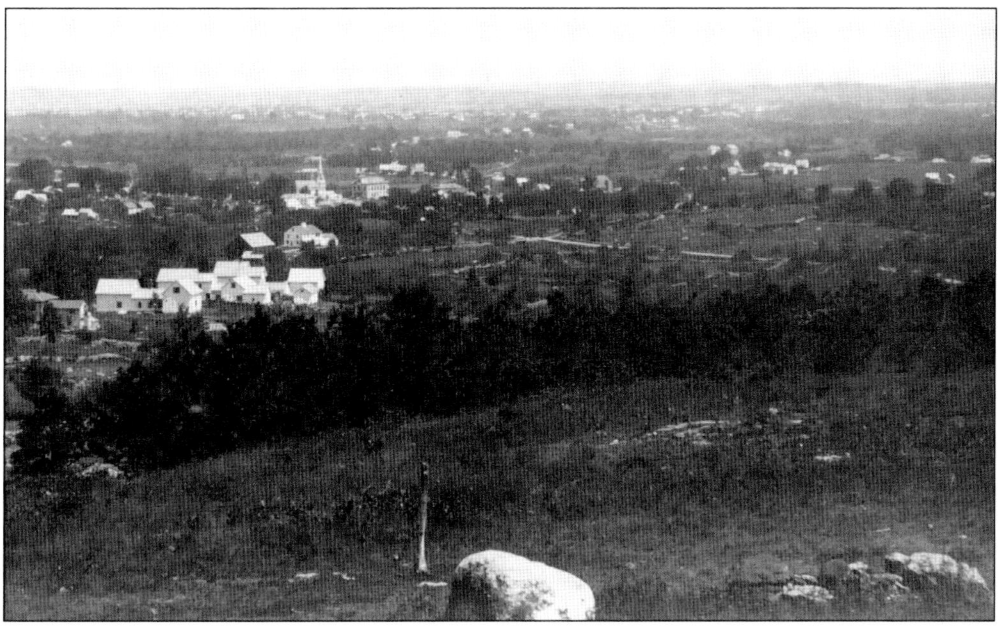

There were no houses at the intersection of High Street and Acton Road (directly above the rock) when this photograph was taken from Robins Hill in August 1887. The Parkhurst family owned most of the land on High Street, and Dr. John C. Bartlett owned most of the land seen here on Acton Road. Subdivision began after train service to Lowell started in 1871. (Chelmsford Historical Society Collection.)

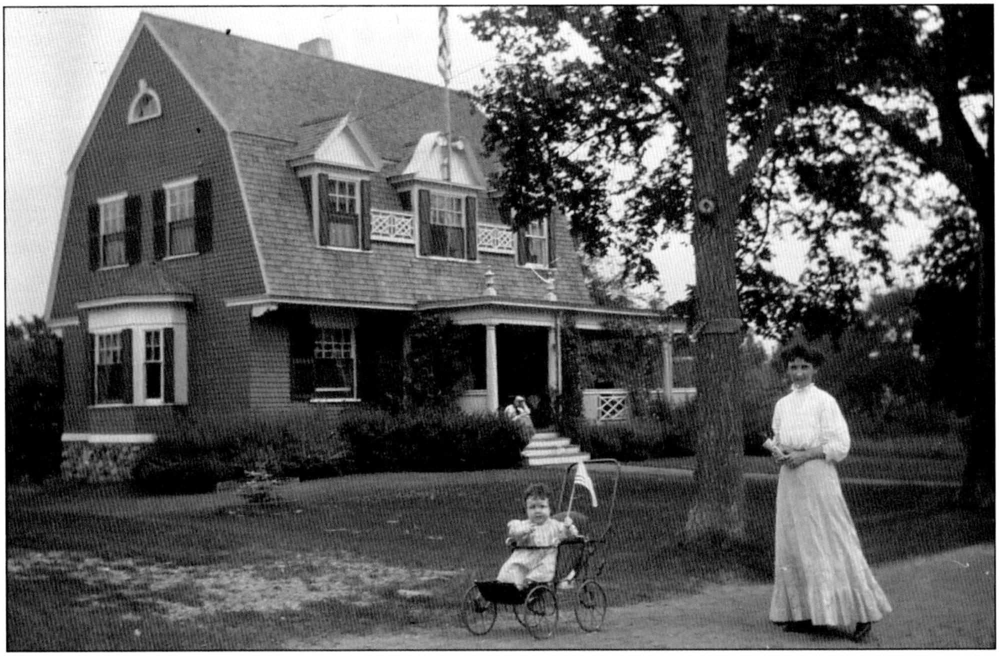

Millie May Parkhurst and her daughter Barbara Alice are in front of 15 Acton Road with Flora H. Jefts sitting on the front steps in this 1908 image. Millie and Winthrop Adams Parkhurst were married in 1900 and purchased this house in 1901. This home was razed in 1973, and the site became a parking lot for the brick Bowl-O-Rama Building constructed next door. (Chelmsford Historical Society Collection.)

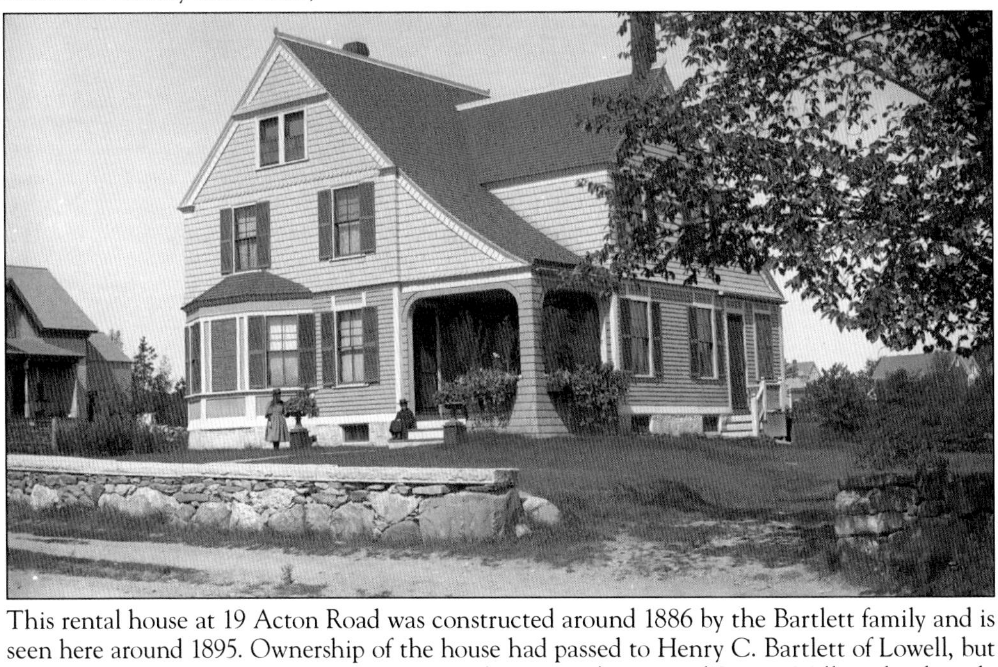

This rental house at 19 Acton Road was constructed around 1886 by the Bartlett family and is seen here around 1895. Ownership of the house had passed to Henry C. Bartlett of Lowell, but there was no indication of who was renting at this time. The Central Square Millpond is directly behind the house, and houses on Littleton Road are seen on the right. (Chelmsford Historical Society Collection.)

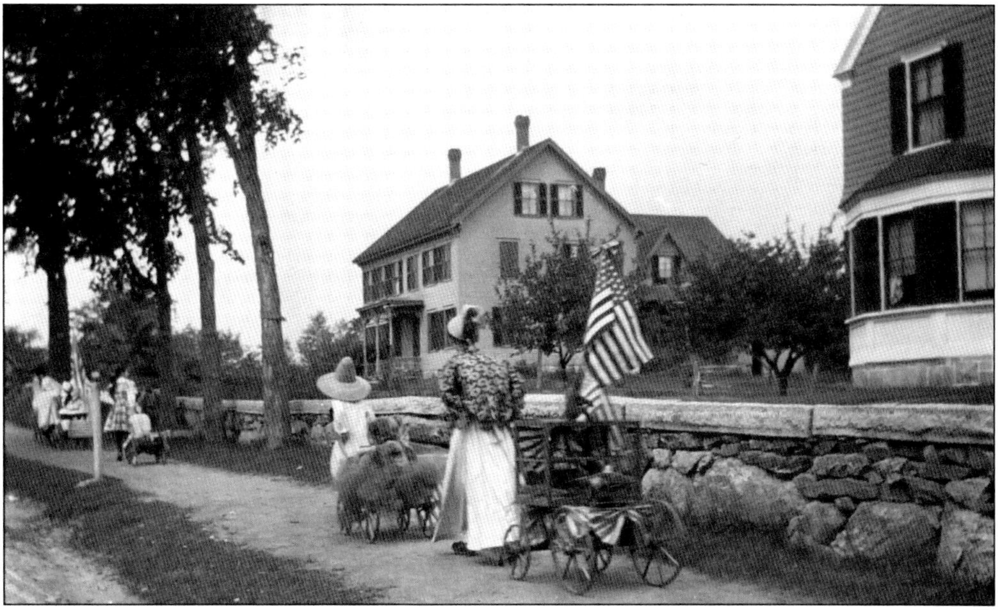

In this 1908 photograph taken in front of 19 Acton Road, neighbors pulling wagon floats with teddy bears and pets are returning from a Fourth of July parade. The 23–25 Acton Road two-family tenement at center was constructed in 1890 by builder Almon Holt for Jasper Elliott to take advantage of what was considered a prime location just a short walk from the train station and post office. (Chelmsford Historical Society Collection.)

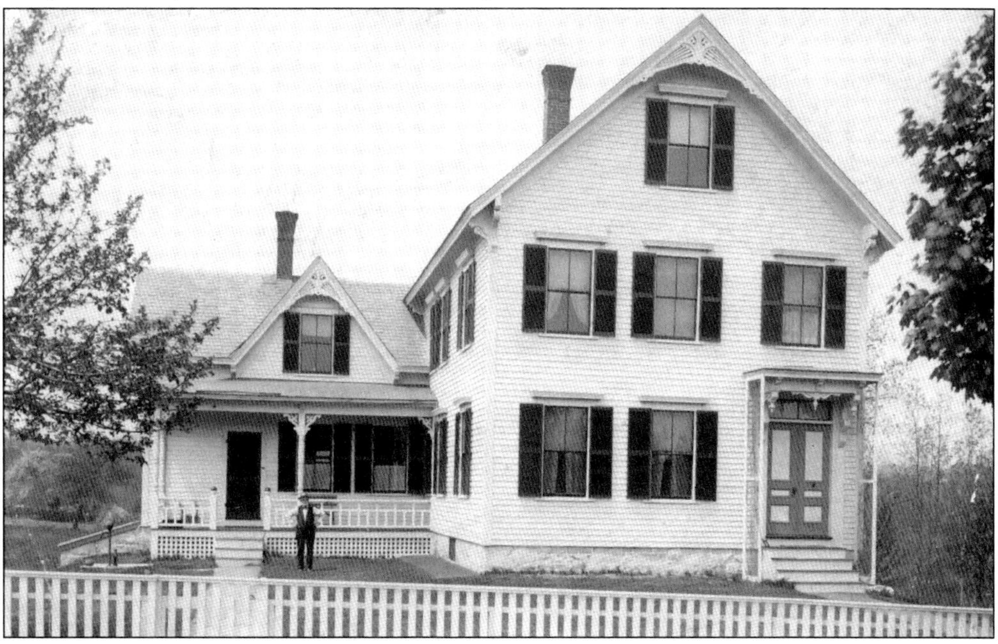

William H. Jefts had this house at 43 Acton Road built by Almon Holt in 1890 on a lot subdivided from the Sewall Parkhurst farm at 35 High Street by new owner Paul F. Litchfield. William supervised the brass molding department in the Lowell Machine Shop foundry for 40 years and retired in 1895; his daughter Millie May married Winthrop A. Parkhurst in 1900. (Chelmsford Historical Society Collection.)

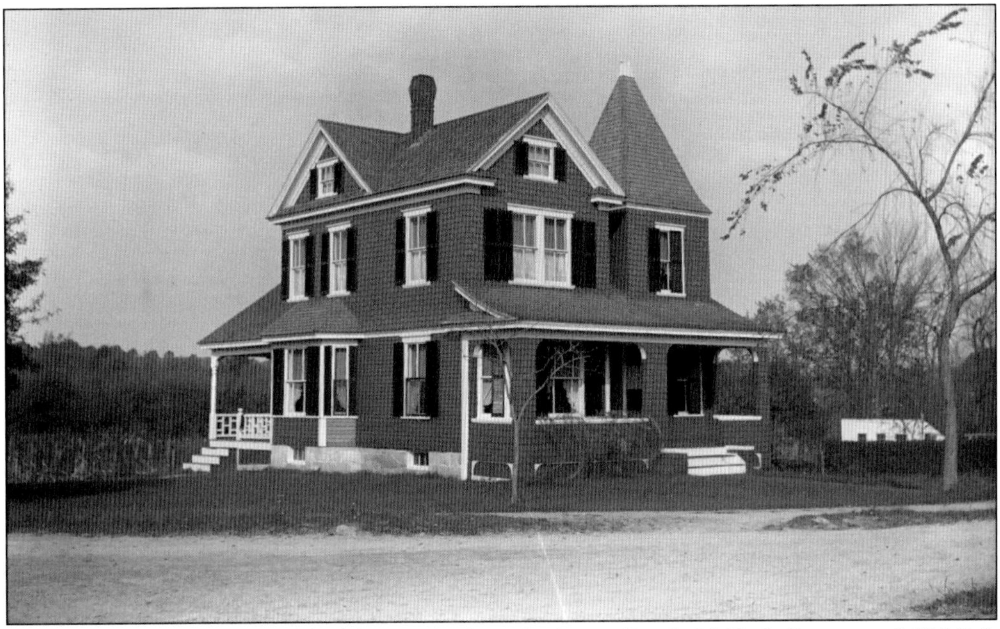

Paul F. and Sarah Litchfield had houses built at 51 Acton Road, 26 High Street, and 29 High Street on speculation in 1893. These were sold in 1895 to William Boland, a developer from Lynn, who planned a 60-house development on the former farm but sold off 51 Acton Road the same year. The large development, which would have included three new streets, was never built. (Chelmsford Historical Society Collection.)

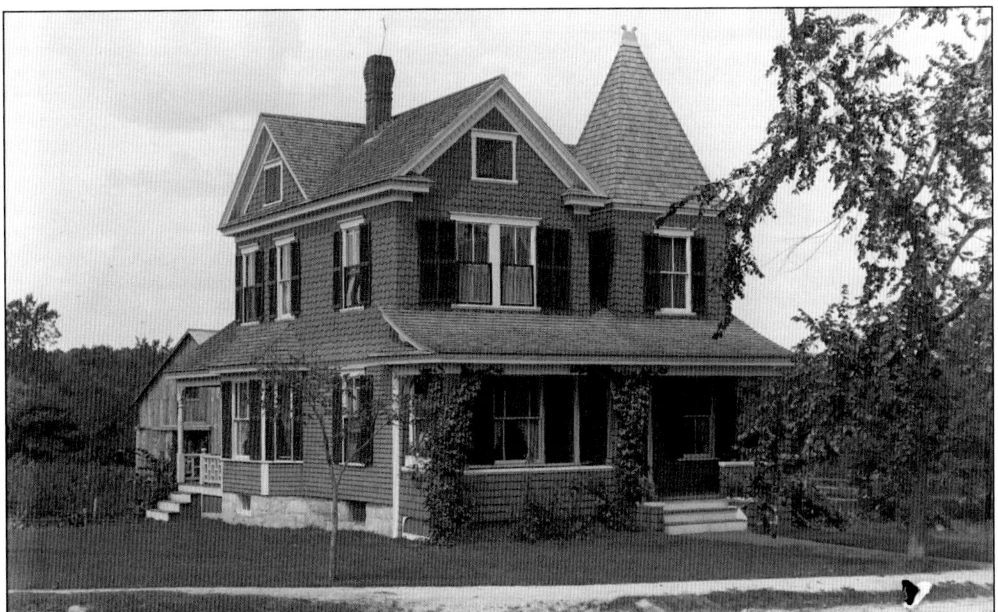

G. Thomas Parkhurst grew up on High Street and married Ednah Byam, daughter of South Chelmsford Civil War veteran Daniel P. Byam, in September 1902. That same year, he purchased the 51 Acton Road house. Their daughter Eleanor Parkhurst inherited the house in 1961, and it remained in the family until 2001. The new barn, seen here on the left, was built behind 29 High Street. (Chelmsford Historical Society Collection.)

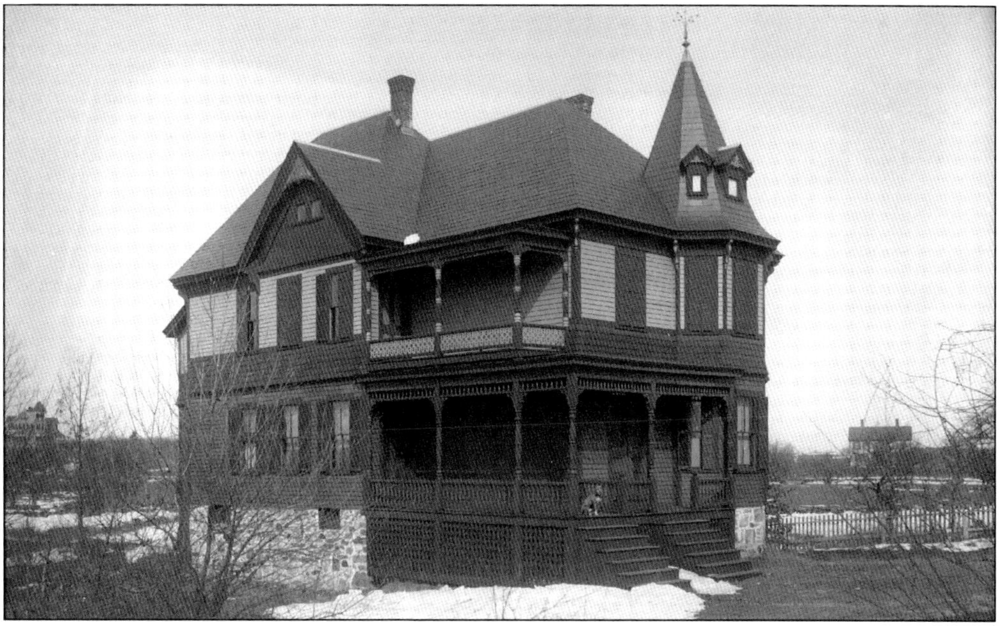

In 1888, Louis A. Young contracted Eugene Prescott to build this substantial Victorian two-family tenement at 77 Acton Road. The 55 High Street house, seen at left, was built for Dr. Frank R. Rix in 1893. The 35 High Street house is on the right, and in this c. 1895 view, Paul Litchfield has removed its center chimney and replaced it with two smaller ones. (Chelmsford Historical Society Collection.)

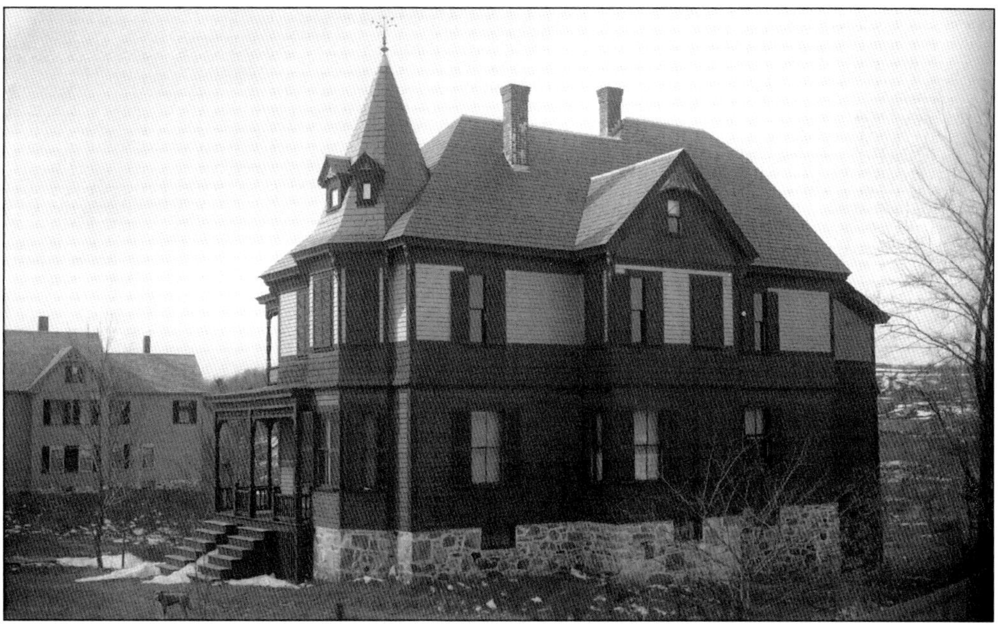

The first tenants in the 77 Acton Road rental were Chelmsford Center blacksmith George M. Wright and railroad flagman Philip Donahoe. Eugene Prescott built the 85 Acton Road house at left in 1887 as a single-family rental for Louis A. Young. The first tenant in that house was a Mr. Burdett who worked for the Byfield Company on Littleton Road. (Chelmsford Historical Society Collection.)

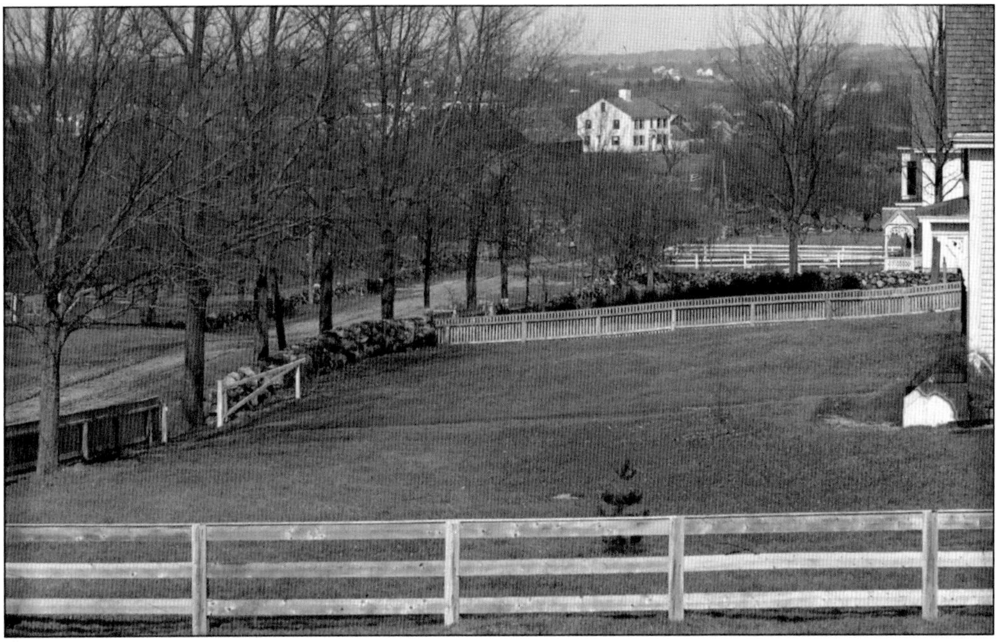

Sewall Parkhurst had teamed Chelmsford lime from the quarry on Littleton Road to Lowell during the heyday of mill construction in the 1820s. After his marriage in 1828, he farmed the land at 35 High Street until 1887, when he became ill. This view looking across several front yards on High Street shows the large center chimney later removed by Paul F. Litchfield. (Chelmsford Historical Society Collection.)

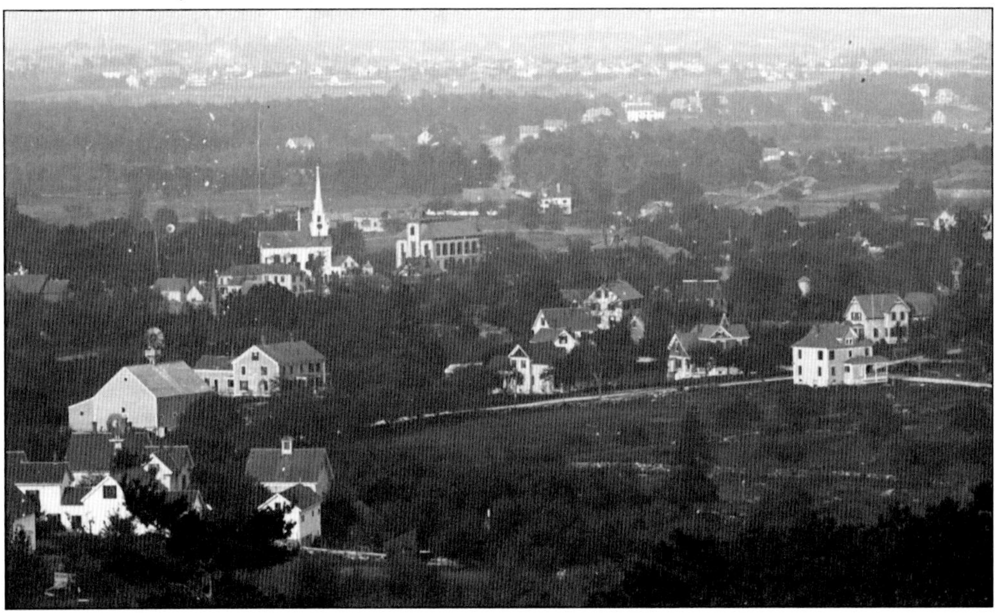

This c. 1895 view from the top of Robins Hill shows 35 High Street with a windmill on the barn roof and the three houses built by Paul F. Litchfield in 1893 at the intersection of High Street and Acton Road. The old farmhouse was converted into a summer residence in 1914 for tenant Harry G. Pollard, with the barn removed for gardens and a tennis court. (Chelmsford Historical Society Collection.)

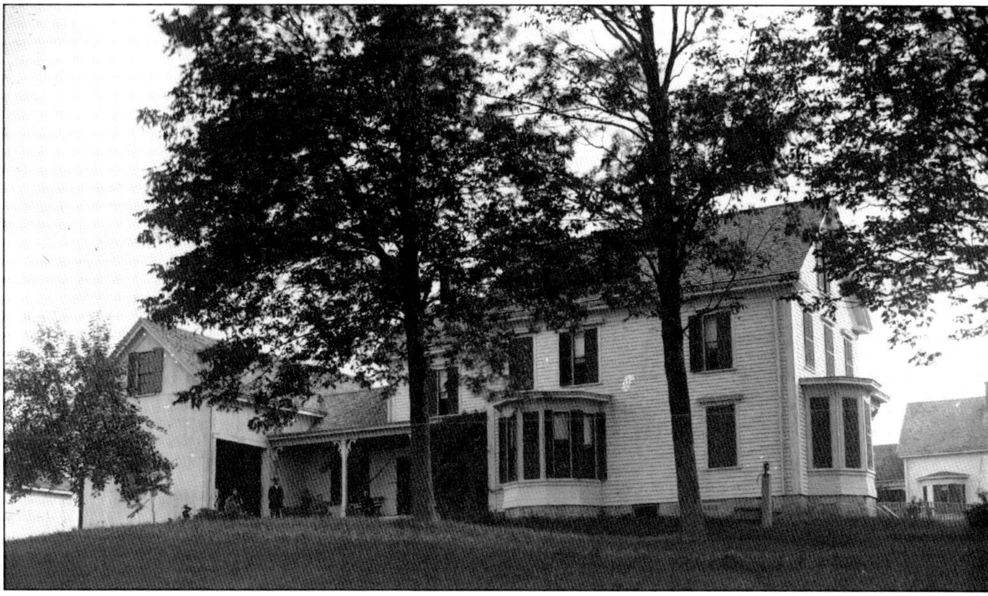

Jasper Elliott had three houses built on High Street. This one at 66 High Street was built in 1876 as his personal residence. Jasper was a retired machinist turned farmer, building rental homes on the side. Lowell Machine Shop contractor William H. Smith and his wife, Mary, purchased 66 High Street from Jasper Elliott in 1885 and are seen here in 1889. (Chelmsford Historical Society Collection.)

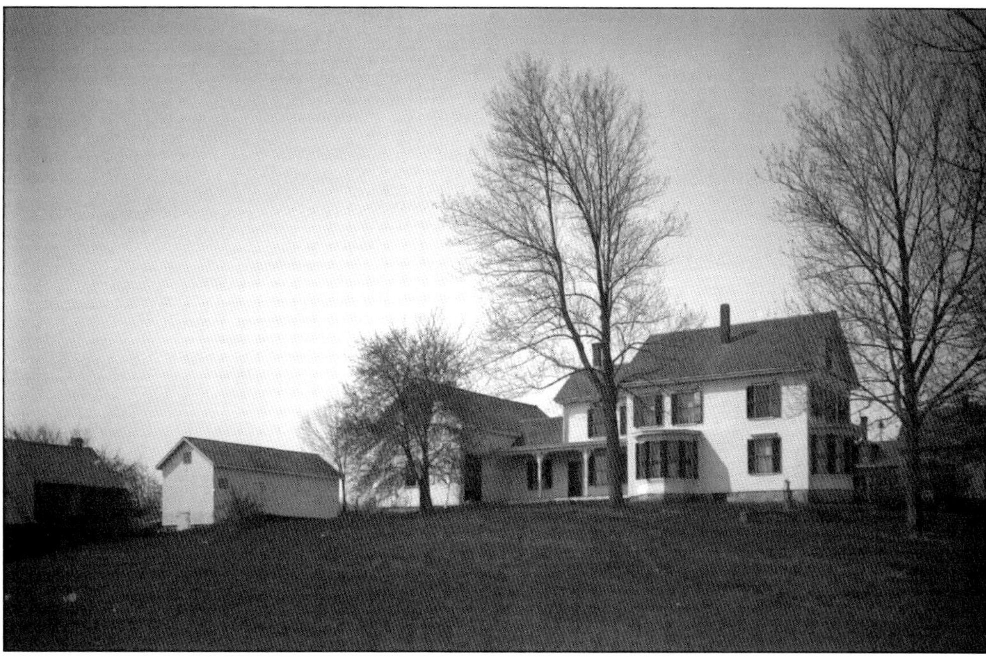

This photograph shows another view of 66 High Street and the house at 72 High Street on the right, which had a similar architectural design and floor plan. Jasper Elliott built 72 High Street in 1882 for his sister Sarah J. and her husband, Enos H. Hanson. Enos was employed by the Merrimack Corporation and later was a watchman in Lowell, but then took up farming in Chelmsford. (Chelmsford Historical Society Collection.)

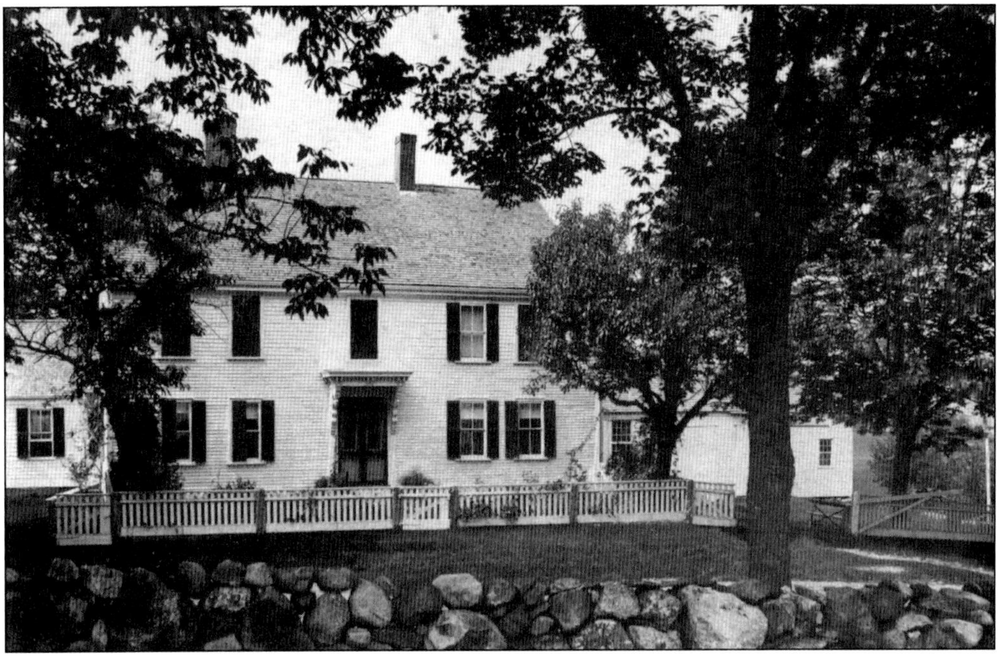

This August 1889 photograph, taken from across the street, shows the Solomon Parkhurst house at 67 High Street with its carriage house ell on the right. Solomon's father Josiah Parkhurst raised his family near what is now 75 High Street, and at one time, the family owned most of the land on High Street from there to Acton Road. (Linda Prescott.)

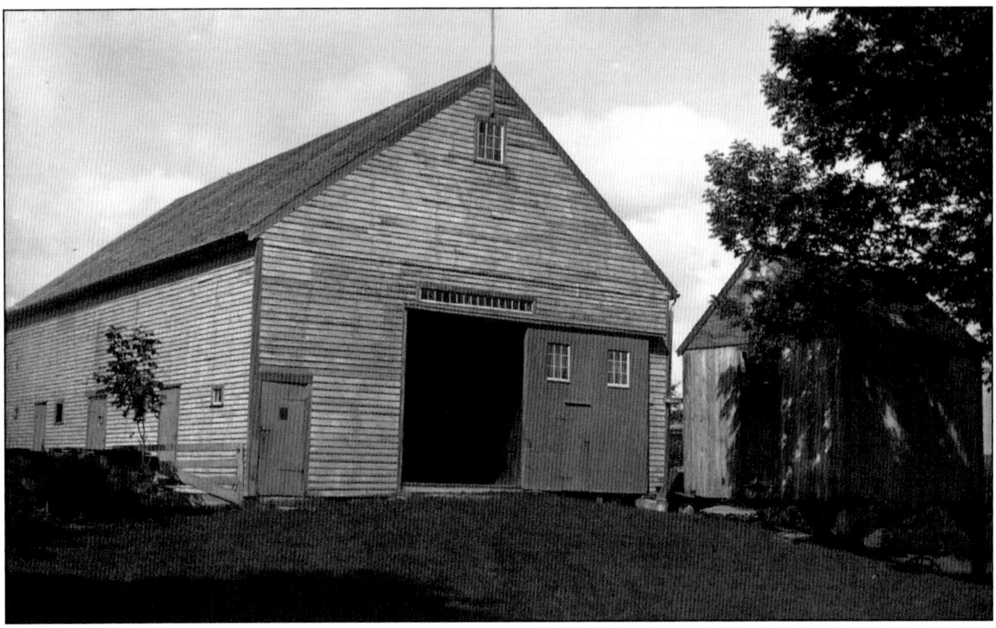

Corncribs, like this one at 67 High Street, had to be well ventilated all around because the fermentation process that creates the silage from chopped up corn stalks also generated nitric oxide, with resulting toxic by-products of nitrogen dioxide and liquid nitric acid. This pollution is carefully controlled on modern farms, and special bacteria are injected to speed up the fermentation process. (Chelmsford Historical Society Collection.)

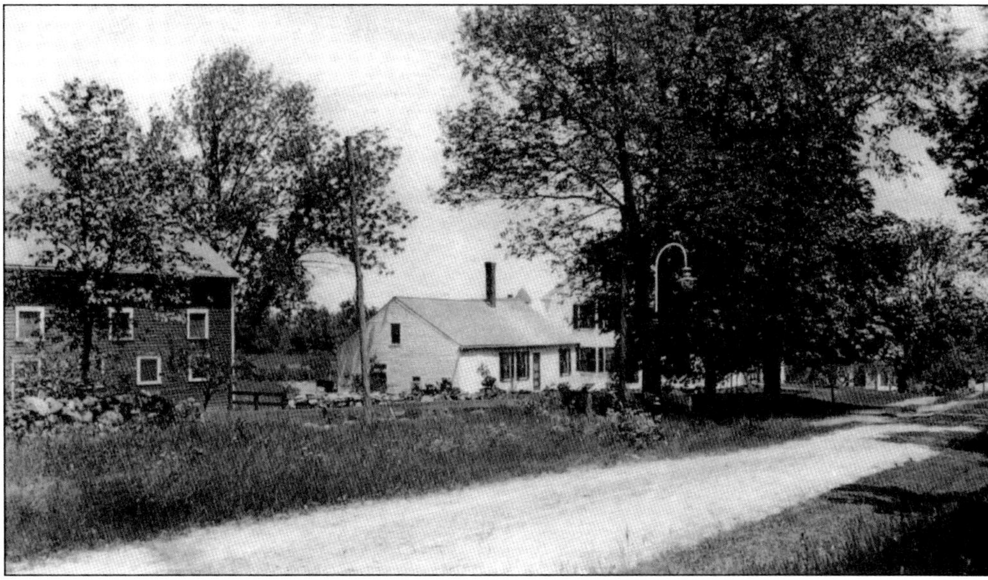

The barn at 67 High Street had been converted to living quarters sometime before 1910. Peter J. Brennan, who was in the business of house finishing and the manufacture of screens and windows, built the house beyond at 61 High Street in 1892. Melvin and Abby Walker lived there at the time of this c. 1910 photograph. (Linda Prescott.)

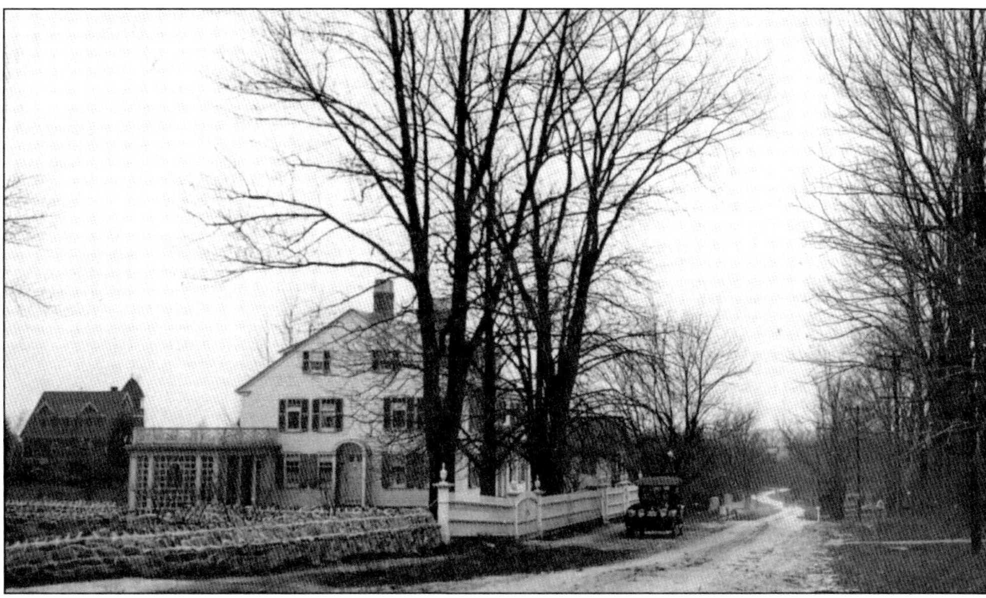

This November 1918 photograph shows significant changes at 67 High Street. The kitchen ell was replaced by a porch and deck, windows were added and relocated on the left end of the house, a mortared stone wall was built around the former barnyard, and three gables were added in the front of the third floor. The Dr. Rix house at 55 High Street is at left. (Linda Prescott.)

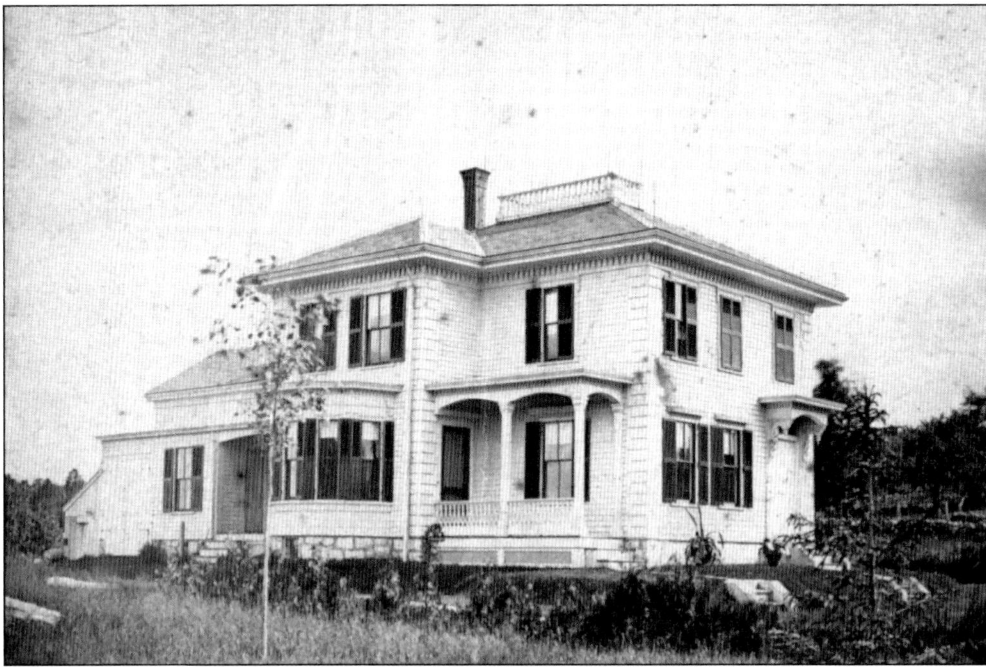

Solomon Parkhurst's son S. Waldo Parkhurst built the house at 78 High Street in the spring of 1876, and this photograph was taken about a year later. High Street was on an exposed ridge with frequent lightning strikes, so S. Waldo installed a lightning arrestor system with rods on the roof and heavy copper grounding wires as soon as the house was built. (John Crawford III.)

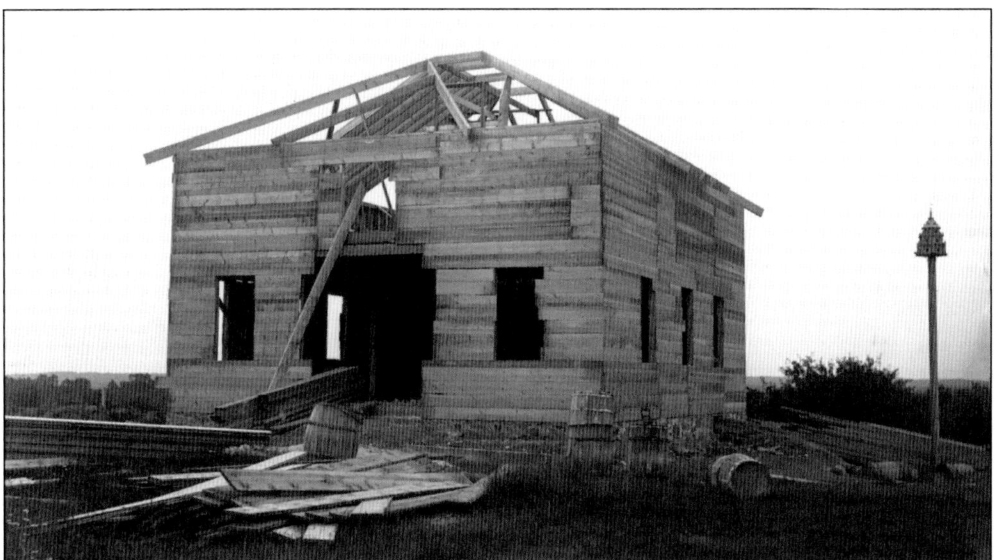

In 1891, S. Waldo Parkhurst constructed this carriage house for the family's transportation needs. The first floor had a workshop, tack room, and three horse stalls on the left side and open vehicle space on the right. Hay and water were stored on the second floor with a trap door and piping to deliver them to horse stalls. The basement had storage space and a chicken coop. (Chelmsford Historical Society Collection.)

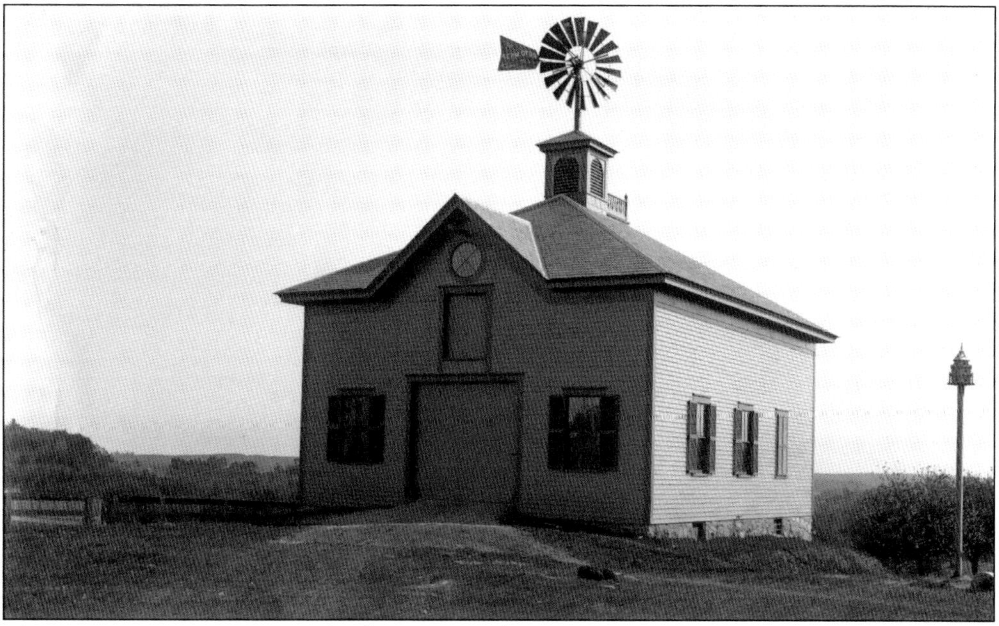

This Aermotor Company windmill transmitted up-and-down motion through a long wooden sucker rod to a pump in the basement, which filled a cistern on the second floor for the horses. There were mechanical cable connections so the owner could pull a lever to lock the sail and pull in the tail when power was not needed and read the water level in the cistern. (Chelmsford Historical Society Collection.)

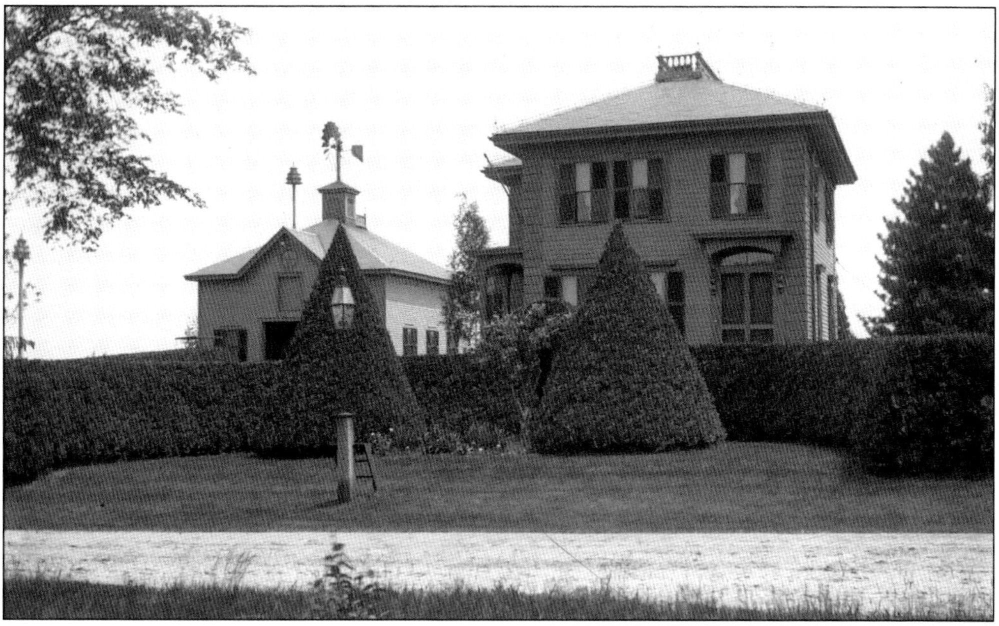

These well-manicured cone-shaped arborvitae bushes and apartment-style martin houses were a long-running tradition at 78 High Street. There was a heart-shaped garden at the center of the semicircle. The kerosene streetlamp on the front lawn had a permanent ladder for the convenience of the Village Improvement Association (VIA) lamplighter on his daily rounds. (John Crawford III.)

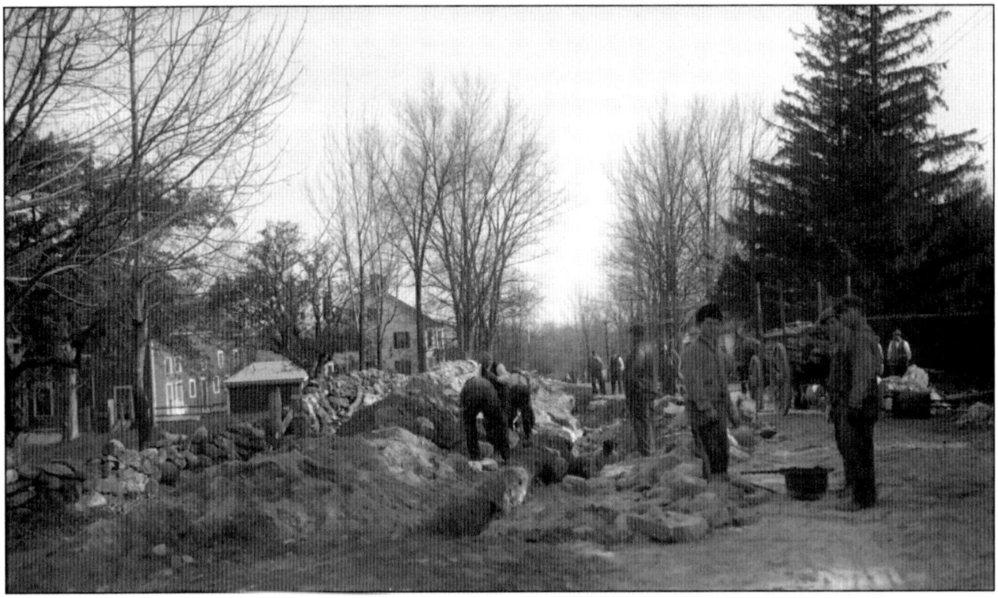

S. Waldo Parkhurst was one of the petitioners in 1895 to see if Baptist Pond, Newfield Pond, or a reservoir on high ground such as Robins Hill could be used to make a water supply system for domestic and fire protection use. No plan was adopted at this time. In 1911, a water district using well water from the River Meadow Brook watershed area and storage on Robins Hill was studied, and in 1913, the annual town meeting voted to authorize and the state legislature approved establishment of the Chelmsford Water District. These 1913 images show the crew hired by the newly formed Chelmsford Water District to install water mains, connecting a new water tower on the side of Robins Hill to a pumping station on Warren Avenue. (Both, Chelmsford Historical Society Collection.)

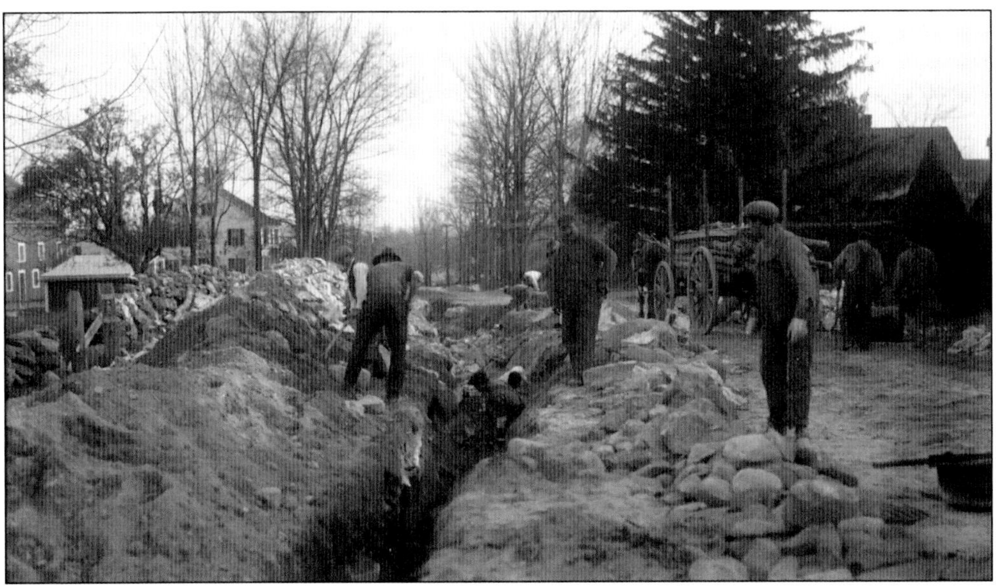

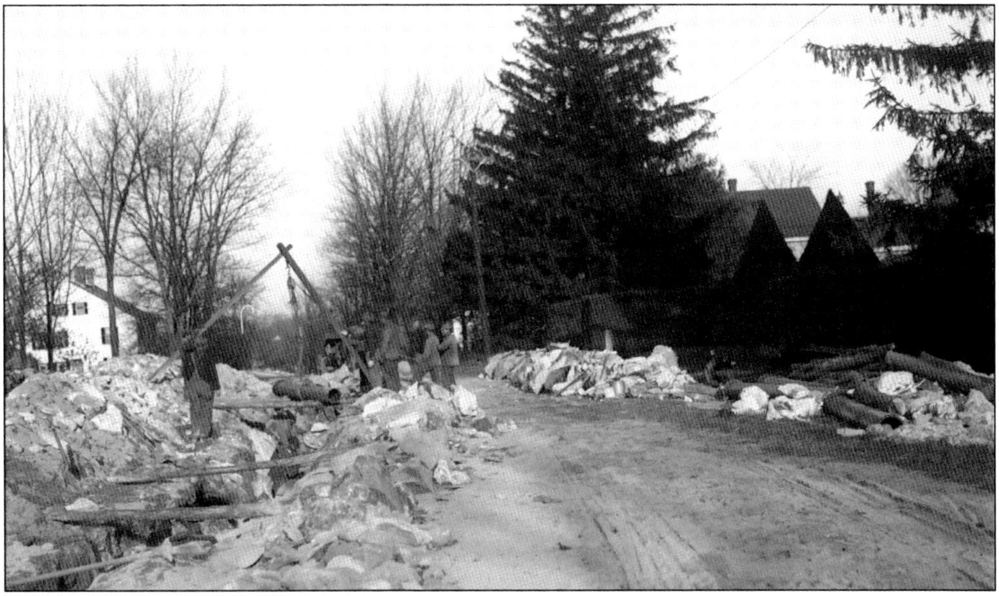

All the work was done by hand labor with shovels, iron bars, and, occasionally, dynamite to cut through the ledges and wooden poles and block and tackle to position the pipe. The image above shows that the soil under this section of High Street was extremely rocky. High Street residents were some of the first to get municipal water service, and the Dr. Rix house at 55 High Street had the first water meter installed in town. The VIA kerosene lamp in front of 78 High Street and the gas lamp at 67 High Street, seen under the pipe handling tripod in the photograph above, had been replaced by electric streetlamps, such as the one attached to the utility pole in the photograph below. (Above, Chelmsford Historical Society Collection; below, John Crawford III.)

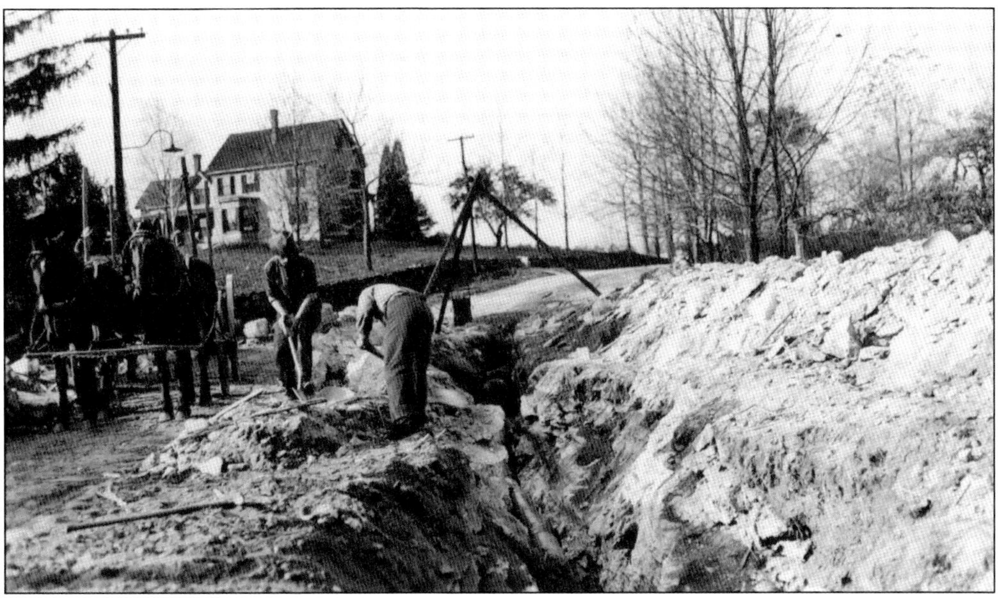

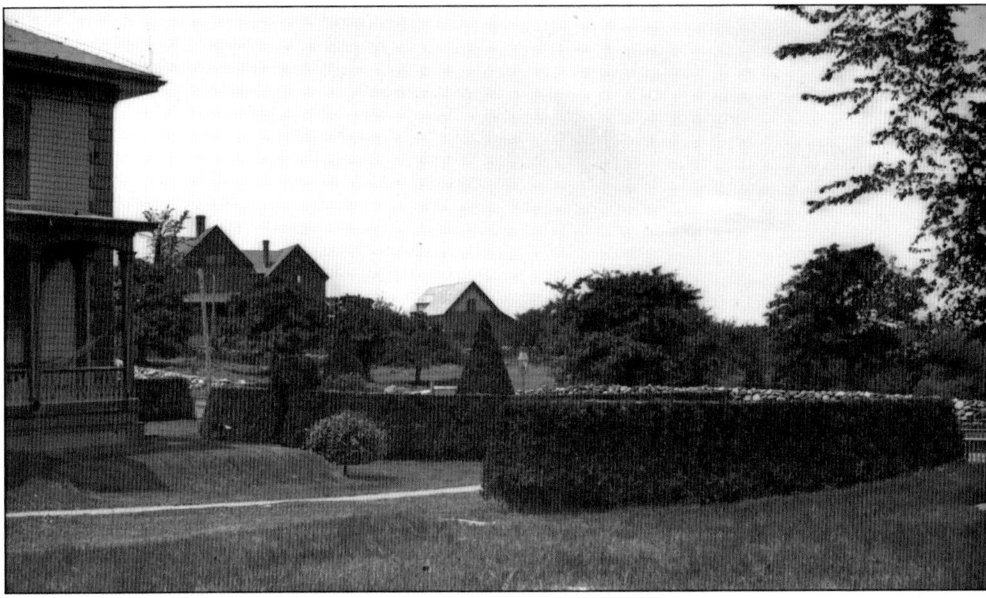

The Victorian house and barn at 85 High Street are seen here beyond the hedges. This was built in 1883 for Lucia and Artemas Woodworth of Lowell, and from 1905 to 1919, Nettie and Robert Barbour lived there. Robert ran the Eclipse Chemical Manufacturing Company in the barn, making indelible inks and aniline dyes, but World War I cut off his raw material source in Germany. (Chelmsford Historical Society Collection.)

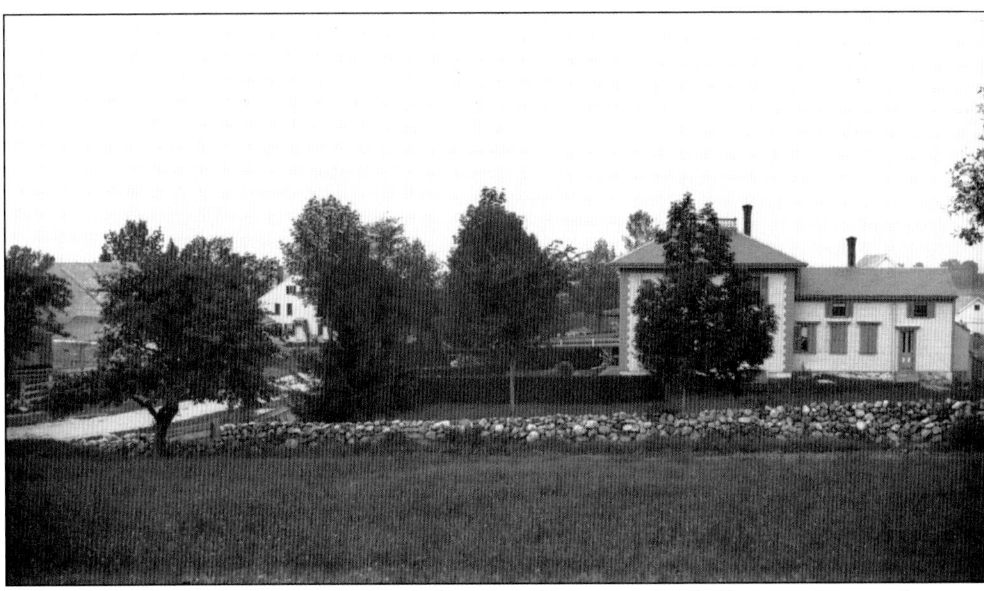

There is a lane that runs between 84 High Street, where this 1888 photograph was taken, and 78 High Street, seen on the other side. Shedd Lane went all the way through to Acton Road and allowed John S. Shedd access to his land and home on the north side of the lane. Several neighbors had deeded rights to use the lane to access their woodlots. (Chelmsford Historical Society Collection.)

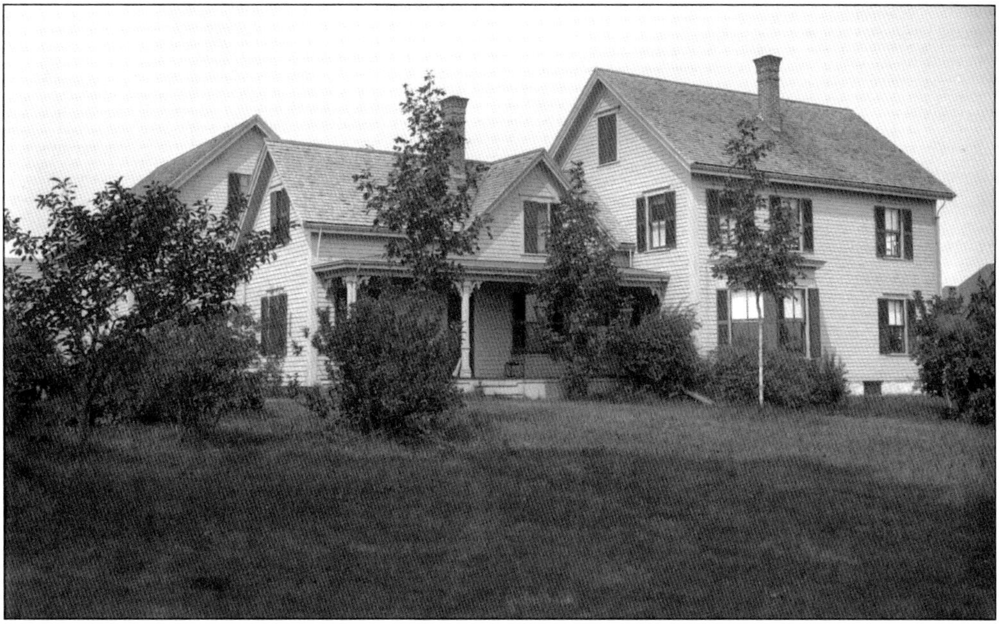

Jasper Elliott built this house at 84 High Street in 1881 for his brother Ephraim, a Civil War veteran, mechanic, and inventor. Among his patented inventions was a weed-pulverizing garden wheel hoe he manufactured on the second floor of E.R. Marshall's woodworking shop on Warren Avenue. The barn on the left was moved next door in the 1920s to become the house at 90 High Street. (Chelmsford Historical Society Collection.)

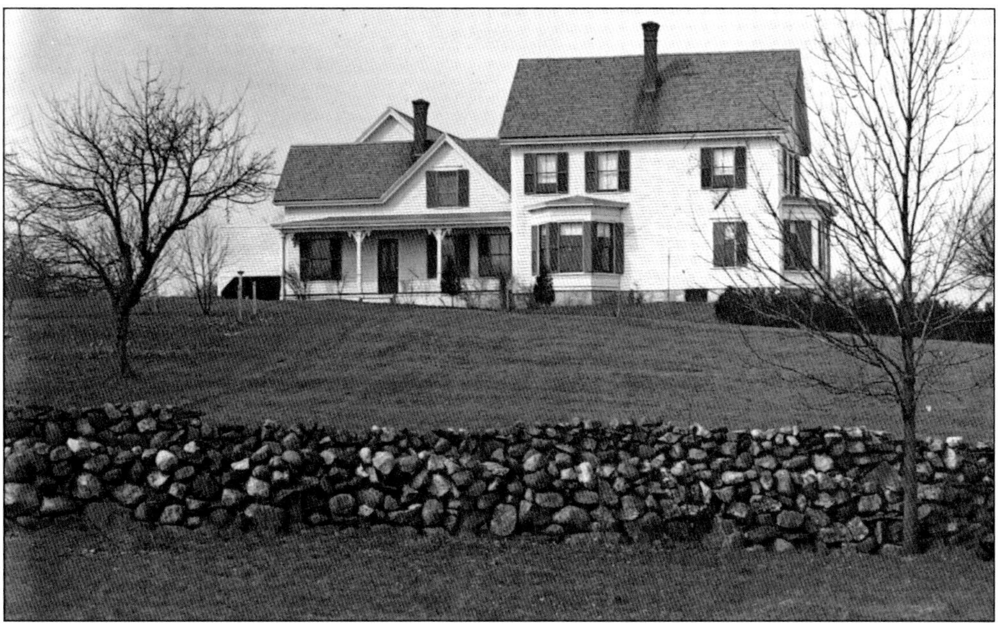

In the 1650s, the colony of Massachusetts enacted legislation requiring farmers to construct fences of wood or stone, such as these bounding Shedd Lane, to separate livestock from neighbors' livestock and crops. Towns were required to hire at least two "fence viewers" to insure that a minimum height of between four and five feet was maintained and to levy a fine in the case of a violation. (Chelmsford Historical Society Collection.)

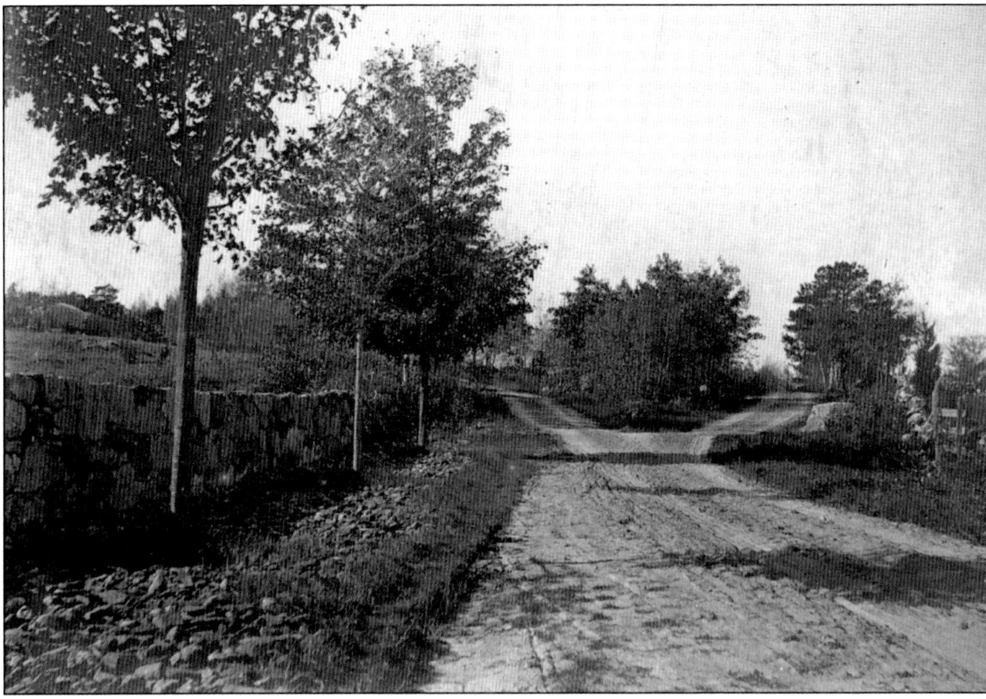

Here are two views of the intersection of Robin Hill Road and High Street around 1900. In the one looking west in the summer, Robin Hill Road goes to the left and High Street goes to the right. Parkhurst's Pulpit is in the field at far left. The source of pure water used by the Chelmsford Ginger Ale Company was out of view on the right side of the road a short distance down the hill. In the view looking east in February 1898, High Street goes ahead and Robin Hill Road comes in from the right. The 85 High Street barn and house are at center, and 94 High Street is on the right. A horse-drawn roller was used to pack down the snow and crews would break through drifts with shovels. (Both, John Crawford III.)

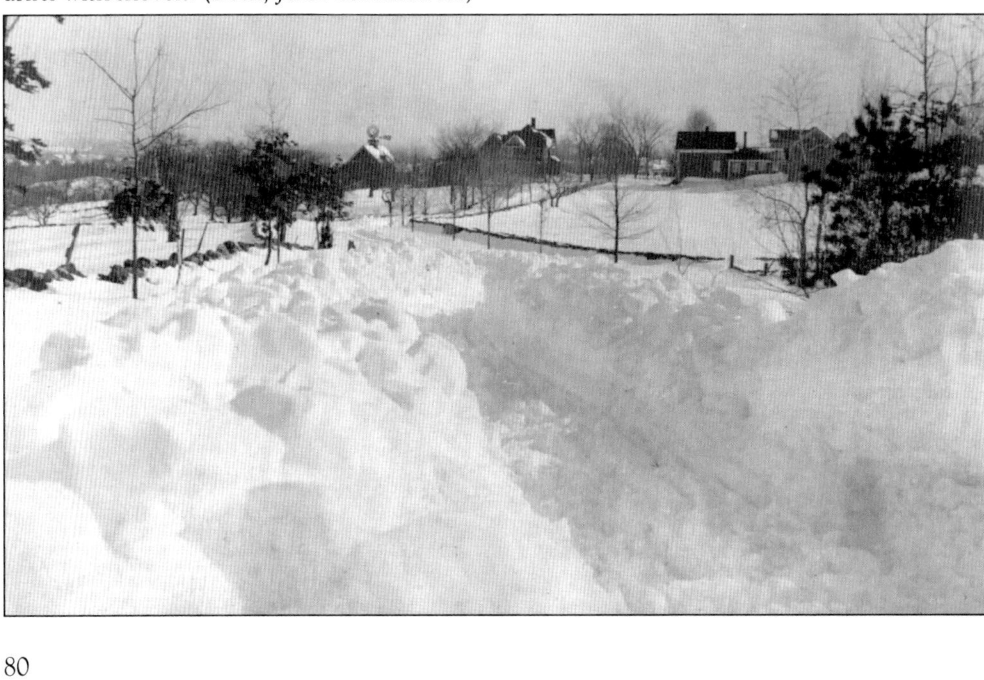

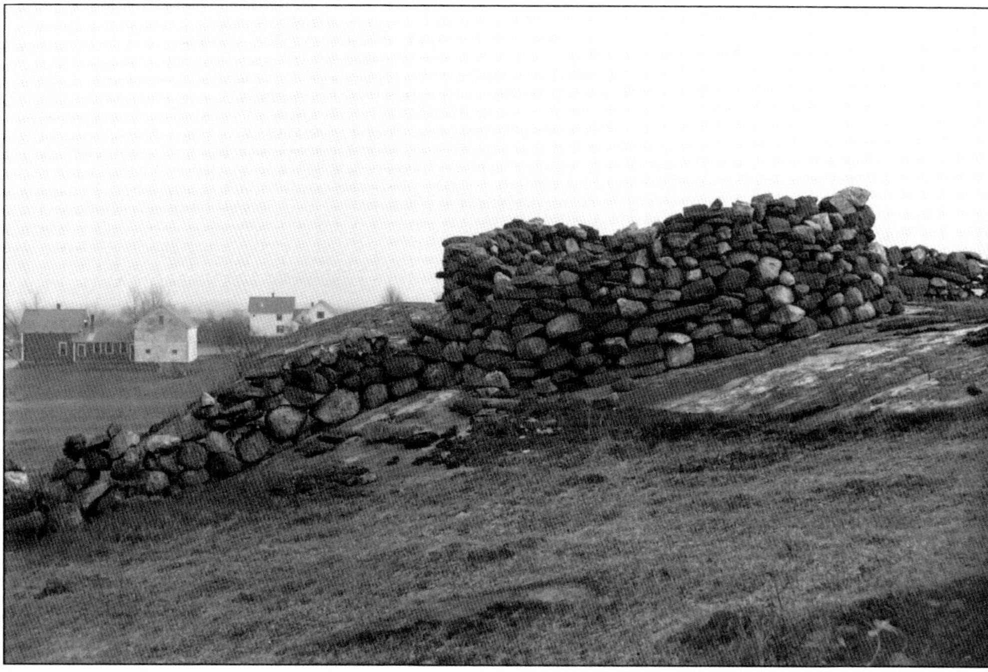

This view is looking across Parkhurst's Pulpit, with 94 High Street on the far left and 84 High Street to its right. Samuel Parkhurst constructed this unique circular rock wall as wind protection for his workmen while eating their dinners. His son Rev. John Parkhurst inherited the land and was in the habit of using the enclosure for meditation and prayer. The structure still exists next to 10 Robin Hill Road. (Chelmsford Historical Society Collection.)

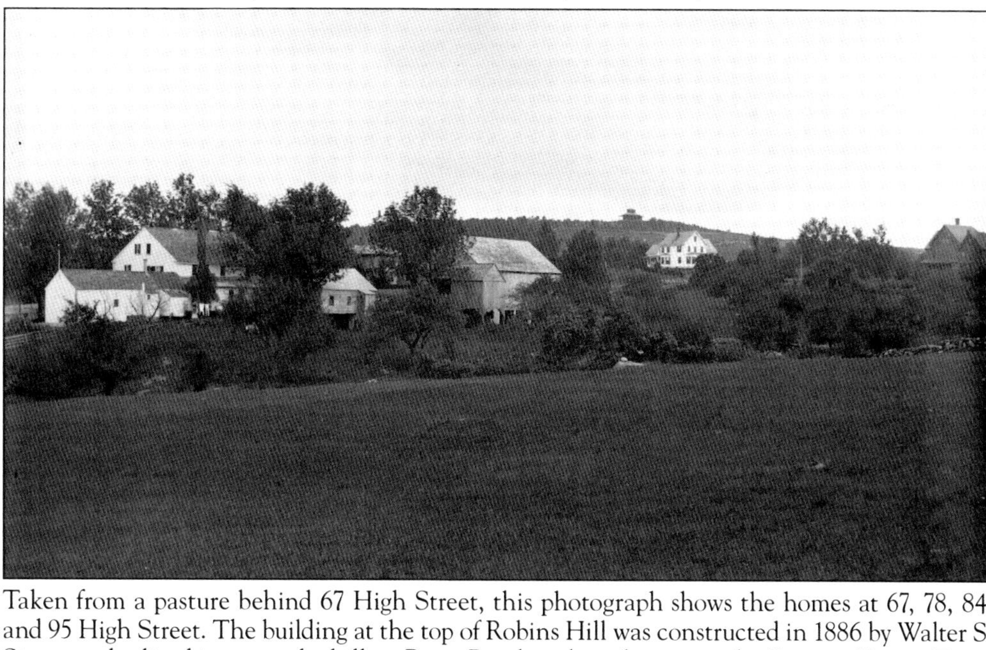

Taken from a pasture behind 67 High Street, this photograph shows the homes at 67, 78, 84, and 95 High Street. The building at the top of Robins Hill was constructed in 1886 by Walter S. Simons, who lived just over the hill on Byam Road, and was known as the Summit House. Trees, no longer harvested for firewood and lumber, now cover Robins Hill. (Chelmsford Historical Society Collection.)

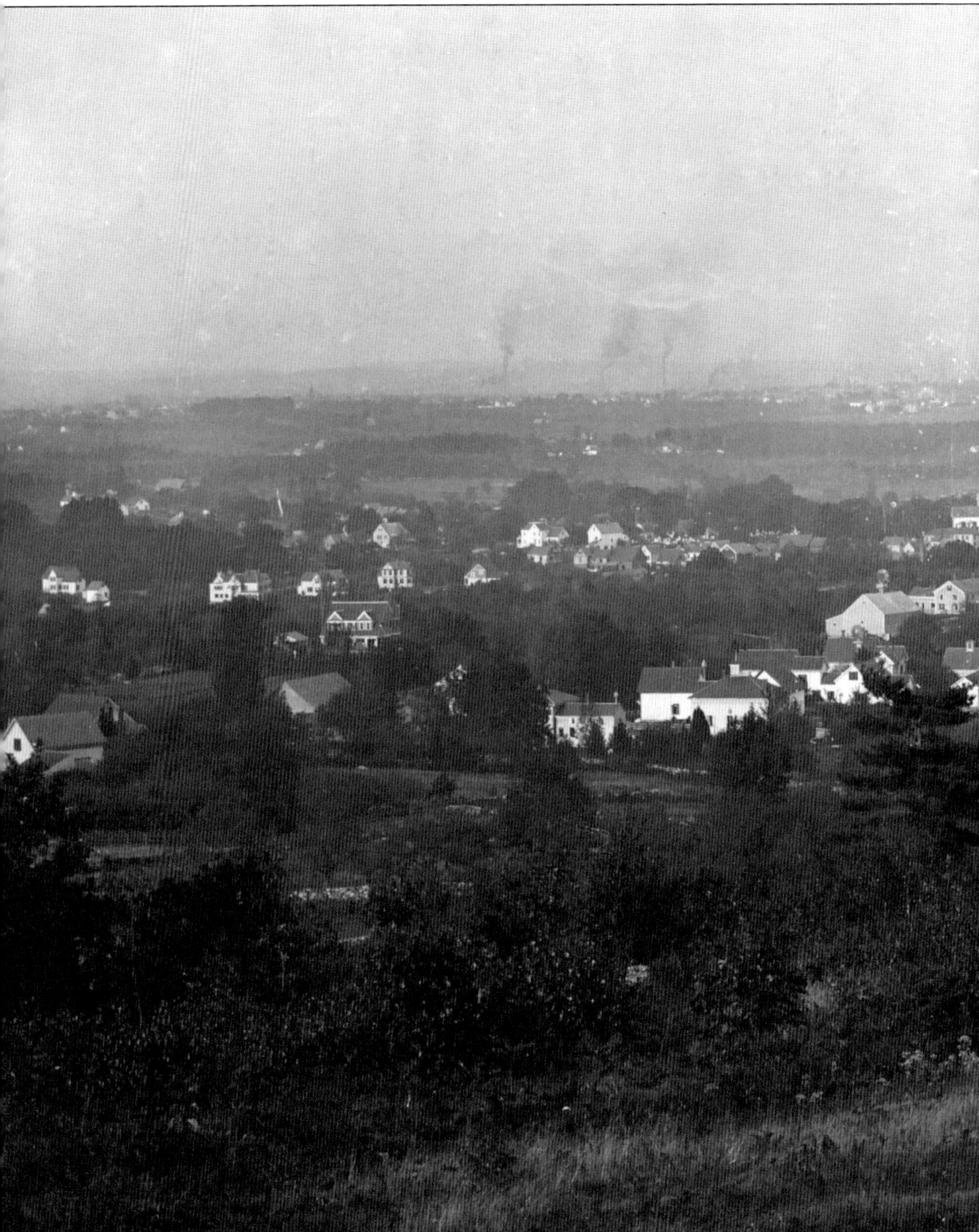

Cairns like this one near the top of Robins Hill have been built by man since ancient times. Houses on Littleton Road, Bridge Street, Chelmsford Street, Acton Road, High Street, Boston Road, and Billerica Road can be seen here, many with windmills. The First Parish Church and

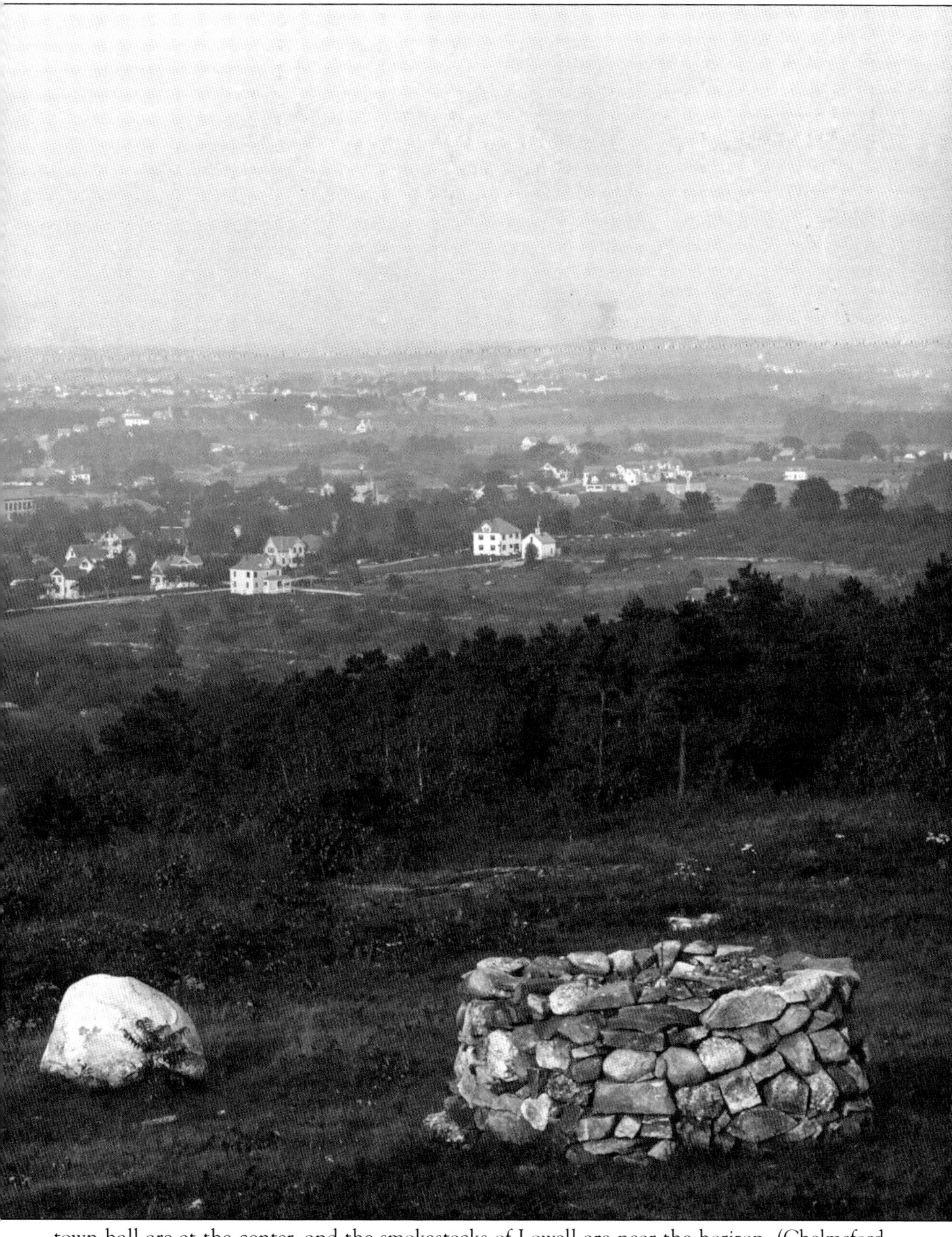

town hall are at the center, and the smokestacks of Lowell are near the horizon. (Chelmsford Historical Society Collection.)

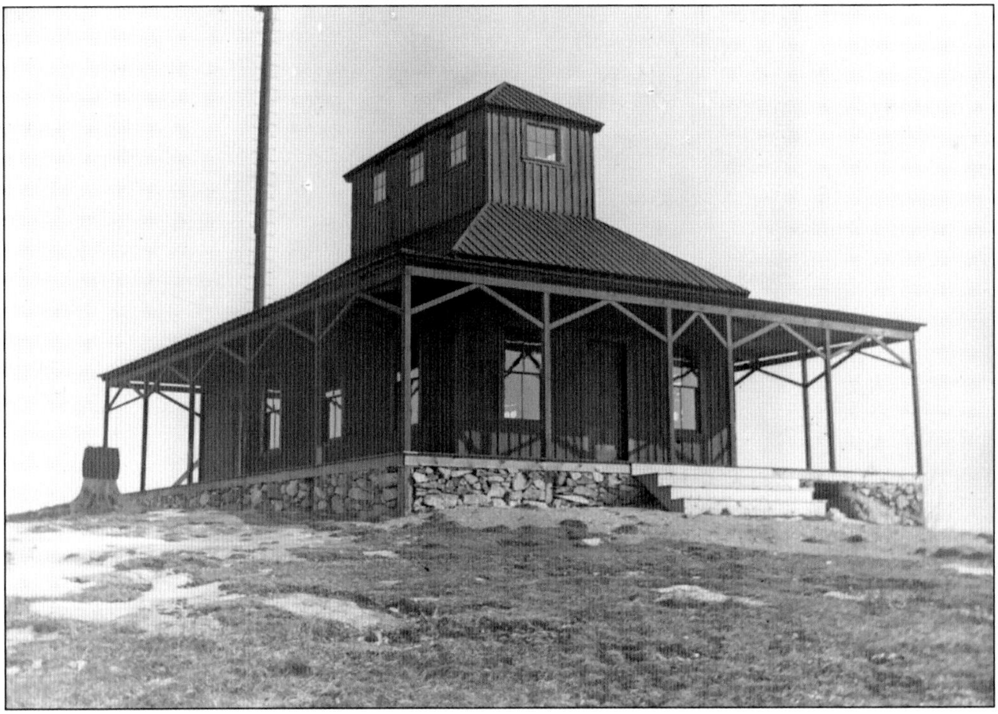

Walter S. Simons Summit House was new, with some winter snow still on the ground when this image was taken around 1887. Walter sold refreshments and ice cream on the first floor in summer and transported visitors from the Central House where he managed the hotel for George H. Wilson Sr. The tall flagpole in back must have drawn frequent lightning strikes during a thunderstorm. (Chelmsford Historical Society Collection.)

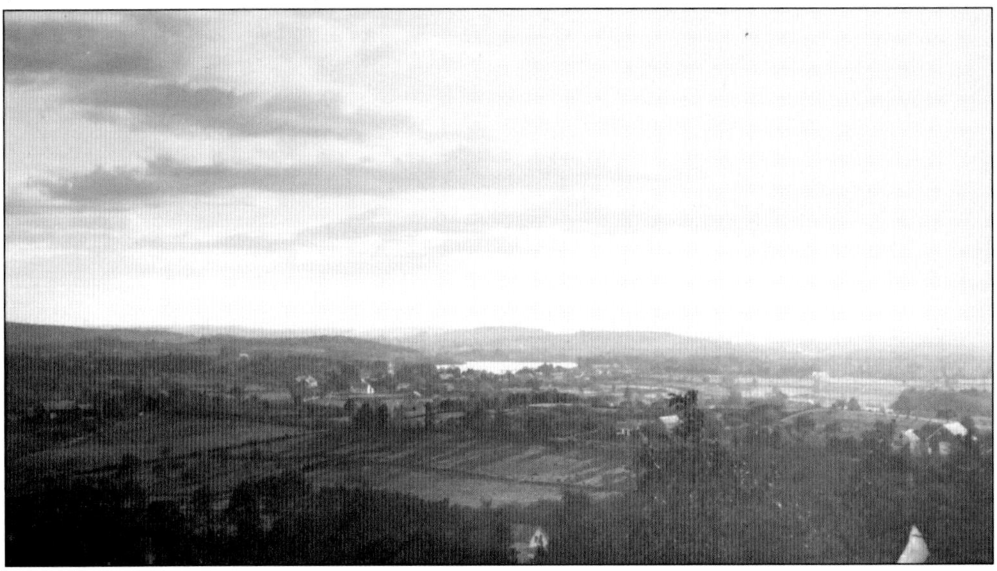

This view from the other side of Robins Hill features Heart Pond (historically known as Hart Pond on postcards and maps) at the center. South Chelmsford was mostly rural in the 1890s, and fortunately, some of the farms and farming heritage have been preserved. The village center can be located by finding the First Baptist Church steeple at 2 Maple Road. (Linda Prescott.)

Seven

More Homes

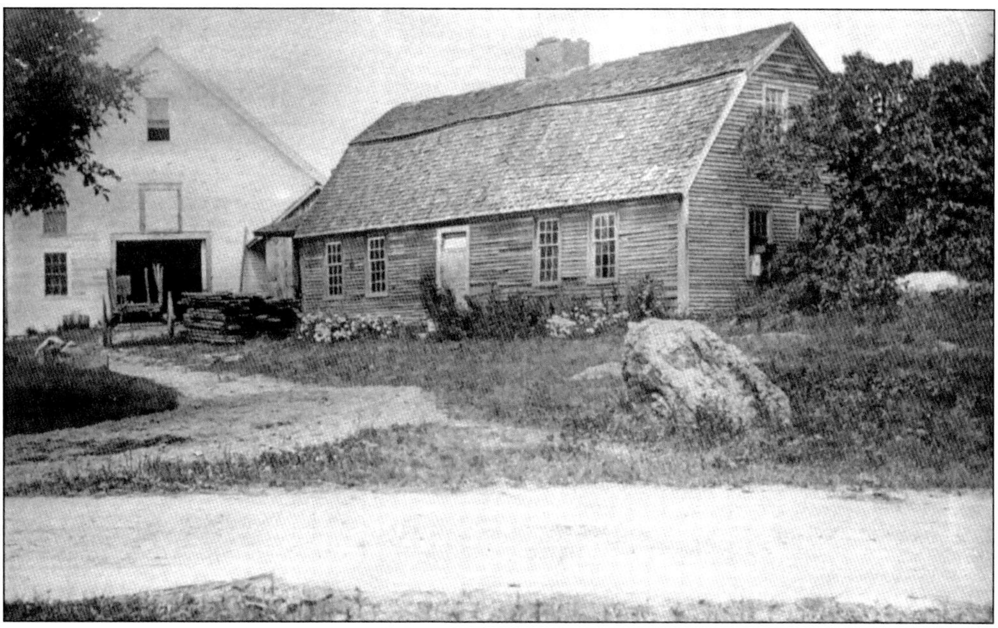

Many generations of William Fletchers lived near Crosby Lane and North Road—from the William who held the first town meeting at his house on September 22, 1654, to the William who graduated from Centre High School in 1888. The William who lived in this house in 1775, known as "Uncle Billy" Fletcher, answered the April 19 call to arms as part of Col. Moses Parker's company. (Chelmsford Historical Society Collection.)

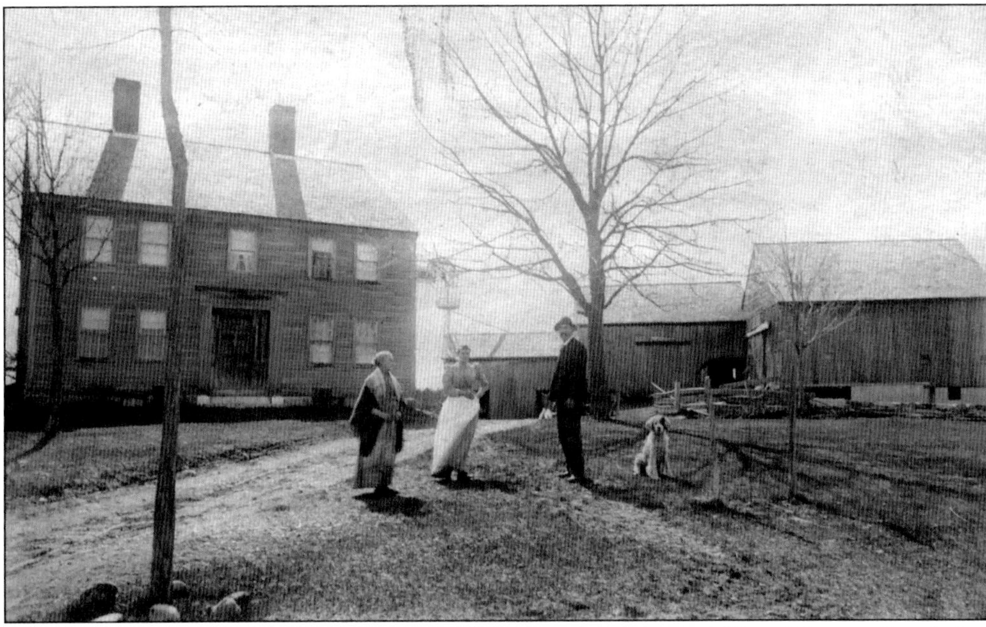

Charles and Mary Sweetser raised seven children on this farm at 187–189 Boston Road. Son Herbert C. Sweetser was active in town government and, with George W. Day, operated the Sweetser and Day mill complex in Central Square. Son Ervin W. Sweetser was town treasurer and tax collector, ran a meat and provision store at Central House, and later built Sweetser's Market at 10 Chelmsford Street. (Chelmsford Historical Society Collection.)

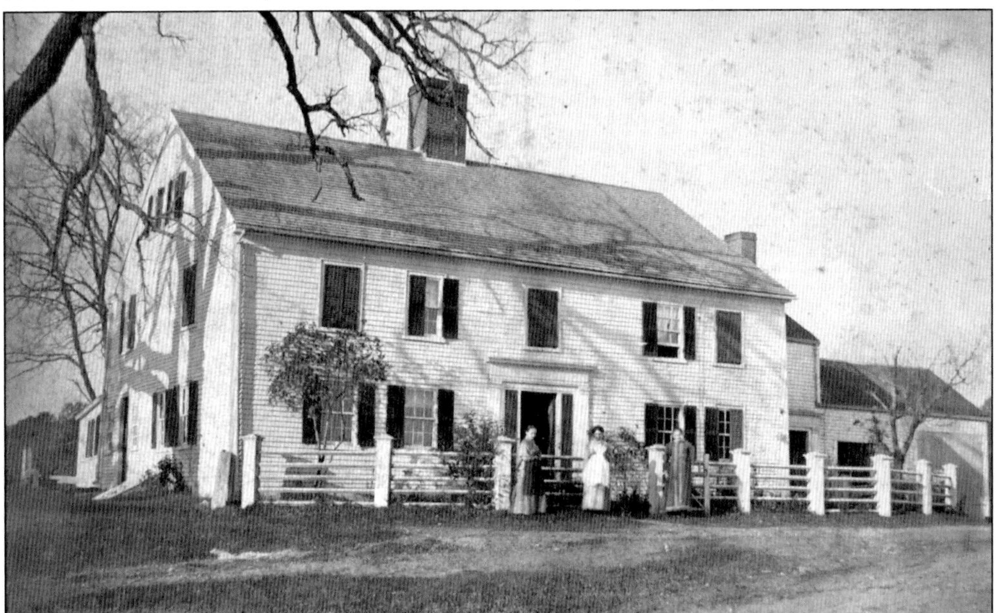

Mary Hatch, a Mrs. White, and Miriam Warren are identified from left to right in this c. 1890 photograph of 101 Boston Road. The house was in the Warren family from 1699 to 1910, and various Joseph Warrens lived there for 200 years. The third Joseph, a selectman, was the man who fired the guns to call the minutemen to assemble in Central Square on April 19, 1775. (Chelmsford Historical Society Collection.)

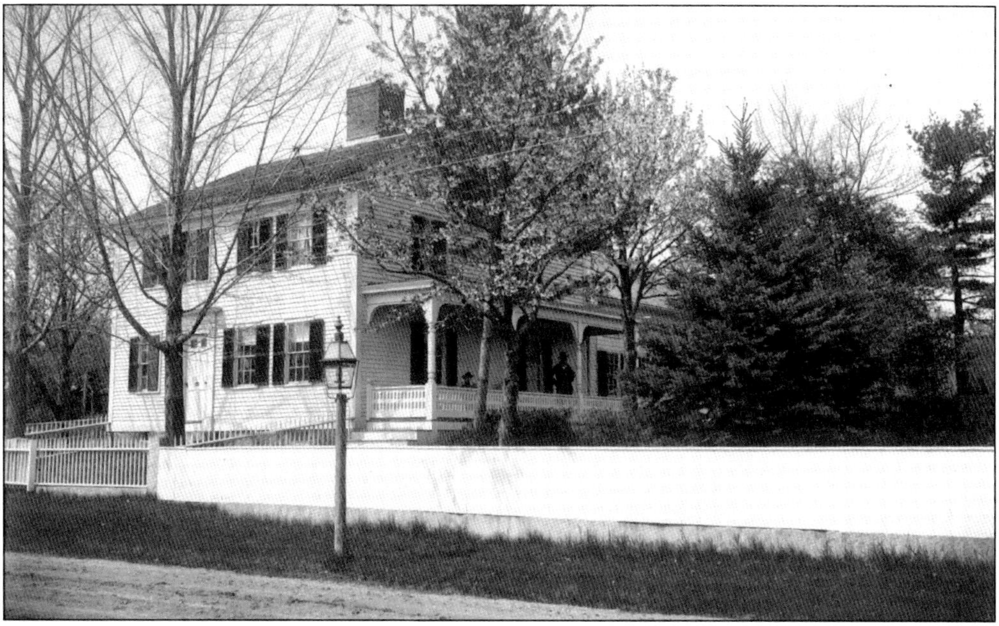

Julia M. Warren and Edwin H. Warren are on their porch at 77 Boston Road around 1891. Their granddaughter Elizabeth Fiske Warren unveiled the Concord Battle Monument (Minuteman Boulder) on Central Square on June 17, 1899. Eight-year-old Elizabeth was the daughter of their eldest son Joseph E. Warren. The VIA kerosene streetlamp in the foreground has "Warren Av" painted on the glass. (Chelmsford Historical Society Collection.)

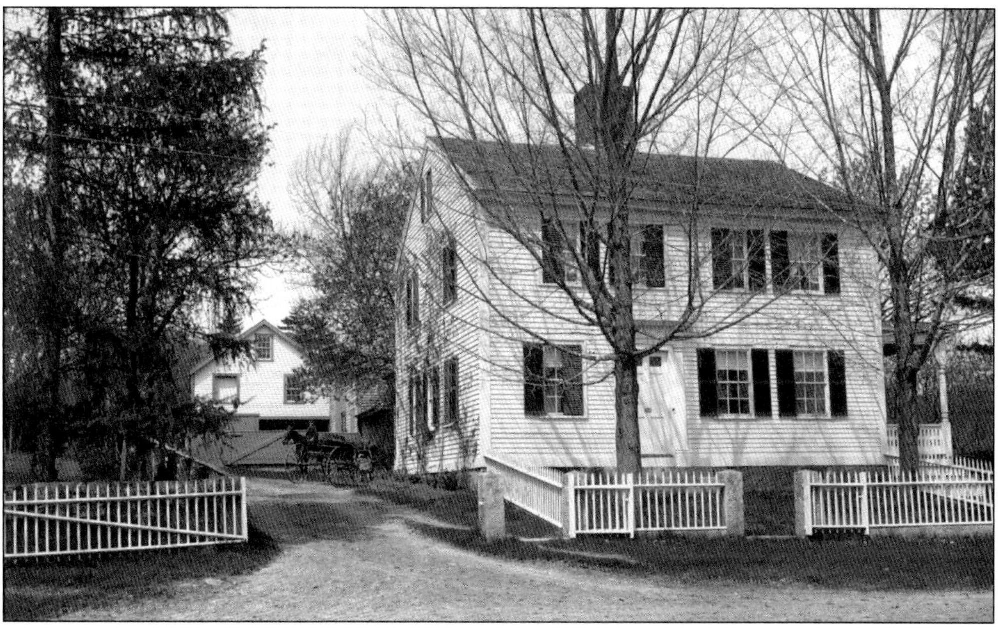

In this c. 1891 photograph of 77 Boston Road, built in 1815, it is likely that Joseph E. Warren is on horseback and his daughter Elizabeth is in the baby carriage. The farmland behind the house extends west to Acton Road, and at one time, the Warren homestead also included all the land on Warren Avenue east to River Meadow Brook. That land was subdivided into 43 house lots in the 1880s for a development called Homestead. (Chelmsford Historical Society Collection.)

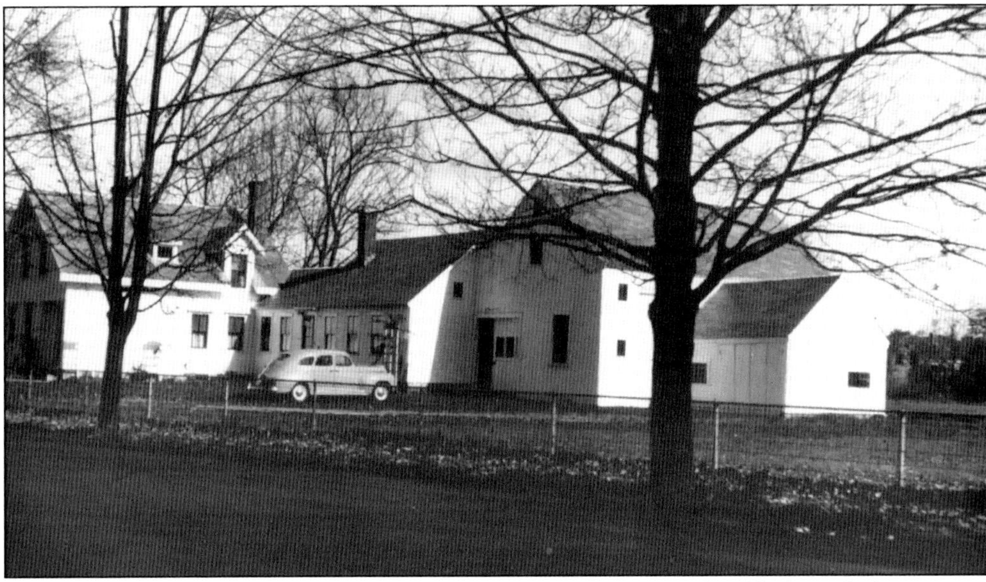

Eben H. Marshall built this 72 Boston Road house around 1845 with a blacksmith shop around the corner on Warren Avenue. His son Eben R. Marshall converted the blacksmith shop to a planing and sawmill after a fire in 1893. The home, seen here around 1945, was demolished in 1972 and replaced with a 5,808-square-foot day care facility now operated by Springboard Schools. (Linda Prescott.)

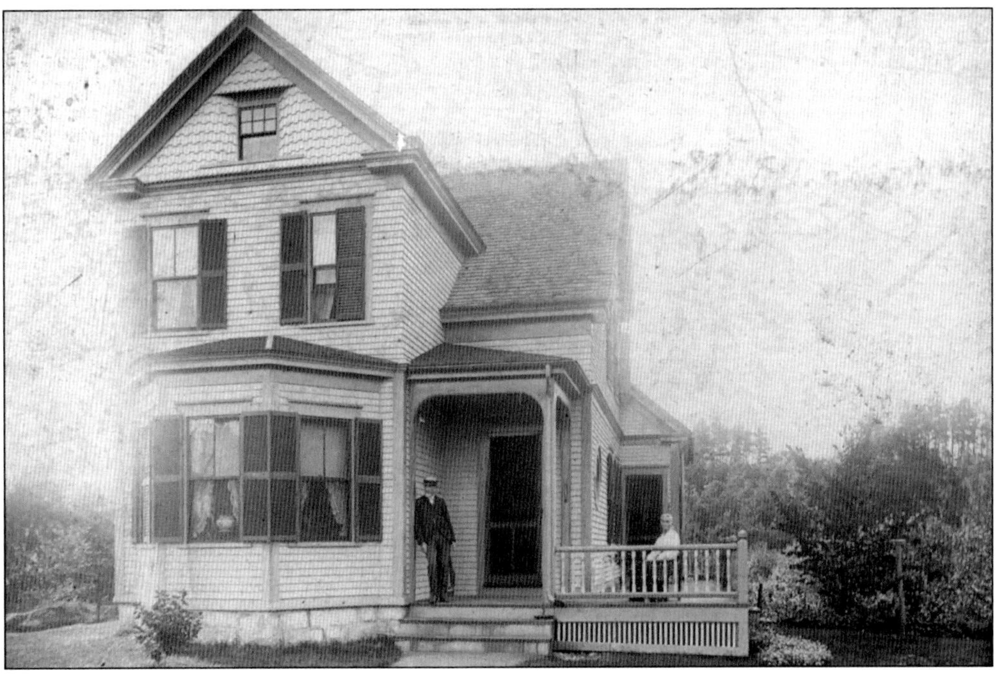

Civil War veteran George A. Parkhurst is standing on the porch at 63 Littleton Road in 1892 with his wife, Clorinda H. Parkhurst (seated). He joined Charles E.A. Bartlett's Company K but was sick the first three months. In spite of this, he signed up for another campaign in 1864–1865 with Daniel P. Byam. George was a journalist and served as Chelmsford's town clerk for 33 years. (Chelmsford Historical Society Collection.)

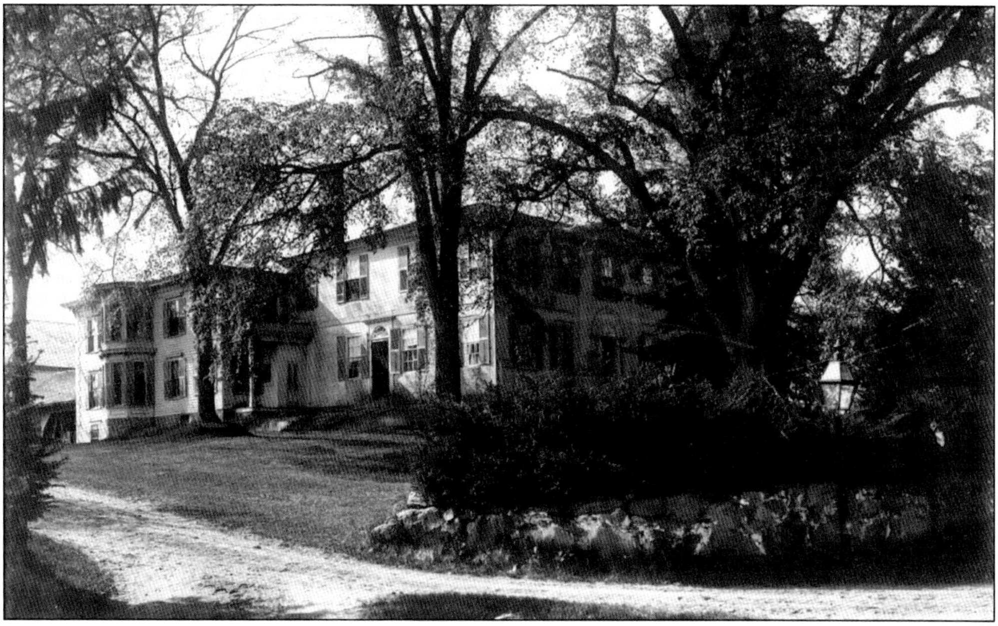

This Georgian house at 10 Worthen Street was built during a time of prosperity by Boston merchant Samuel Prince around 1799. David Perham purchased the property in 1869 and sold it in 1873 to fellow Baptist Ezekiel B. Worthen and his wife, Sarah. Ezekiel was a well-respected grocer in Lowell, and "the Tyngsboro Road" passing by his house was renamed Worthen Street in his honor. (Chelmsford Historical Society Collection.)

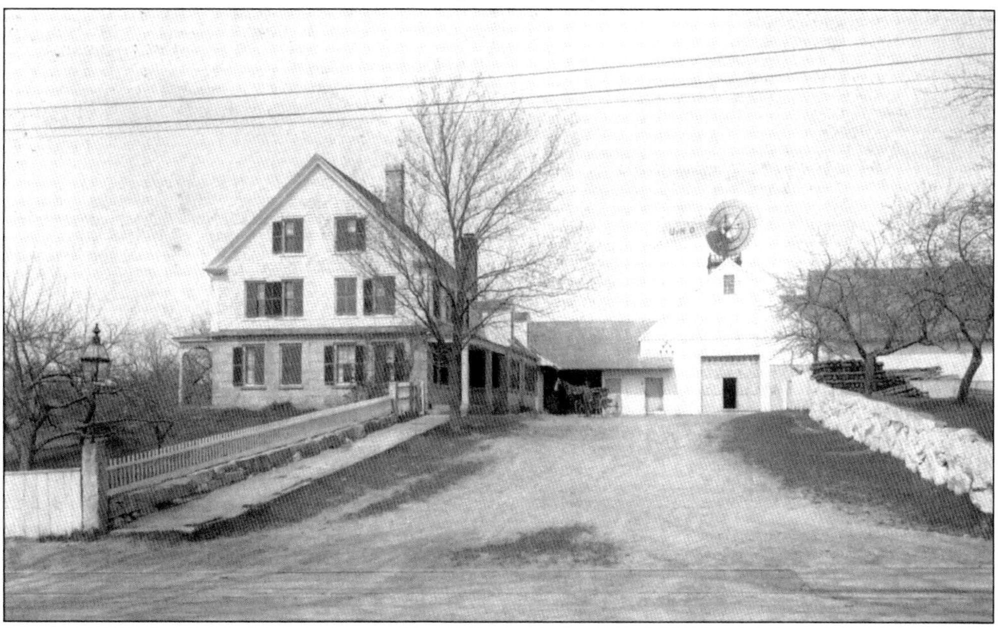

Amos B. Adams (not to be confused with donor of the Adams Library, Amos F. Adams) is standing in the yard of his farm at the corner of Chelmsford and Fletcher Streets around 1900. Amos was a wood and lumber dealer specializing in posts, poles, and railroad ties. This house was purchased and demolished by Standard Oil in 1961 and the site is now home to a Sunoco station. (Chelmsford Historical Society Collection.)

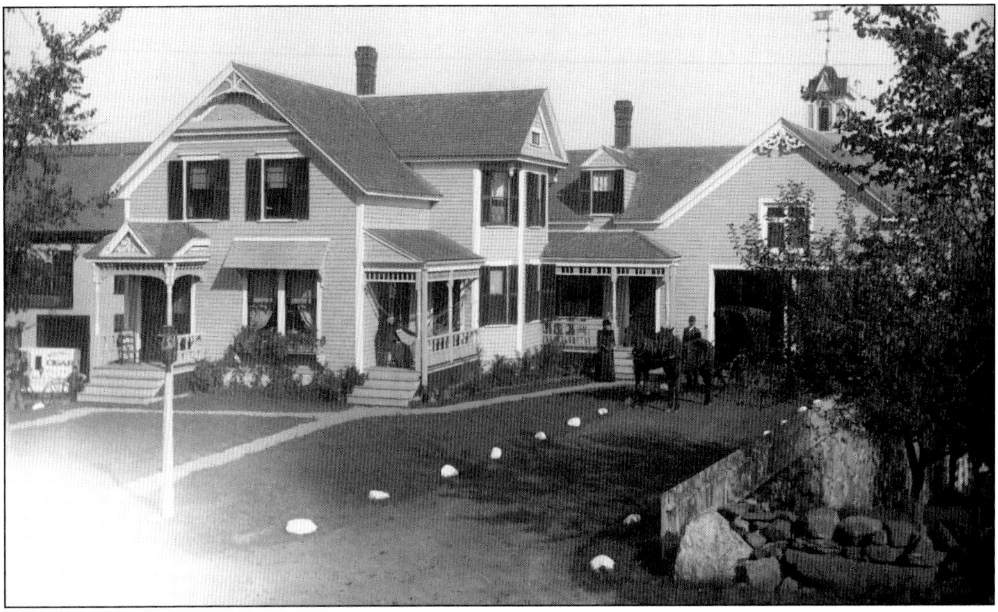

Carriage manufacturer Floyer J. Whittemore opened his shop on North Road in January 1890 and built this house, barn, and stable at 127 North Road later the same year. The barn was also used for storage of carriages from the shop. In this c. 1892 photograph are, from left to right, Floyer's mother-in-law, Elmira W. Upham, on the porch; his wife, Clara M. Whittemore; and Floyer J. Whittemore. (Chelmsford Historical Society Collection.)

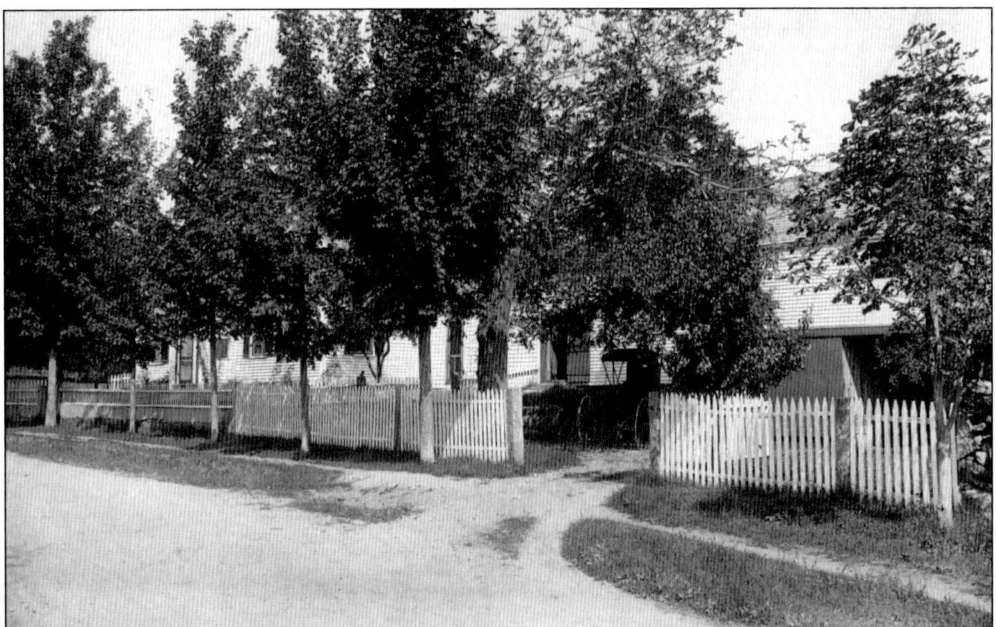

This is the 41 Westford Street home where Rufus F. and Adelaide D. Emerson raised their three children—Arthur I., Susan M., and Frank A. Emerson. A fourth child, named Lewis, died in 1876 at the age of 18 when he was accidentally hit by a baseball on Chelmsford Common. Frank, a blueberry wholesaler, sold the house out of the family in 1942. (Chelmsford Historical Society Collection.)

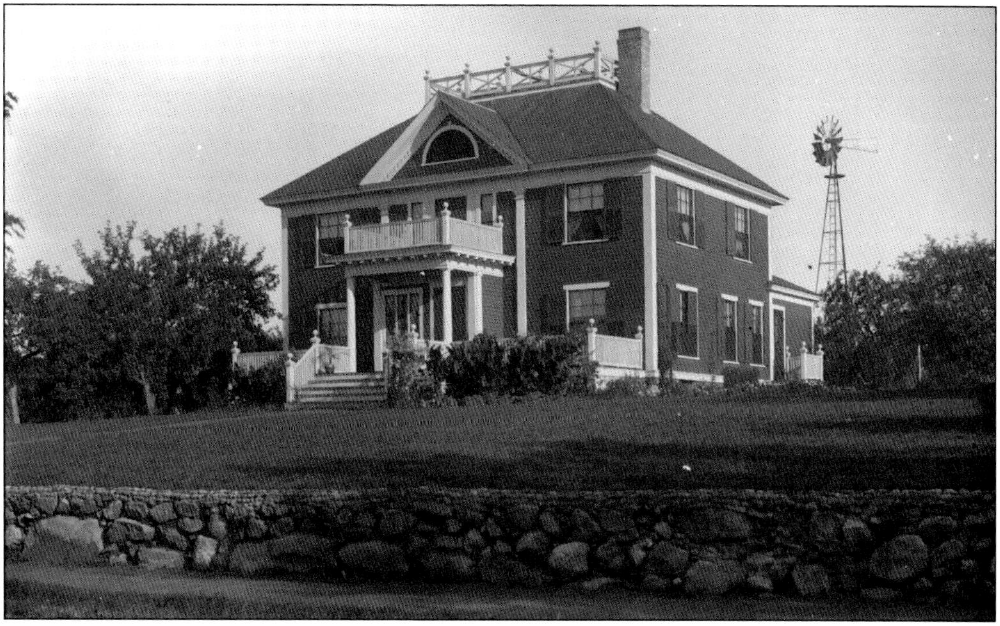

Walter Perham returned to Chelmsford in 1892 to help his father, Henry S. Perham, run the family cider mill on Westford Street. In 1897, Walter and his wife, Grace, hired architect Charles E. Parkhurst to build this house at 45 Westford Street to Grace's specifications. Walter operated a funeral home here starting in 1899 and was always on call for funeral duty. (Chelmsford Historical Society Collection.)

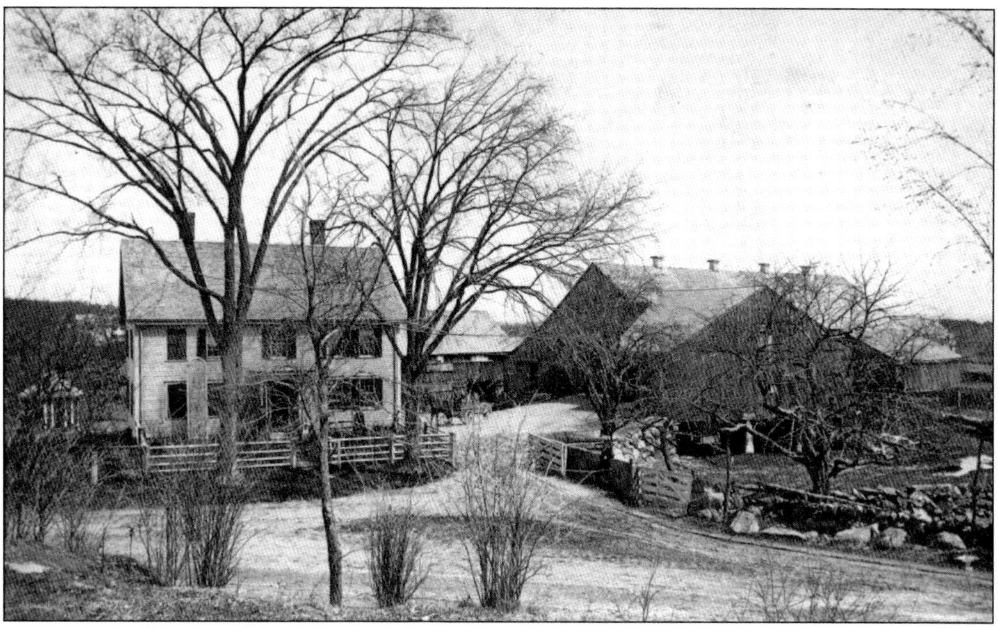

Deacon David Perham (the son of another David Perham) started the Perham Cider Mill in 1840. At the time of this c. 1890 photograph, David's son Henry S. Perham was running the business. When Henry died in 1906, his son Walter Perham continued to run the mill from his home at 45 Westford Street and rented out the old family home as a two-family residence. (Chelmsford Historical Society Collection.)

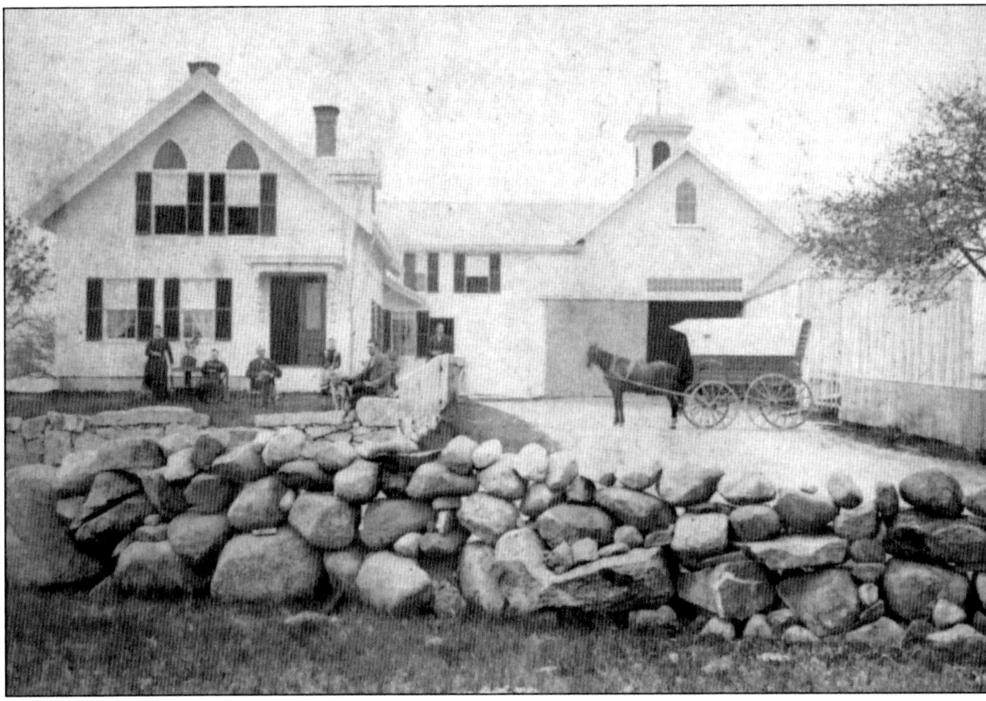

David C. Perham, a butcher from Wilton, New Hampshire, married Maria A. Byam from 19 Maple Road in Chelmsford in 1853 and purchased land and buildings on Westford Street from his third cousin Deacon David Perham in April 1873. His house at 76 Westford Street is seen above in a Simon Towle stereopticon slide, dated May 14, 1879. Pictured, from left to right, are Emma J., Maria A., David C., Lottie L., and Edwin C. Perham, and Herbert C. Sweetser. David C. also owned the old 1730 house across the street at 77 Westford Street and, in 1883, built a large barn out back on what is now Skyview Drive. The photograph below shows the farm at 76 Westford Street, as owned by son Edwin C. Perham in 1937, with the end of Dalton Road showing in the foreground. (Both, Brad Perham.)

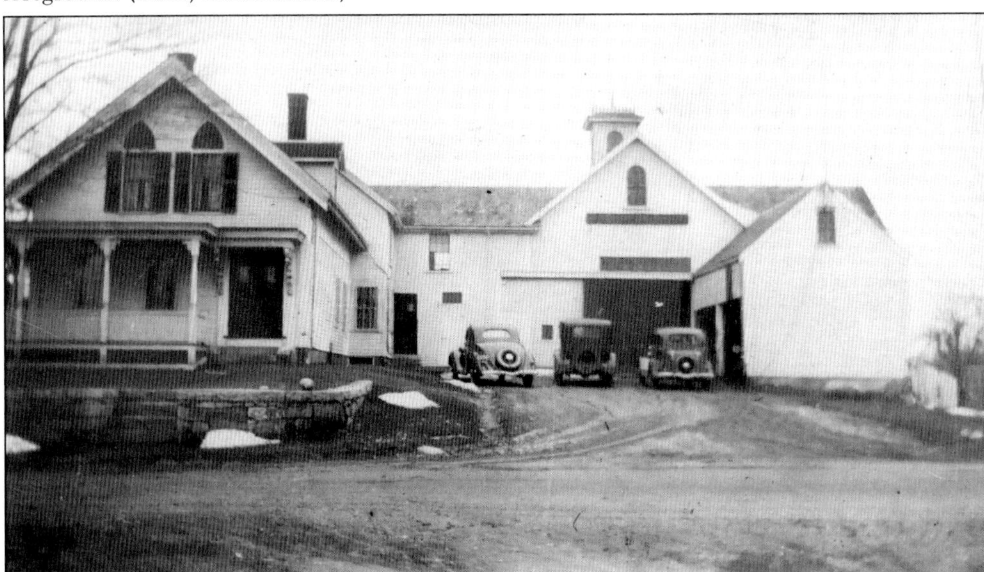

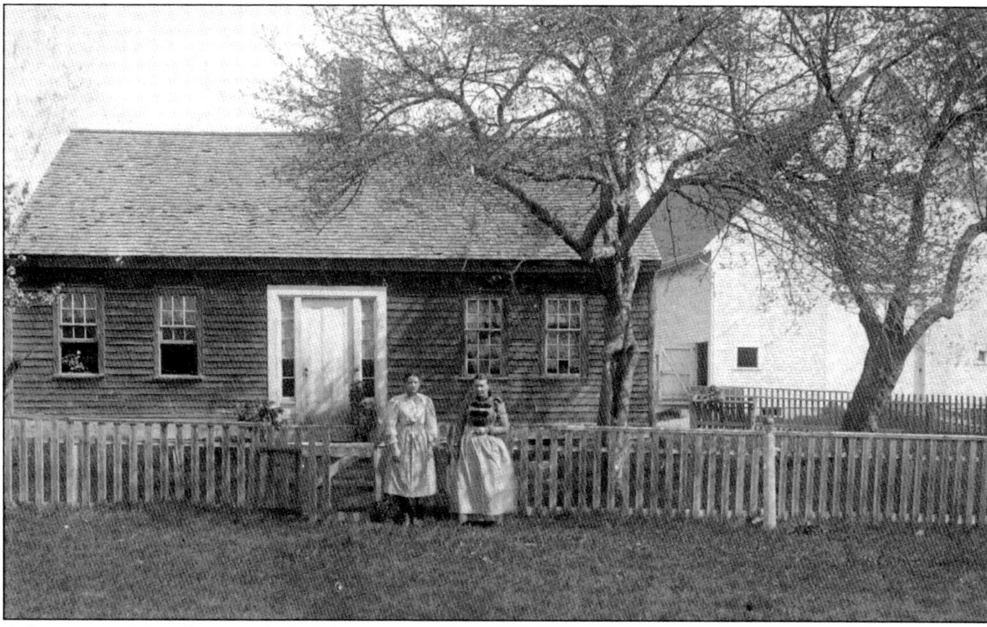

After 1894, David C. Perham's house at 77 Westford Street was rented to Edward P. Dryden, a fellow butcher, who had emigrated from Canada. In this 1899 photograph are, from left to right, Edward's daughter Hattie M. at age 15 and wife, Bertha A. Dryden. The Perham's large barn is seen on the right, and a smaller barn is hidden from view behind the house. (Brad Perham.)

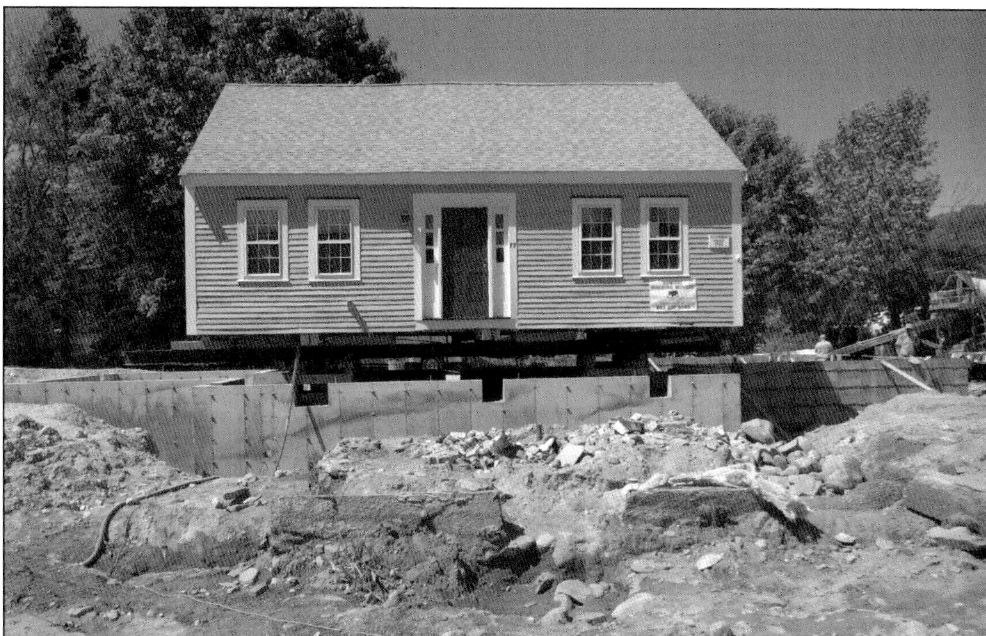

Donald and Nancy Patch of Chelmsford purchased the 77 Westford Street house in 2012 to preserve the historic home and make it more functional with a full basement. The house was moved back about 25 feet, and a new foundation was poured to include a master bedroom on the left and a two-car garage on the right, as seen in this May 2013 photograph. (Photograph by the author.)

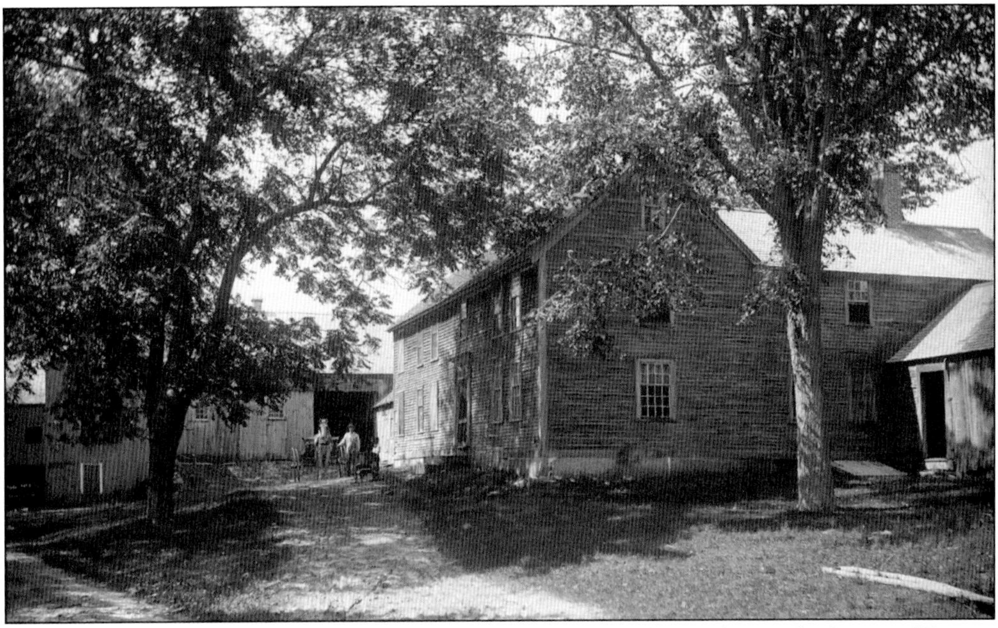

The Emerson farm, located on Dalton Road just west of North Road, was the home of Bryant Emerson and his five sons—Burt, Rufus W., J. Bradford, Henry H., and James P. Emerson. Bradford's son Walter and grandson Breck are shown in this c. 1893 photograph. The farm burned on November 5, 1905, and two Dutch Colonial–style homes were built on the site in 1922. (Chelmsford Historical Society Collection.)

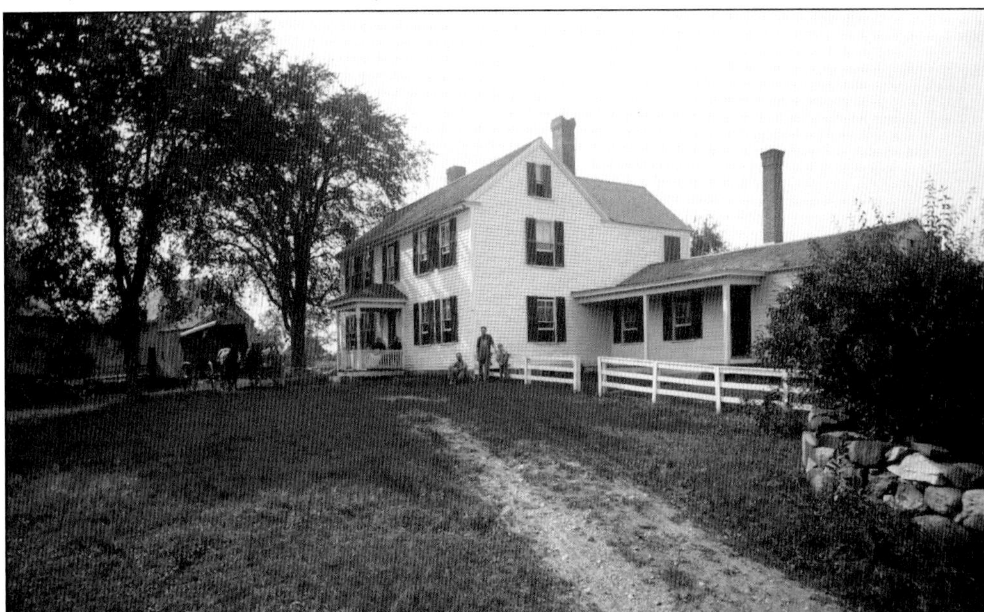

The builder of this c. 1775 house was Joseph Spaulding, who served in the Revolutionary War. He fired the first shot of the Battle of Bunker Hill against Gen. Israel Putnam's orders and received a whack on the head in reprimand. In this c. 1900 photograph are, from left to right, George Spaulding, Emily Aldrich, Julia A. Spaulding, George O. Spaulding (widowed), James Murray, and Clarence L. Spaulding. (Chelmsford Historical Society Collection.)

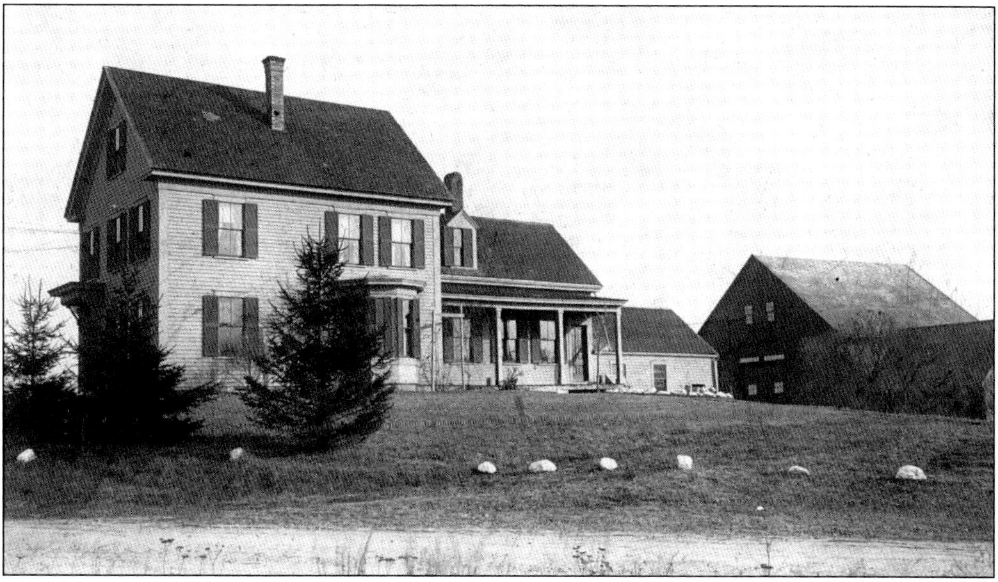

James and Susannah McFarlin operated this 195 Riverneck Road farm, and their daughter Susan S. McFarlin taught the seventh and eighth grades in the East and Centre Schools from 1879 to 1929. In honor of her 50-year distinguished teaching career, the 1926 Centre Grammar School on Wilson Street was renamed the Susan S. McFarlin School, and in 1979, it became the Chelmsford Housing Authority's McFarlin Manor senior housing. (Chelmsford Historical Society Collection.)

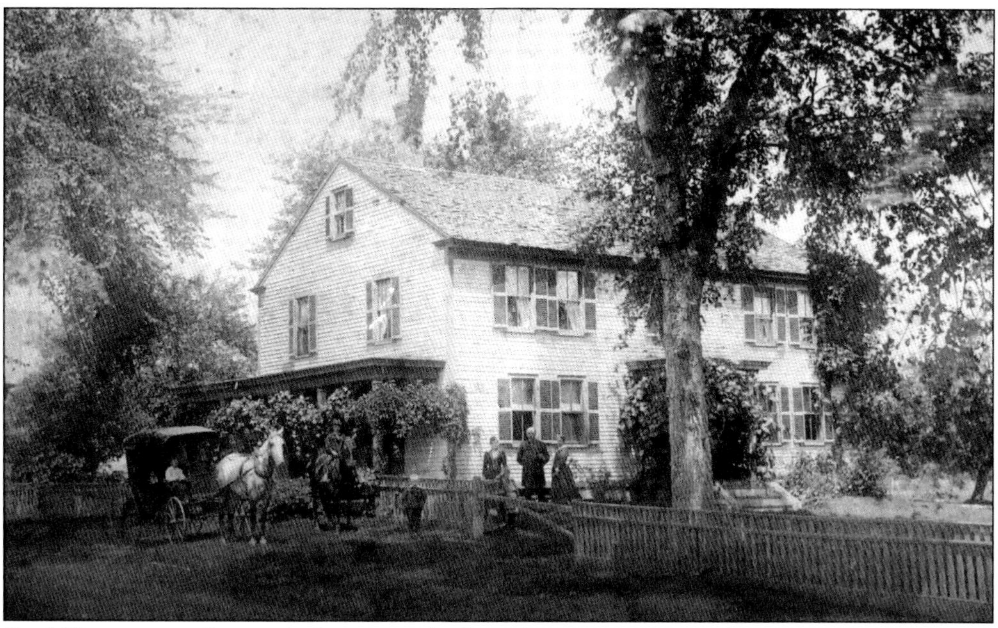

Civil War veteran George A. Byam was the last of nine generations of Byams to live at 50 Hunt Road. This house, a part of which was built in 1656, is the oldest in Chelmsford. Seen here around 1890 are, from left to right, George A. Jr., Bernard H., Ray L.S., Rebecca C. Emerson (an extended family member), Arnold A., George A., and Mary S. Byam. (Richard Bump.)

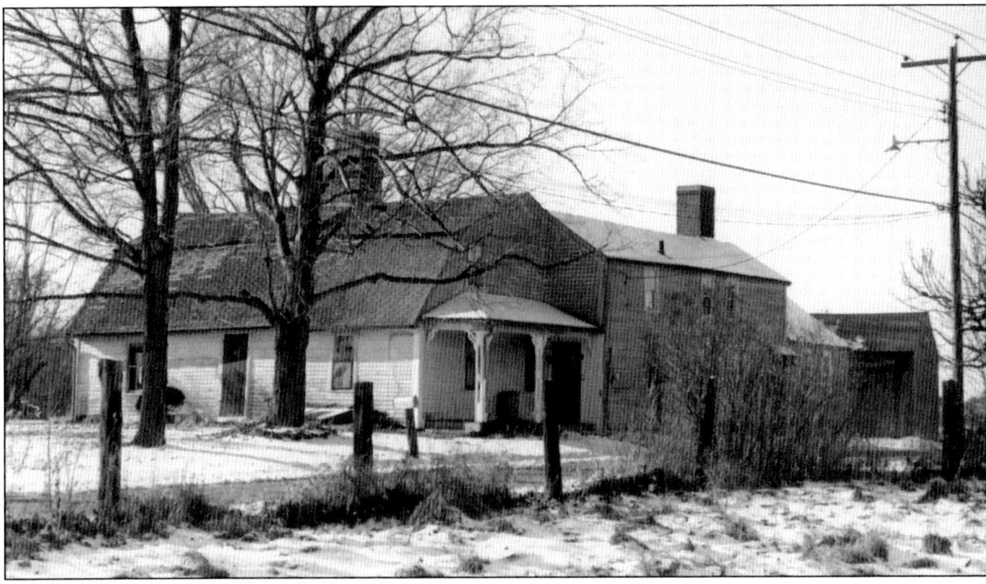

Annie Clarke and son David S. Clarke lived in the house at 50 Garrison Road, built by Jacob Warren around 1680 and seen in the undated photograph above. After David died in 1988, his son Kevin Clarke wanted a new house but also wanted the historic home preserved. Chelmsford historic restoration specialist Dana Gray took up the challenge by cataloging and dismantling the house in October and November 1989, storing the pieces at his family's home on Chamberlain Road, and assisting Kevin in the construction of his new house. Dana was unable to find a suitable lot in Chelmsford and instead purchased a 3.7-acre parcel of land in Littleton, Massachusetts, in October 1993. From April 1994 to January 1998, he reconstructed the house at its new location, as seen below in April 2013. (Above, Chelmsford Historical Commission; below, photograph by the author.)

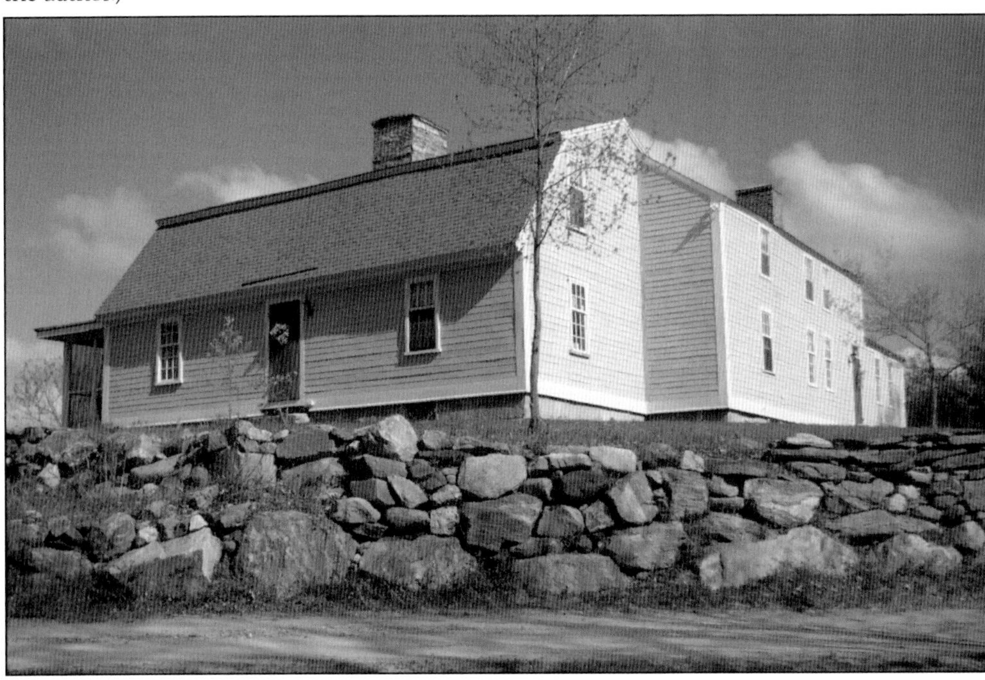

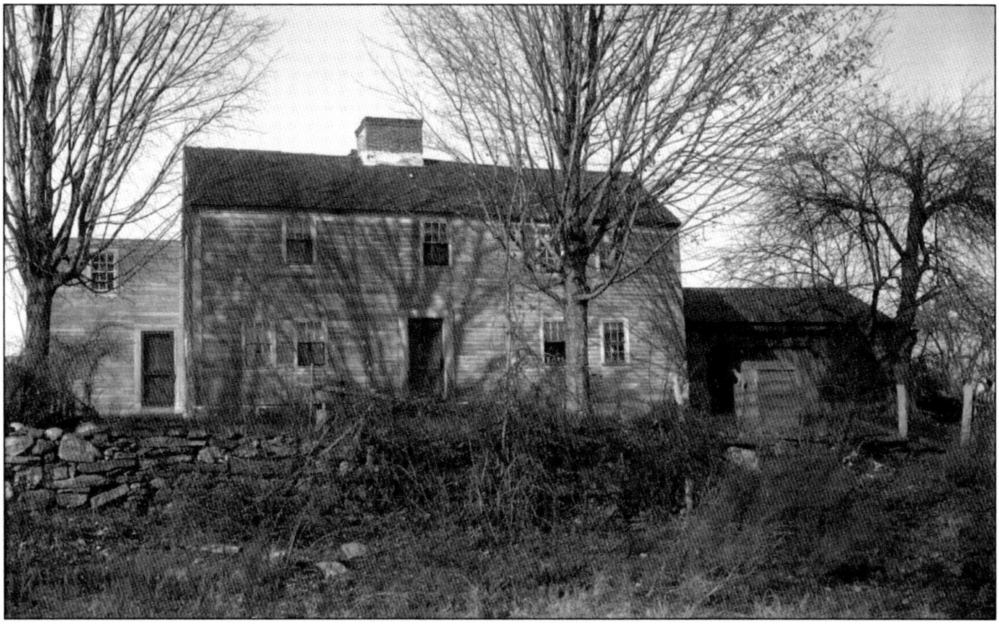

This c. 1702 house located at 105 Garrison Road was sold to developer Warren C. Lahue in 1959. Concerned citizens took action to prevent its demolition, and when the Chelmsford Historical Society Board of Directors turned it down as too large a rehabilitation project, the "Old Chelmsford" Garrison House Association was formed. Warren C. Lahue and Charlotte Park DeWolf were among 28 co-incorporators on December 3, 1959. (Chelmsford Historical Society Collection.)

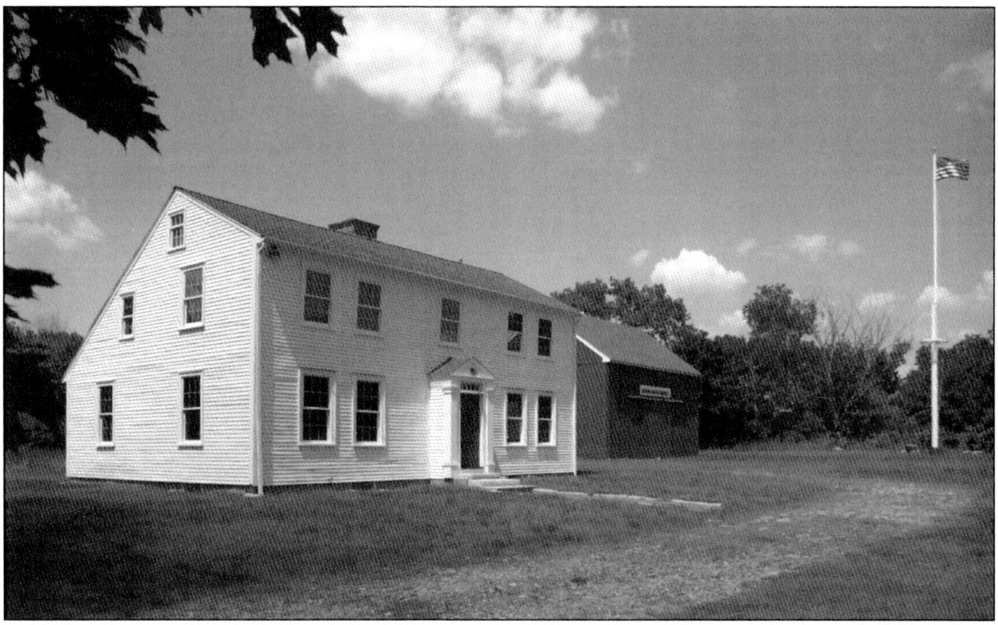

This June 2013 photograph shows other historic artifacts preserved on the Garrison House grounds. The Hill Jock House at left was moved from 155 Boston Road in April 2004, the Fiske Barn at center was dismantled at 1 Billerica Road in June 2004 and reconstructed in 2006, and the 1905 flagpole removed from Center Common in September 2011 was installed here on Flag Day 2013. (Photograph by the author.)

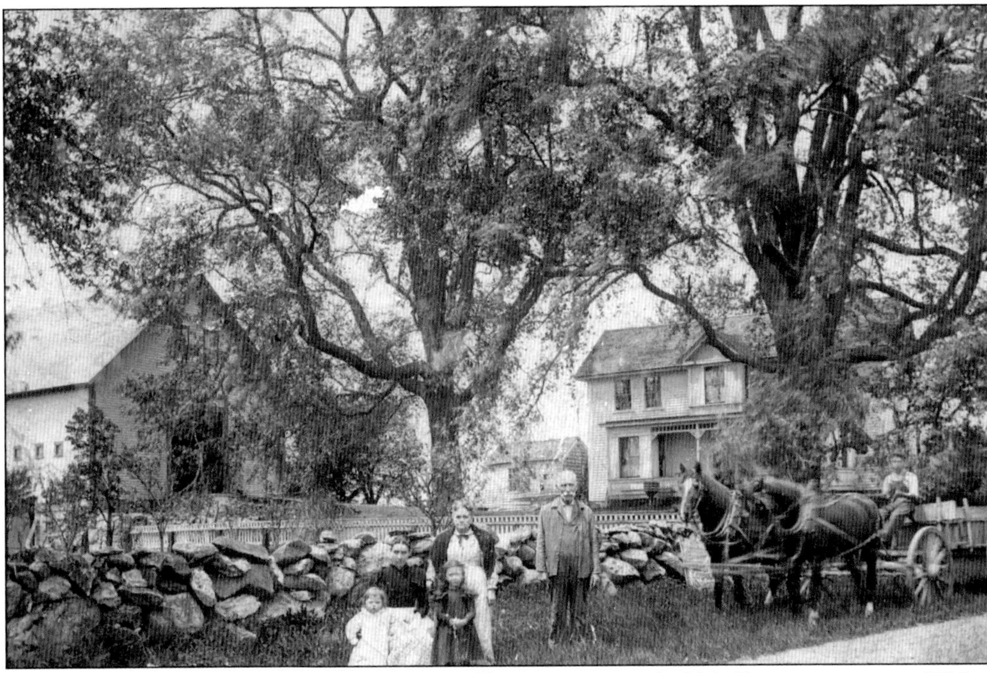

This is the farm of Walter R. Winning at 19 Elm Street around 1900. For extra income, Walter hauled gravel for the town using a heavy-duty teamster wagon like that shown in this photograph and broke snowdrifts in the winter. Pictured, from left to right, are daughter Gladys E.; wife, Julia A.; daughter Mildred C.; mother, Elizabeth Winning; "servant" George Walker; and an unidentified wagon driver. (Chelmsford Historical Society Collection.)

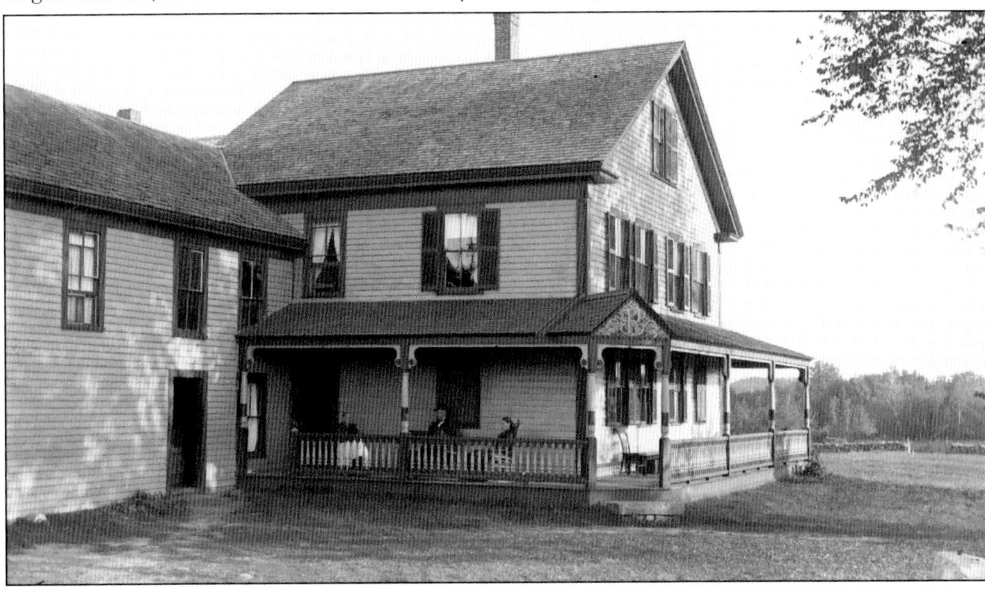

Fred W. Park's father, Andrew H. Park, who was blind and had studied at the Perkins School for the Blind, lived at 50 Billerica Road before purchasing this house at 12 Park Place. Shown, from left to right, in this c. 1895 photograph are Andrew's sister-in-law Mary Allen, Andrew H. Park, and his wife, Sarah T. Park. This house, located next to the Chelmsford Country Club, was demolished in 2005. (Chelmsford Historical Society Collection.)

Eight

PEOPLE

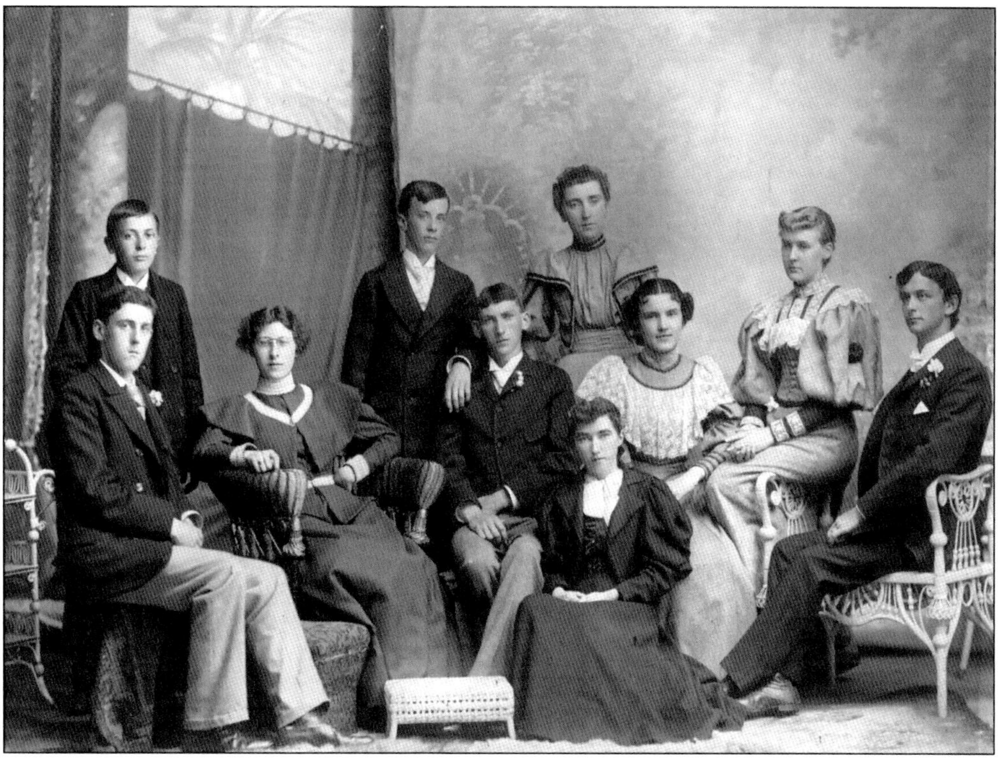

The Centre High School class of 1894 poses for an Emerson portrait. Pictured are, from left to right, (sitting) Edward J. Robbins (class president), Agnes L. Nichols, Edwin L. Stearns, Alice M. Stearns (class valedictorian), Mabel F. Fenderson (married Ralph W. Emerson), Ednah F. Byam (class secretary and treasurer), and Ralph W. Emerson (class salutatorian); (standing) William H. Fulton, Harry A. Dutton, and Jessie M. Holt. (Linda Prescott.)

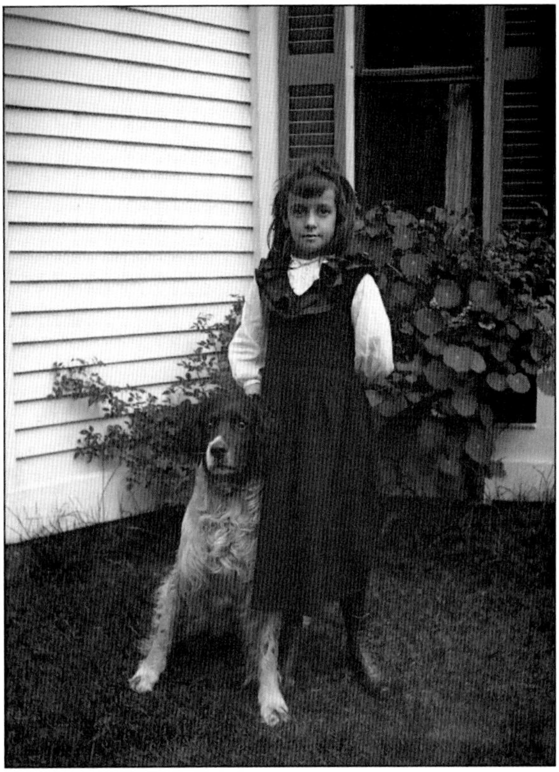

Bertha G. Bartlett was the youngest daughter of J. Adams Bartlett and is seen here at age eight with her dog Spot at 4 Bartlett Street in 1892. Her sister Mary B. Bartlett married Dr. Arthur G. Scoboria, and her sister Emma M. Bartlett married salesman and journalist Paul Dutton. Bertha married Warren H. Blaisdell of Carlisle and moved to Belmont, Massachusetts, where they raised three children. (Chelmsford Historical Society Collection.)

This 1908 photograph shows two-year-old Marjorie B. Scoboria, daughter of Dr. Arthur G. and Mary B. Scoboria, who lived next door to the Adams Library. Marjorie became an educator, was active in numerous Chelmsford organizations, and lived to age 104. Four-year-old Adams B. Dutton was the son of Paul and Emma M. Dutton, who lived next door to the Scoborias. (Chelmsford Historical Society Collection.)

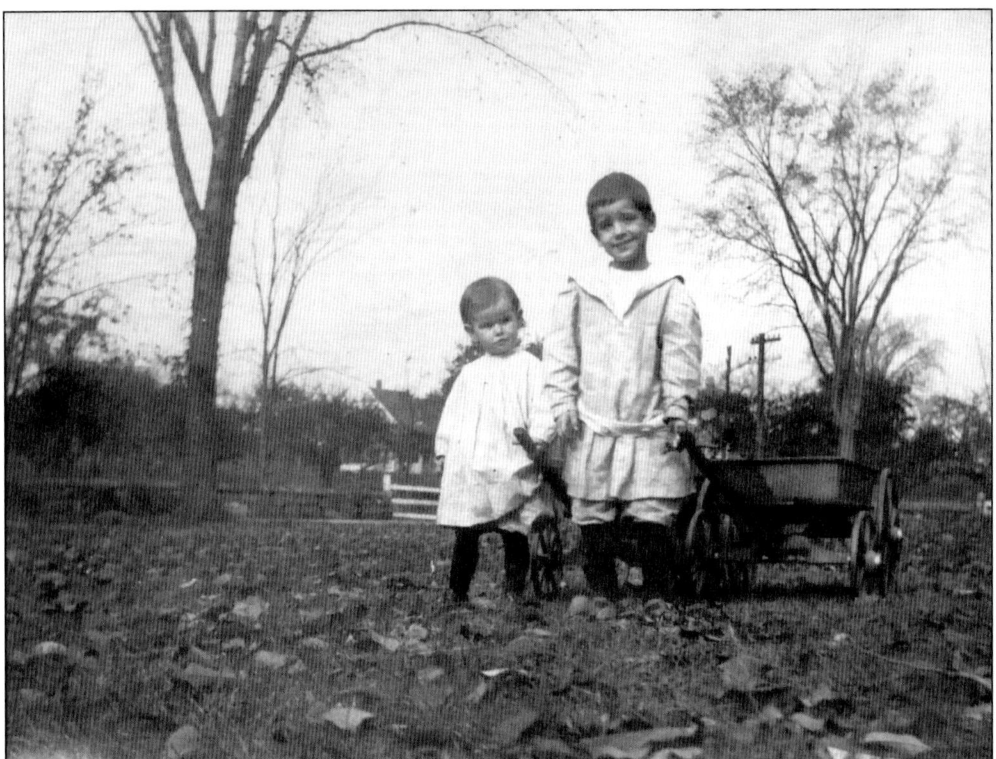

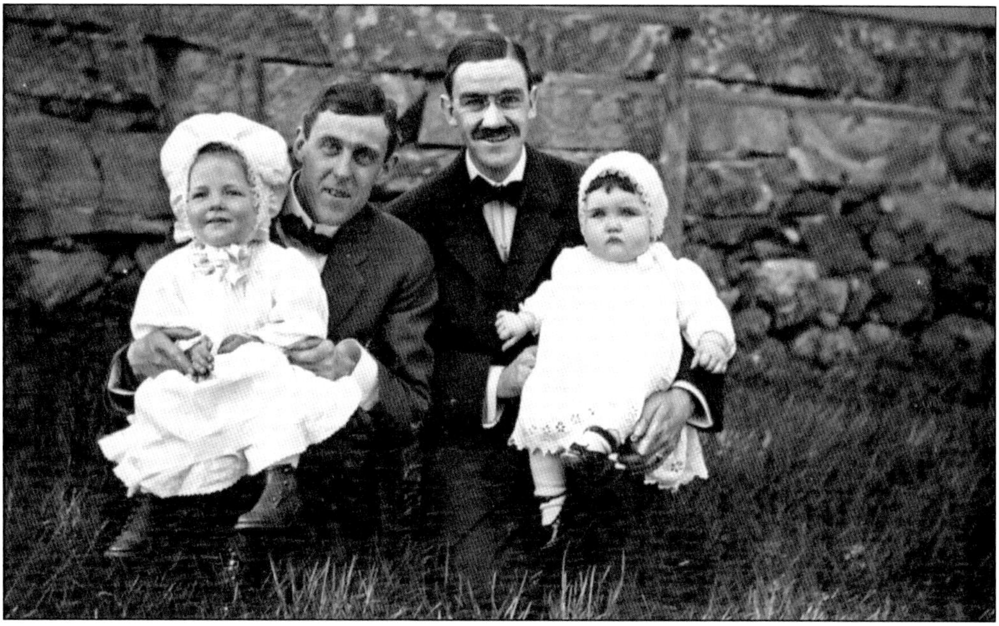

In this 1908 photograph are, from left to right, Margaret Robbins (age two), Edward J. Robbins, Winthrop A. Parkhurst, and Barbara Parkhurst (age one). Margaret Robbins Mills became actively involved in all things historical and conservation in Chelmsford. The Crooked Spring Reservation was dedicated to her with a ceremony held in June 1993. Edward J. was the town clerk from 1904 to 1923. (Chelmsford Historical Society Collection.)

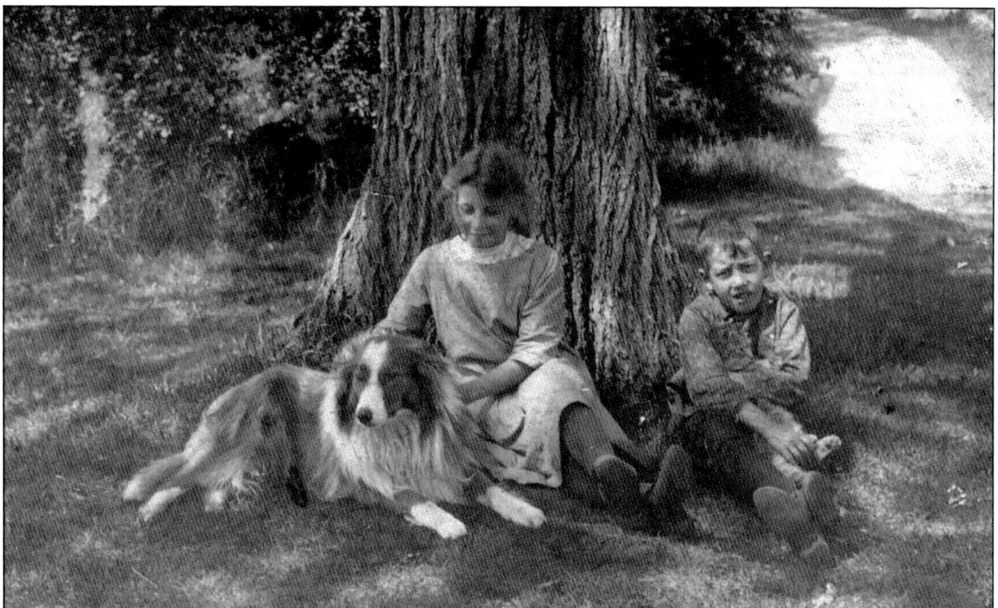

Charlotte H. Park and Phillip W. Park, the children of Fred W. Park, are seen in this c. 1913 photograph at 12 Park Place. As the wife of Gordon P. DeWolf, Charlotte replaced Town Clerk Harold C. Petterson, who died in 1956, and was elected town clerk from 1957 to 1972. Charlotte was a founder and lifelong supporter of the "Old Chelmsford" Garrison House Association. (Chelmsford Historical Society Collection.)

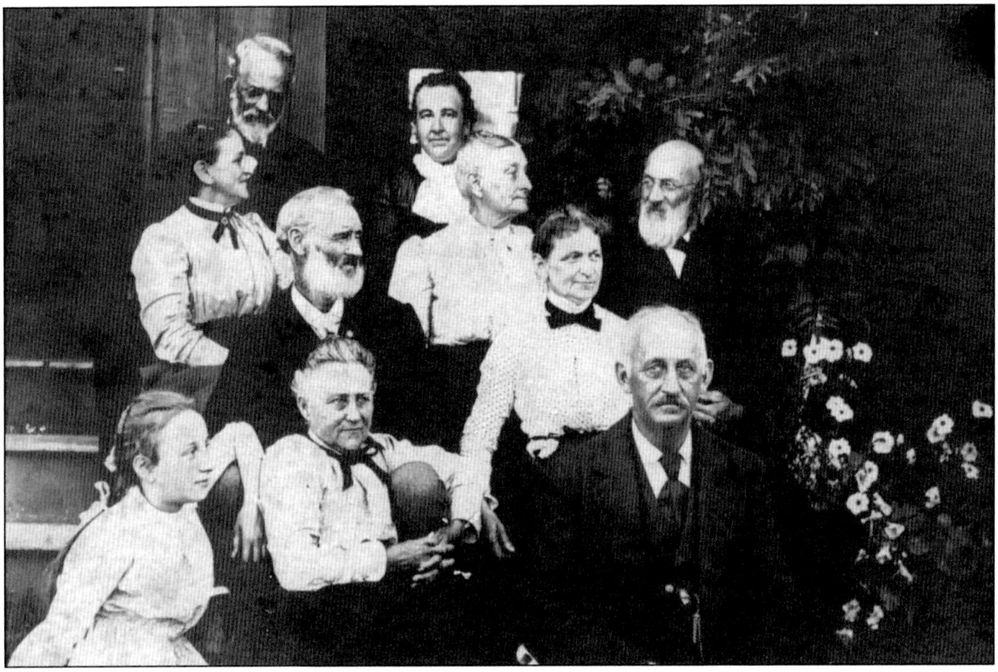

Pictured at a Bryant Emerson family gathering around 1900 are, from left to right, (first row) Abbie M. (servant), Addie E., and James P. Emerson; (second row) Henry H. and Louise F. Emerson; (third row) Bertha E. (wife of Burt), Martha P., and Rufus W. Emerson; (fourth row) Burt and Helen M. Emerson (daughter of Rufus). James, Henry, and Rufus served in the Civil War. (Brad Perham.)

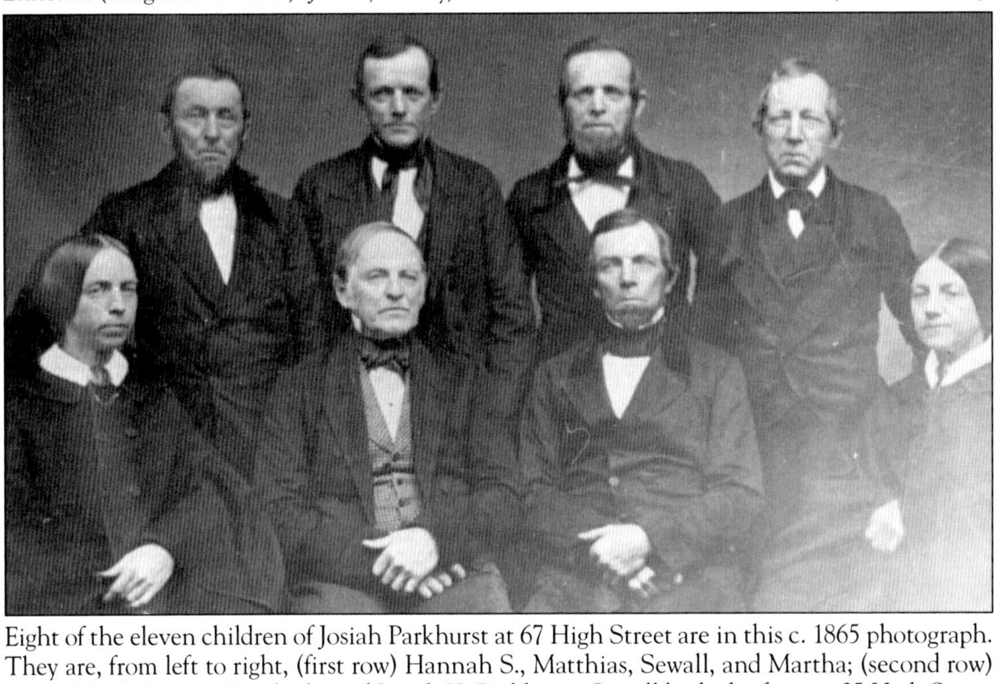

Eight of the eleven children of Josiah Parkhurst at 67 High Street are in this c. 1865 photograph. They are, from left to right, (first row) Hannah S., Matthias, Sewall, and Martha; (second row) Samuel S., Solomon, Hezekiah, and Josiah K. Parkhurst. Sewall built the farm at 35 High Street around 1820, Samuel was a storekeeper in Central Square, and Solomon inherited the farm at 67 High Street. (Linda Prescott.)

Solomon and Lucina A. Parkhurst are at 67 High Street around 1888. Once the railroad came to Chelmsford Center, there was pressure to subdivide the large tracts of Parkhurst farmland on the "Road to Robins Hill." In 1875, nephew Edwin K. Parkhurst had a survey drawn for a five-lot subdivision directly across High Street. Solomon's son S. Waldo Parkhurst built his home on lot No. 5 in 1876. (Chelmsford Historical Society Collection.)

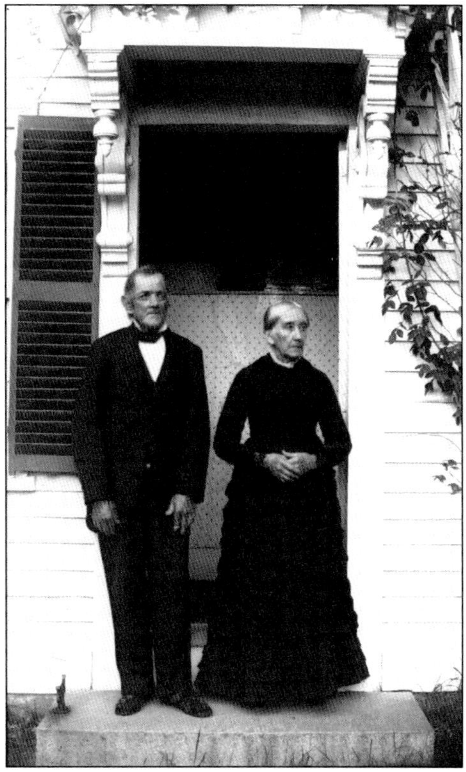

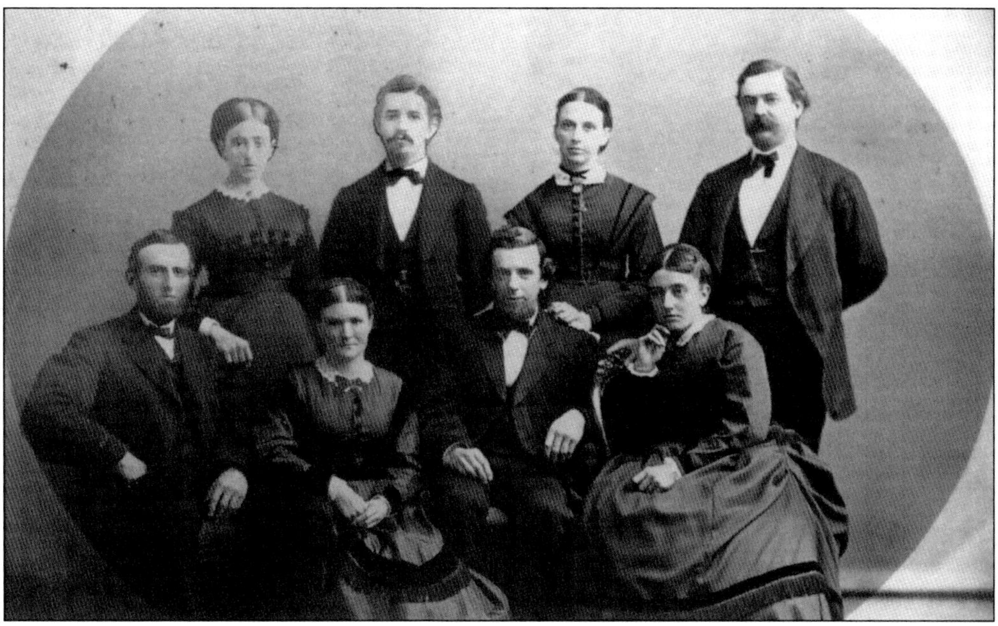

Solomon and Lucina had four married children, seen here around 1870. Pictured are, from left to right, (first row) S. Waldo Parkhurst, Martha Dutton Parkhurst (wife of S. Waldo Parkhurst), George A. Parkhurst, and Ellen Parkhurst Comins (wife of George T. Comins); (second row) Caroline Parkhurst Dutton (wife of Dr. Charles Dutton), Dr. Charles Dutton, Clorinda Hodgman Parkhurst (wife of George A. Parkhurst), and George T. Comins. (Linda Prescott.)

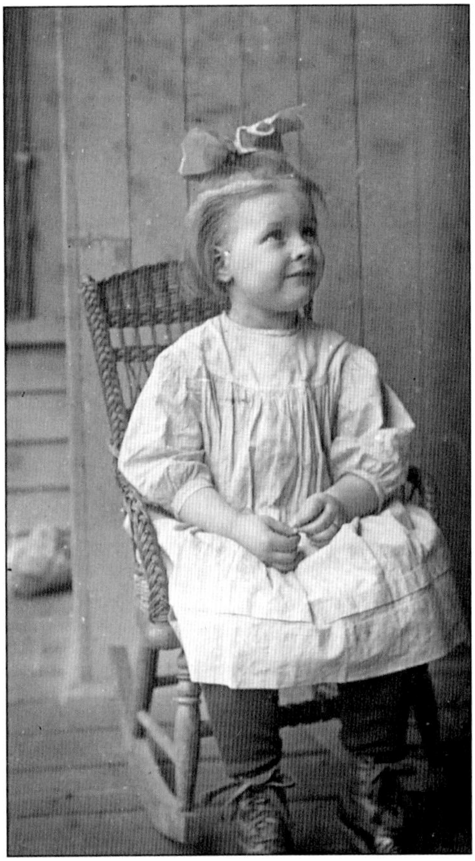

G. Thomas Parkhurst, a son of S. Waldo Parkhurst, married Ednah Byam in September 1902, and their only child, Eleanor, was born in July 1909. She is pictured at left around 1912 visiting her grandparents' home at 78 High Street. In the 1927 photograph below, Ednah, Eleanor, and G. Thomas Parkhurst are at 51 Acton Road. Eleanor is on her way to Wellesley College, where she majored in English and economics and worked part-time as a newspaper reporter. She returned home from the Midwest at the end of World War II, became involved with the *Chelmsford Newsweekly* in 1955, and was selected to write an update to the town history in 1967. Her unpublished manuscript was rediscovered in 2008 and published by this author for the Chelmsford Historical Commission in 2011. (Left, Chelmsford Historical Society Collection; below, Linda Prescott.)

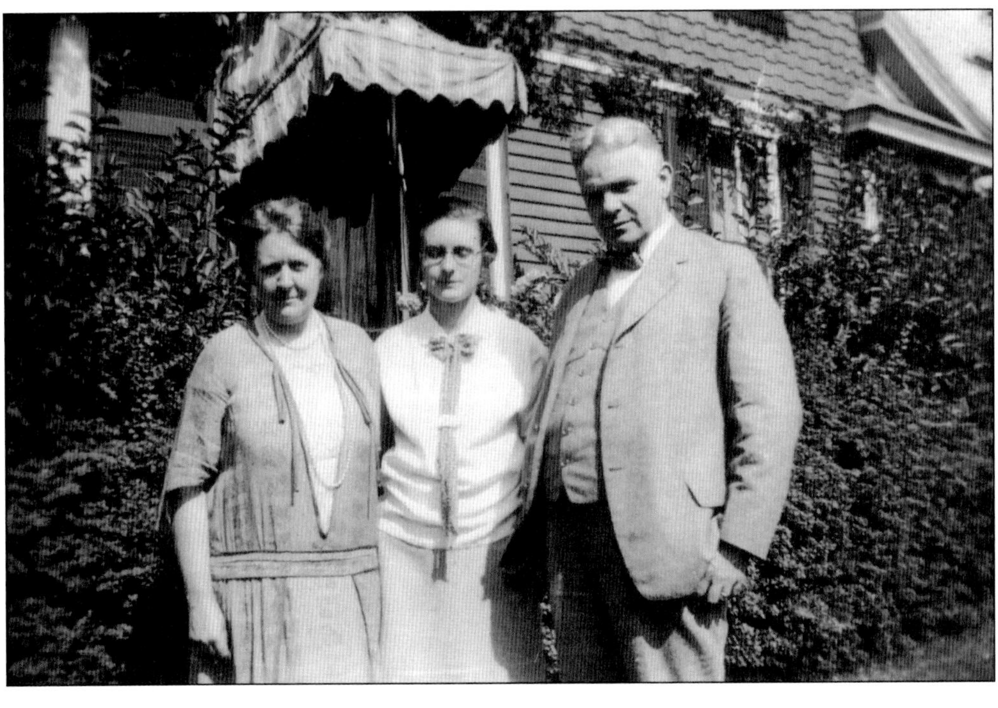

Lumber dealer Amos B. Adams, the grandson of Deacon Otis Adams, had the portrait at right taken at Arthur I. Emerson's studio around 1890. Amos died in 1908, at age 54, living only four years longer than his father, Otis J. Adams, and leaving behind his wife and seven children. The photograph below shows the family with five of the children and their dog around 1900 in front of the Fletcher Street entrance to their farm at 80 Chelmsford Street. Pictured, from left to right, are Hettie E., Edith H., Mabel M., Louise A., Ruth E., Amos B., and Adelbert B. Adams. The siding on the farmhouse, seen in this view, came from the Fletcher quarry on the Westford–North Chelmsford town line, according to a note on the photograph. (Both, Chelmsford Historical Society Collection.)

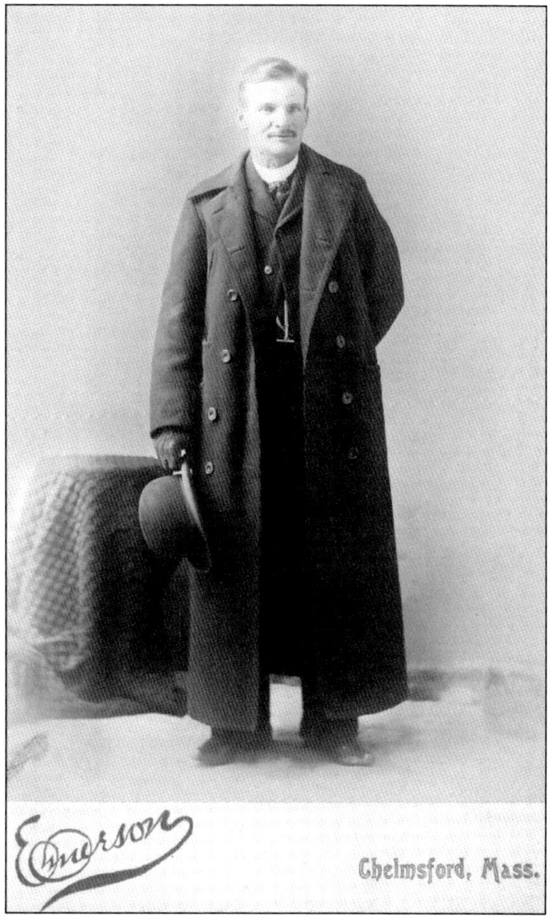

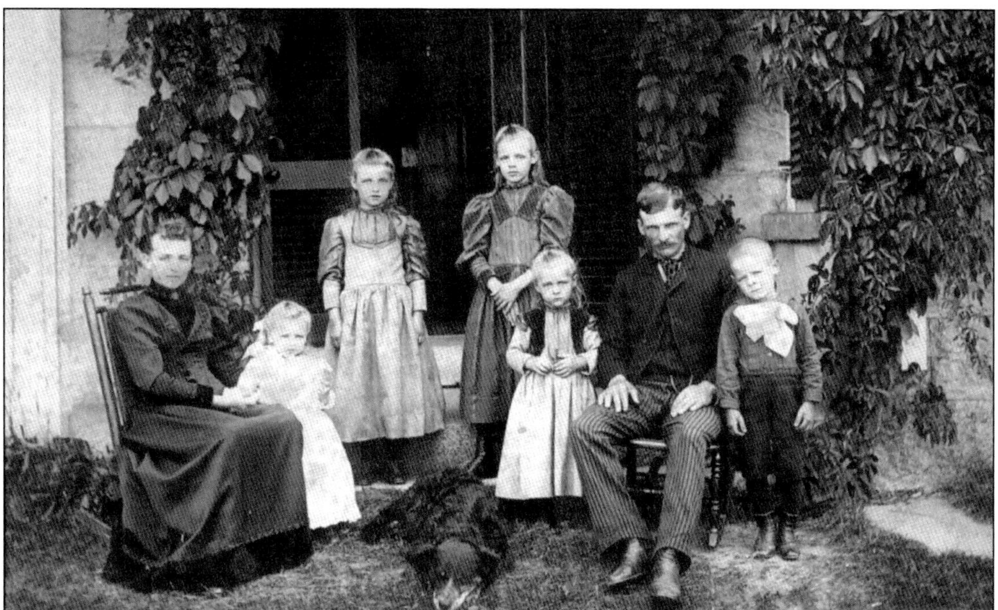

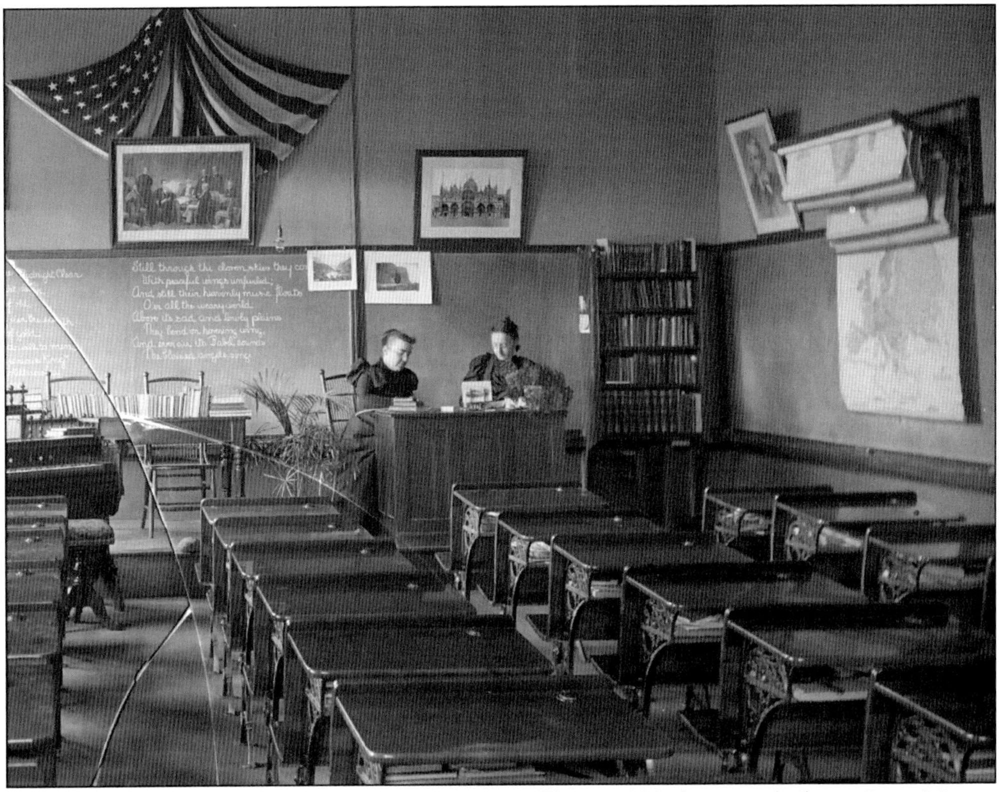

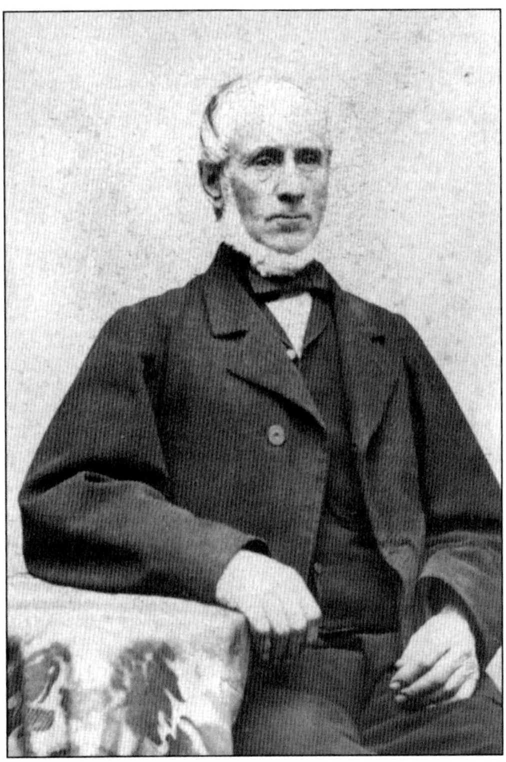

This c. 1891 photograph shows Susie M. Emerson (left) with Frances Clark in Susie's Centre School classroom. Frances at age 21 had just started teaching, and due to the resignation of high school principal B.W. Tinker the previous spring, Susie was asked to take that position. Susie is likely preparing Frances to take over her duties as intermediate class teacher in the fall. (Chelmsford Historical Society Collection.)

Deacon David Perham, shown in this c. 1880 Gilchrest carte de visite, was an astute businessman. He started the Perham Cider Mill in 1840 on the family farm on Westford Street, built the Central Baptist Church in 1868, and, in partnership with Dr. Levi Howard, Edwin K. Parkhurst, and Benjamin M. Fiske, operated the Chelmsford Mill Company and icehouses in Central Square from 1865 to 1884. (Chelmsford Historical Society Collection.)

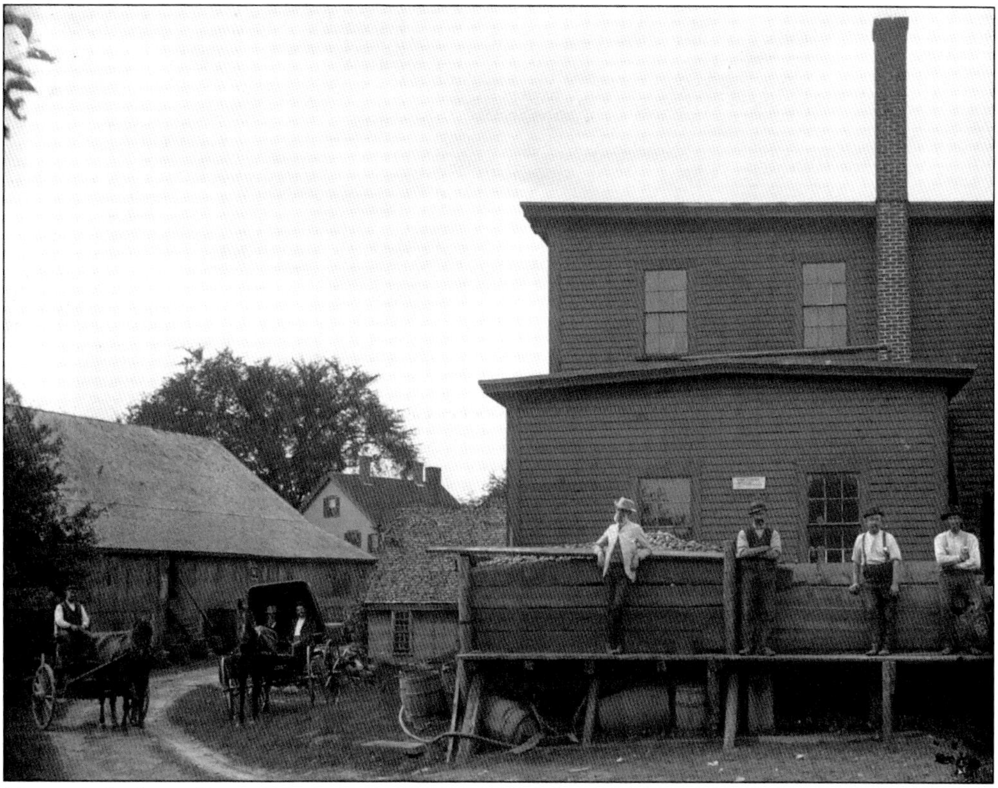

Henry S. Perham, Deacon David's son, continued operating the family cider mill. Henry is wearing the white jacket in this c. 1900 photograph. He was instrumental in the public library and the preservation of town records, was asked to update the town history in 1904, and chaired the 250th anniversary celebration committee in 1905. Henry died in 1906, and Rev. Wilson Waters published the history book in 1917. (Chelmsford Historical Society Collection.)

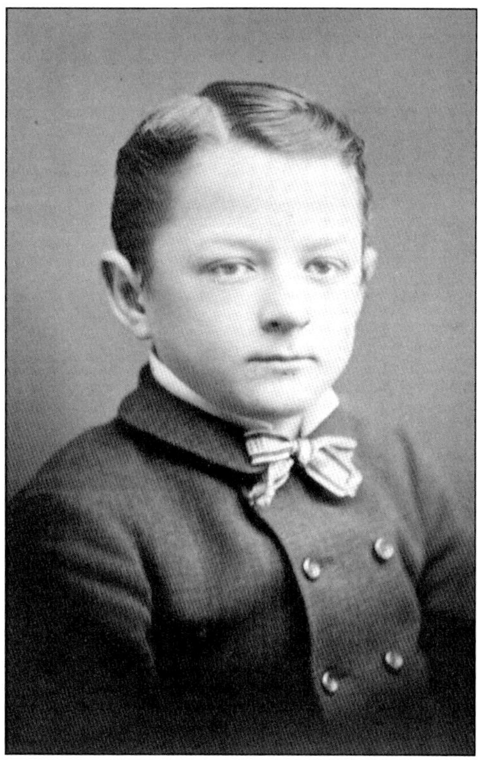

Henry S. Perham's son Walter, seen here as a boy around 1880, went on to run the family cider mill and a funeral home but also branched out into town and state government. He served on several appointed committees and was elected to one term as a selectman, two years as a state representative, and six years as a state senator, and was town moderator from 1915 to 1946. (Chelmsford Historical Society Collection.)

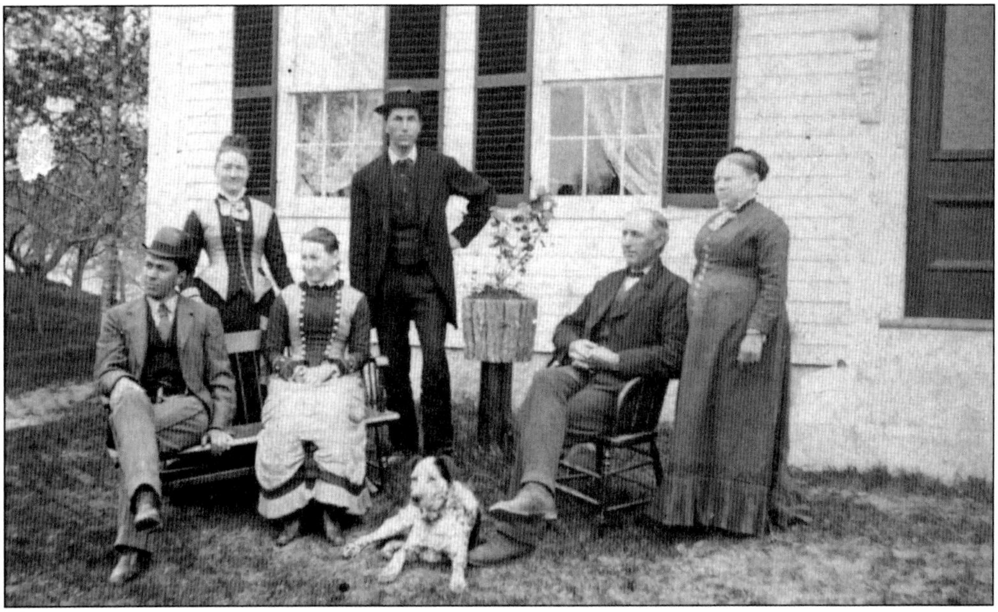

The David C. Perham family is seen here on the right half of a Simon Towle stereopticon slide dated May 14, 1879. Pictured, from left to right, are son Edwin C.; daughter Emma J.; daughter Lottie L.; Herbert C. Sweetser; David C. Perham; and his wife, Maria A. Perham. David was originally Dewitt Clinton Perham from Wilton, New Hampshire, but changed his first name to David at an early age. (Brad Perham.)

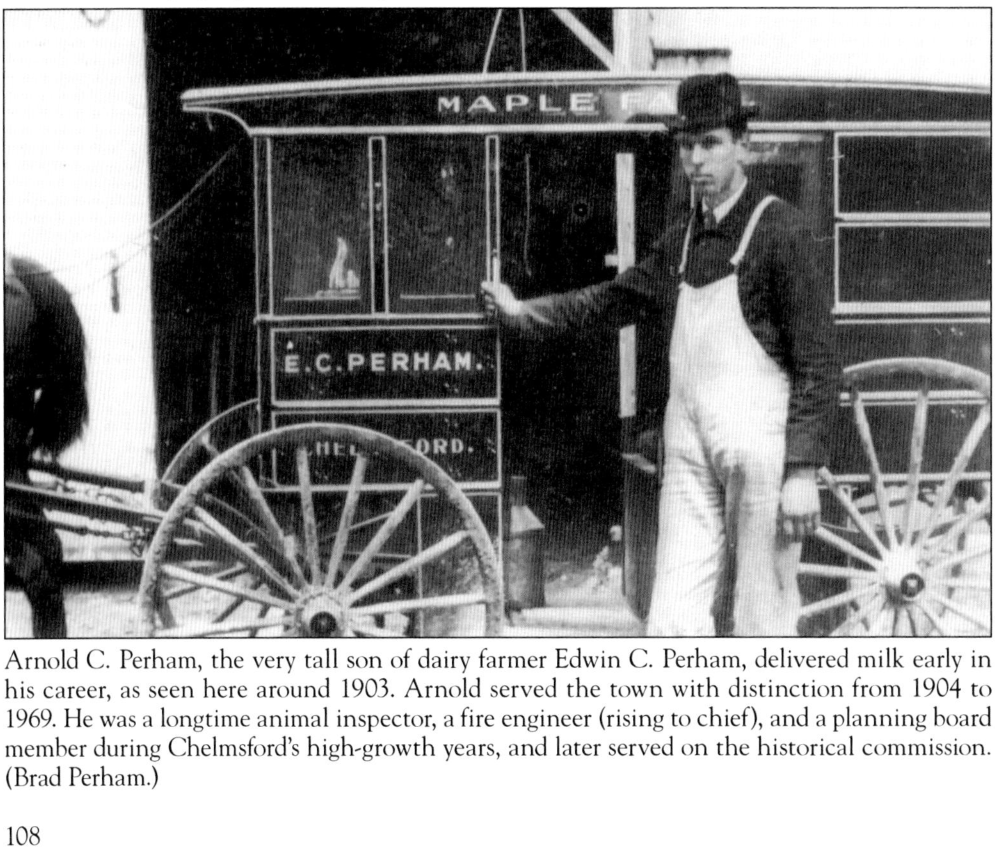

Arnold C. Perham, the very tall son of dairy farmer Edwin C. Perham, delivered milk early in his career, as seen here around 1903. Arnold served the town with distinction from 1904 to 1969. He was a longtime animal inspector, a fire engineer (rising to chief), and a planning board member during Chelmsford's high-growth years, and later served on the historical commission. (Brad Perham.)

Floyer J. and Clara M. Whittemore had this portrait taken in December 1883 after their marriage and just before a wedding trip, presumably to a warmer climate. They bought land in 1889 near Clara's Upham family home, building the carriage shop first and then the house and stable at 127 North Road. Floyer's brother Calvin H. Whittemore went into the carriage business in North Chelmsford. (Chelmsford Historical Society Collection.)

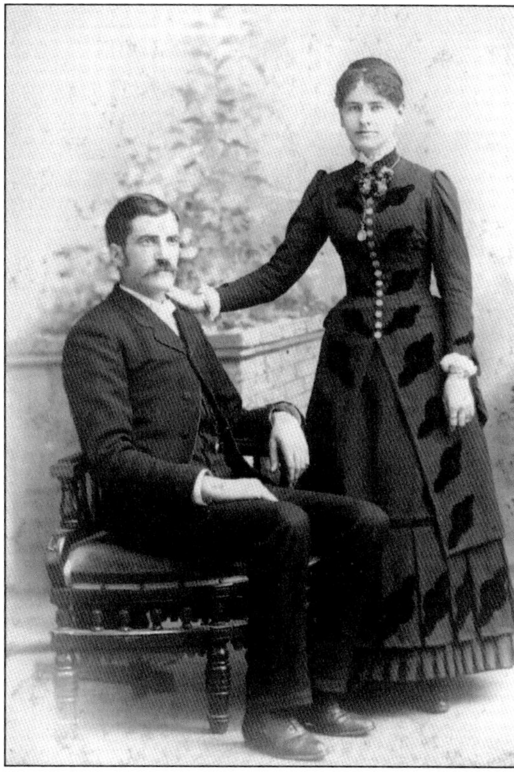

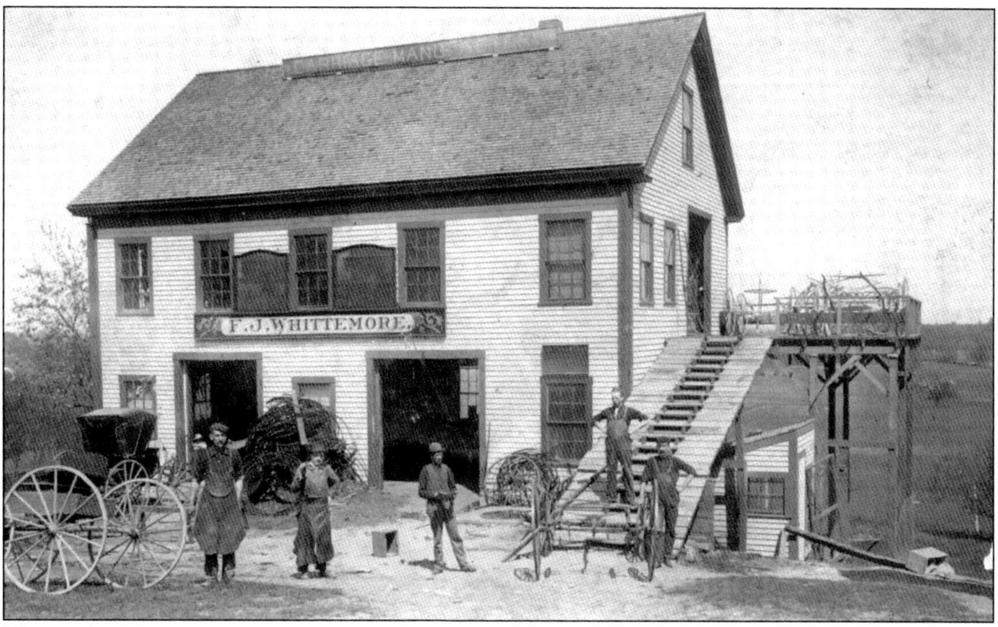

This is the carriage "manufactory" in 1899, with Floyer J. Whittemore standing at center holding some paperwork. The business did not survive the transition to automobiles and service stations, and the shop eventually became derelict. Son F. Earl Whittemore sold the property out of the family in 1946, and Erlin Road (accepted in 1954) was constructed through the site of the shop. (Chelmsford Historical Society Collection.)

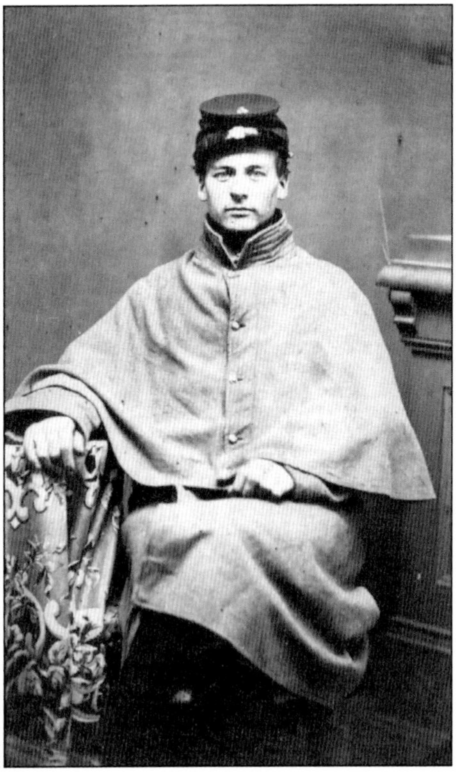

George A. Byam was a Civil War veteran from Charles E.A. Bartlett's Company K and is seen here in his Civil War coat and hat around 1863. George was a town auditor for two years, a selectman for six years, and on the school committee for ten years. In Lowell, he practiced law and founded the Byam Bros. Real Estate and Insurance Company. (Richard Bump.)

The George A. Byam family around 1900 includes, from left to right, Arnold A., Rebecca C. Emerson (extended family member), George A., Bernard H., Ray S., Mary S., and George A. Byam Jr. Mary was a Byam before her 1869 marriage and was a teacher of the deaf along with Harriet B. Rogers at 1 Academy Street in 1866, becoming assistant principal of the Clarke School in 1867. (Chelmsford Historical Society Collection.)

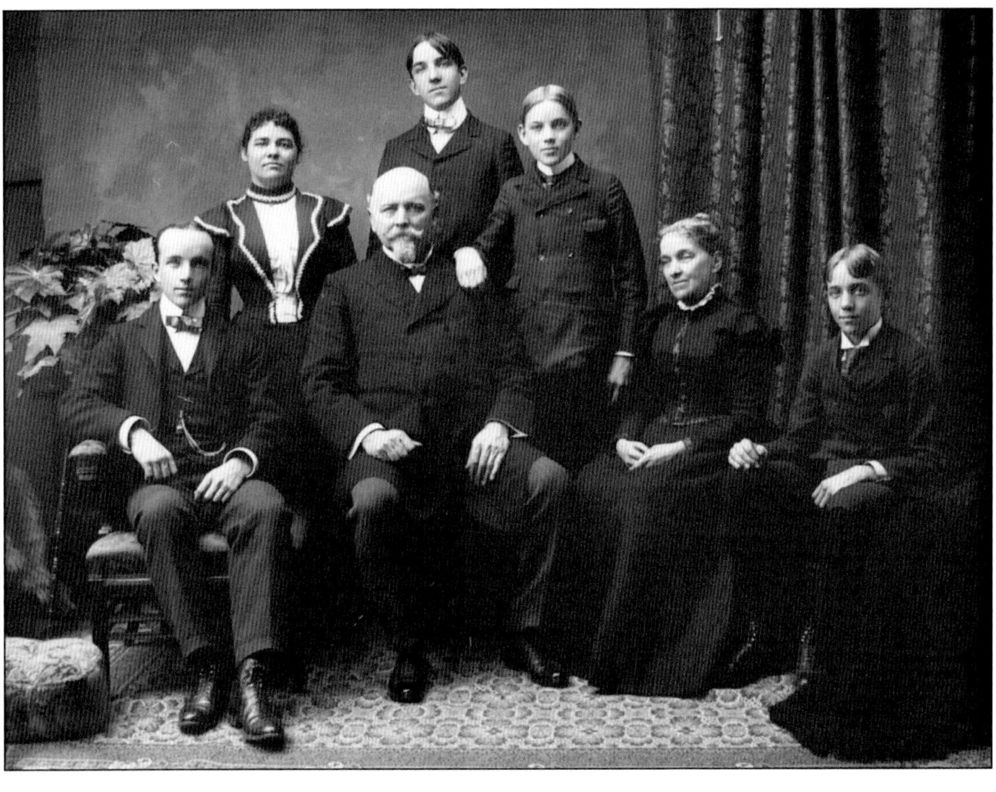

Daniel P. Byam, son of blacksmith Marcus D. Byam at 11 Maple Road, is seen here around 1870. In his second tour of duty in the Civil War, he kept a daily diary. On May 19, 1864, while riding a train from Harper's Ferry with other members of the Signal Corps, his car derailed, rolled over four times, and landed upside down in a creek. Byam survived. (Chelmsford Historical Society Collection.)

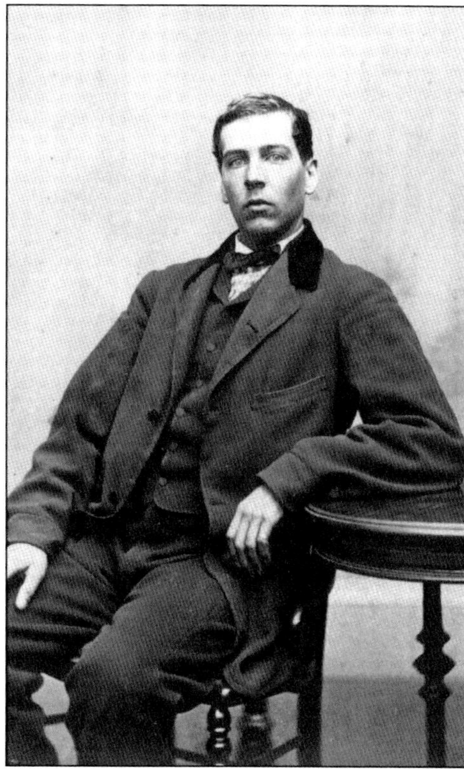

Daniel P. Byam, now the grandfather of Eleanor Parkhurst, has joined the eight other surviving Grand Army of the Republic (Union army veterans) members from South Chelmsford in April 1914 for a 50th-reunion gathering. In this photograph are, from left to right, Samuel J. Garland, Robert Fletcher, Lorenzo Sweetser, Thomas Sullivan, Byam, S.M. Hutchins, Henry H. Emerson, Charles L. Adams, and Benjamin M. Fletcher. (Linda Prescott.)

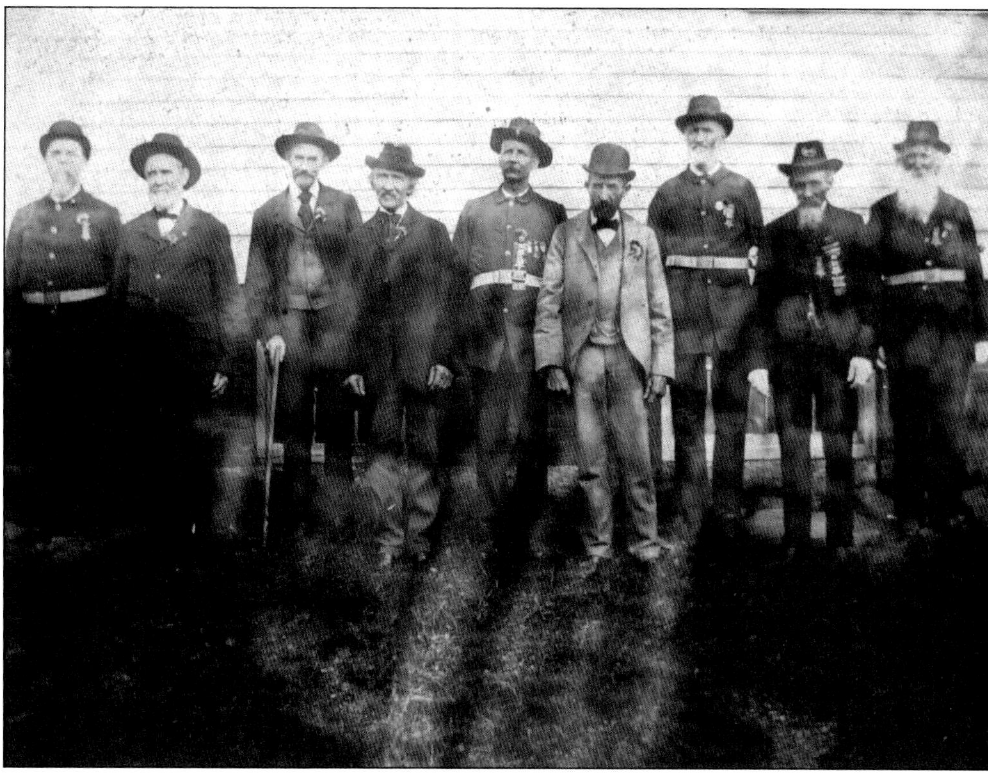

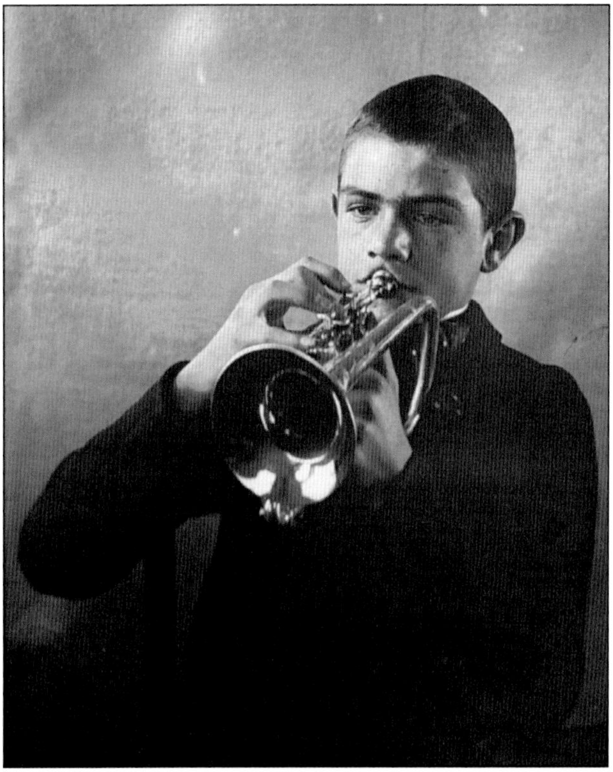

G. Thomas Parkhurst was musically talented, specializing in the cornet, which plays like a trumpet but has a warm mellow tone as opposed to the more penetrating sound of the trumpet, but playing and teaching both instruments. For a short time, he toured with the John Philip Sousa Band, which performed concerts between 1892 and 1931 to sold-out crowds in America and around the world. (Chelmsford Historical Society Collection.)

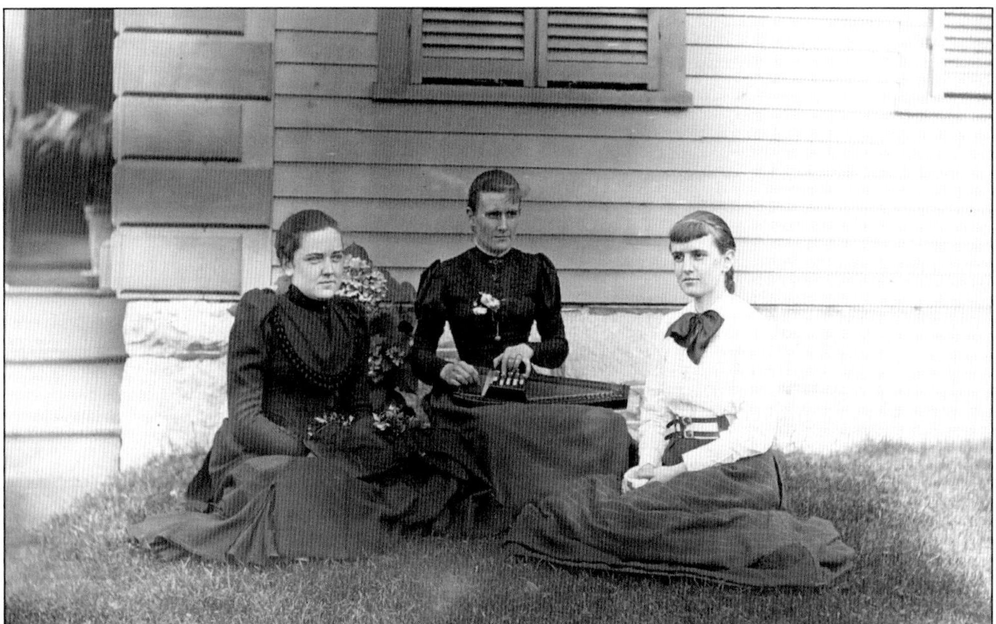

Emma L. Parkhurst shared the family's interest in music and was a music teacher in addition to working in her father's store in Central Square as a clerk. In this c. 1892 photograph, Emma (center) is playing an autoharp, and with her are her first cousin Amy L. Comins (left) and Bertha A. Parkhurst. None of the girls ever married. (Chelmsford Historical Society Collection.)

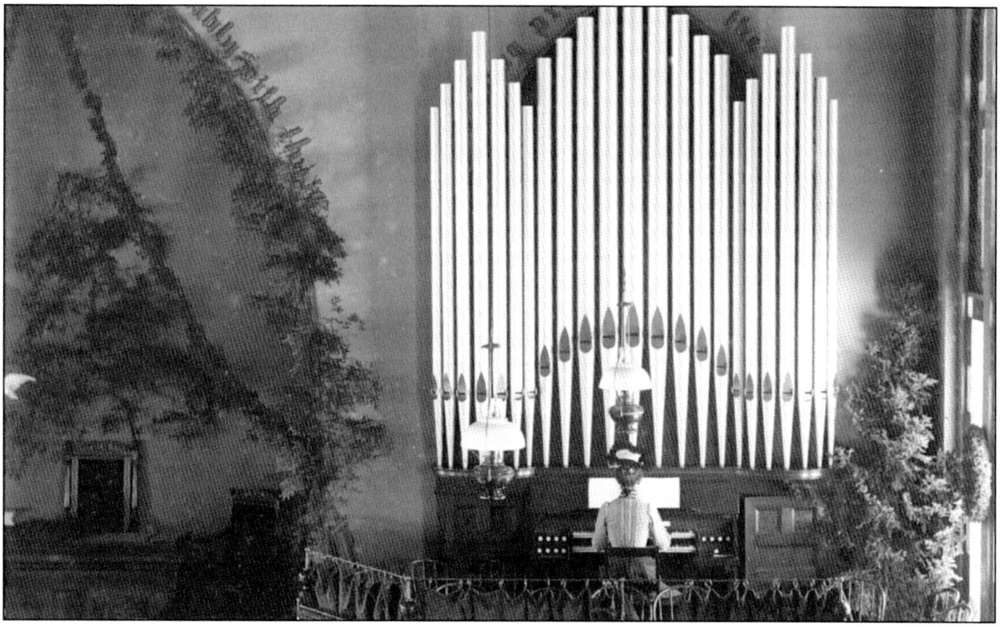

Emma L. Parkhurst was the organist at the First Parish Unitarian Church for 45 years and is seen here at the pipe organ around 1890 surrounded by evergreen Christmas decorations. Amos F. Adams was a contributor to the purchase of this new organ. Two kerosene lamps are hanging from the ceiling to illuminate the keyboard since gas lighting was not installed in the church until 1903. (Chelmsford Historical Society Collection.)

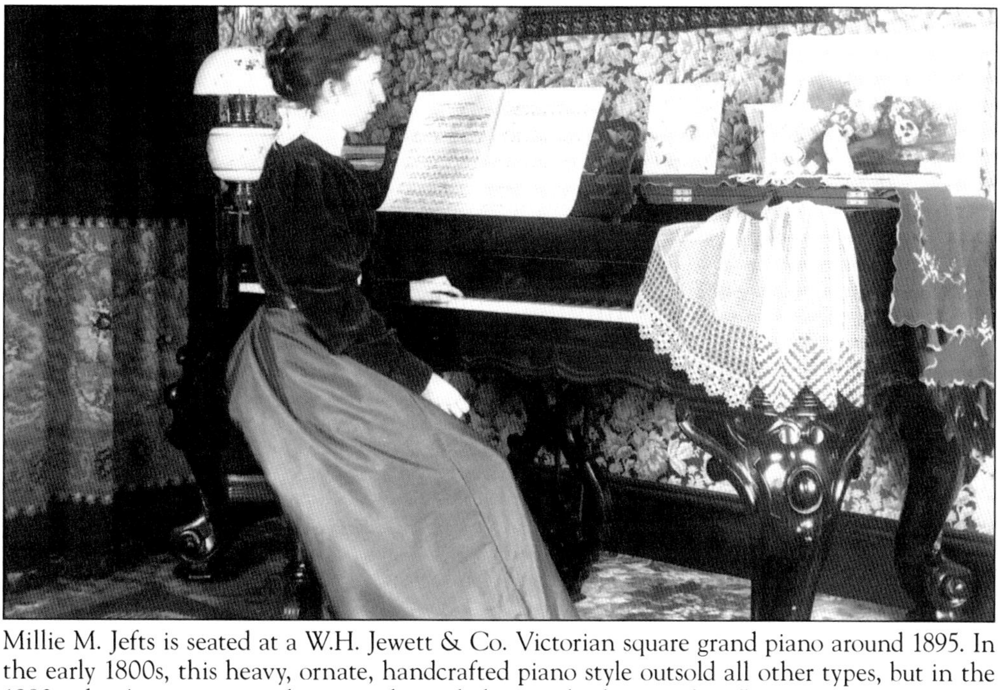

Millie M. Jefts is seated at a W.H. Jewett & Co. Victorian square grand piano around 1895. In the early 1800s, this heavy, ornate, handcrafted piano style outsold all other types, but in the 1880s, the American upright piano, being lighter and taking up less floor space, rendered the square grand obsolete. The square grand became a garish reminder of a gilded age, and most were destroyed. (Chelmsford Historical Society Collection.)

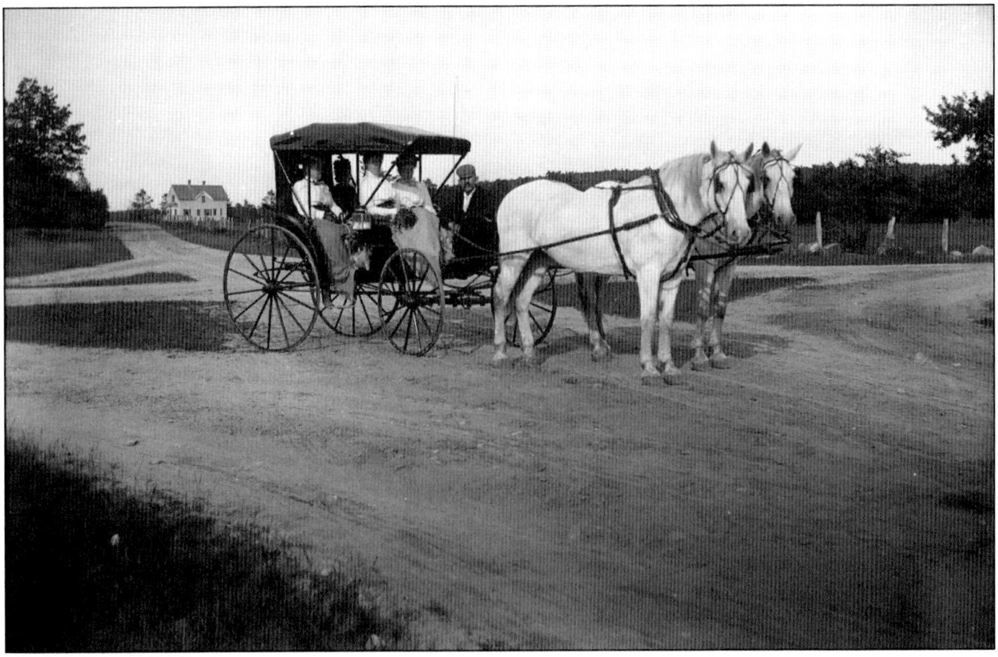

Frank A. Emerson is taking three lady friends and a dog out for a Sunday drive and is stopped at this unidentified intersection so his brother Arthur can take the photograph, around 1890. There are four seats in the carriage, so one lady had to sit on the lap of another. Frank's mother, Adelaide, is sitting in the back left seat as a chaperone. (Chelmsford Historical Society Collection.)

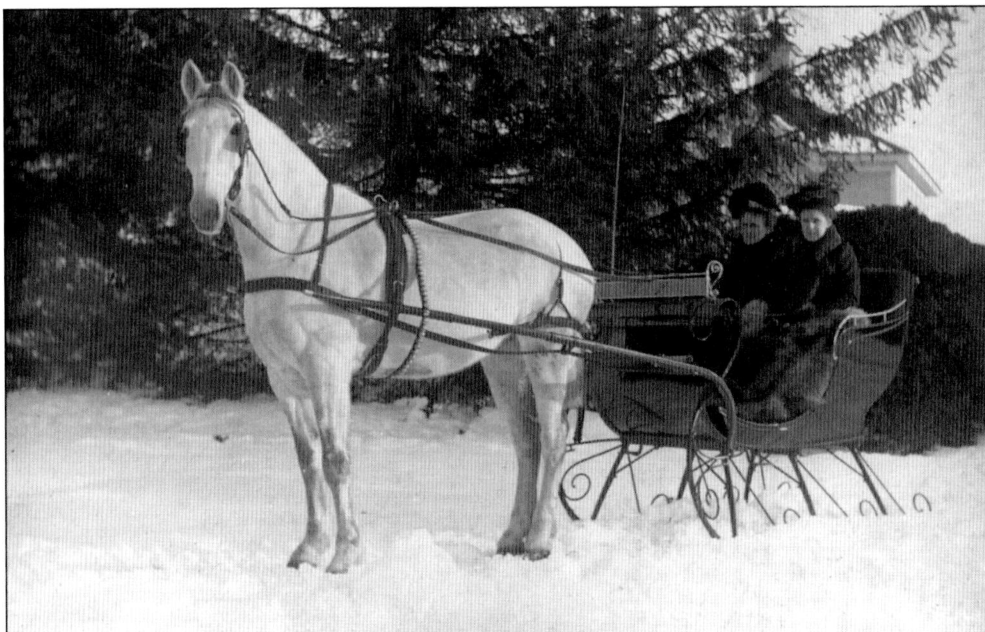

Emma L. and Bertha A. Parkhurst may be heading off to church or trying out a brand new sleigh in January 1902. The heavy coats, fur pieces, and a thick rug or bearskin were needed to keep warm. As organist at the First Parish Church, Emma had to get to church, regardless of weather. The barn and windmill at 78 High Street are in the background. (Linda Prescott.)

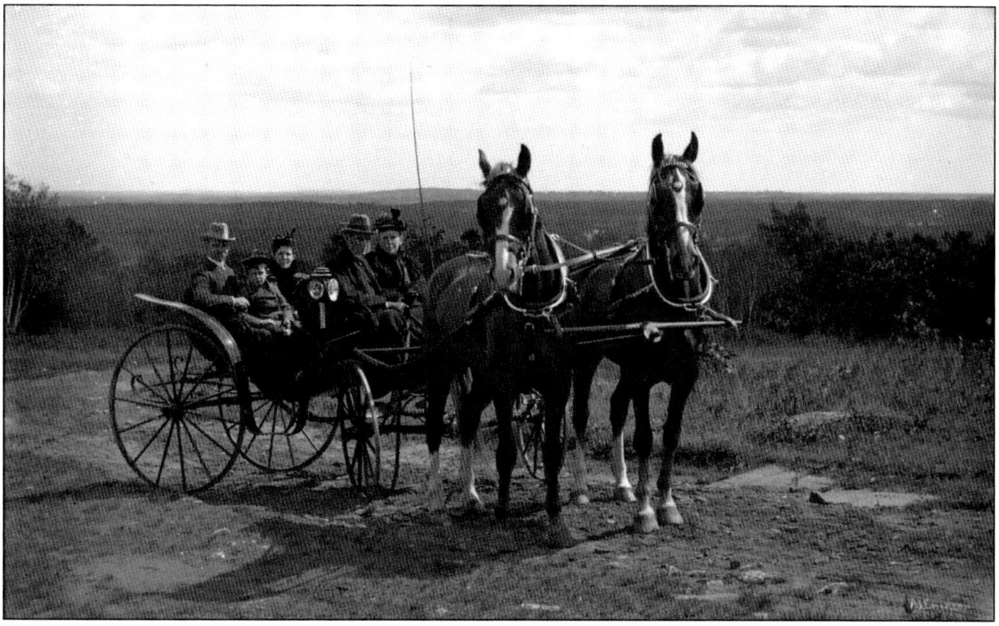

Benjamin M. Fiske is taking an unidentified family group for a pleasure trip to the Summit House on top of Robins Hill around 1895. His wife, Elizabeth A. Fiske, was the daughter of Rev. John Parkhurst, who was minister of the First Baptist Church in South Chelmsford when it split into two factions in 1846. Reverend Parkhurst then became the first minister of the new Central Baptist Church. (Chelmsford Historical Society Collection.)

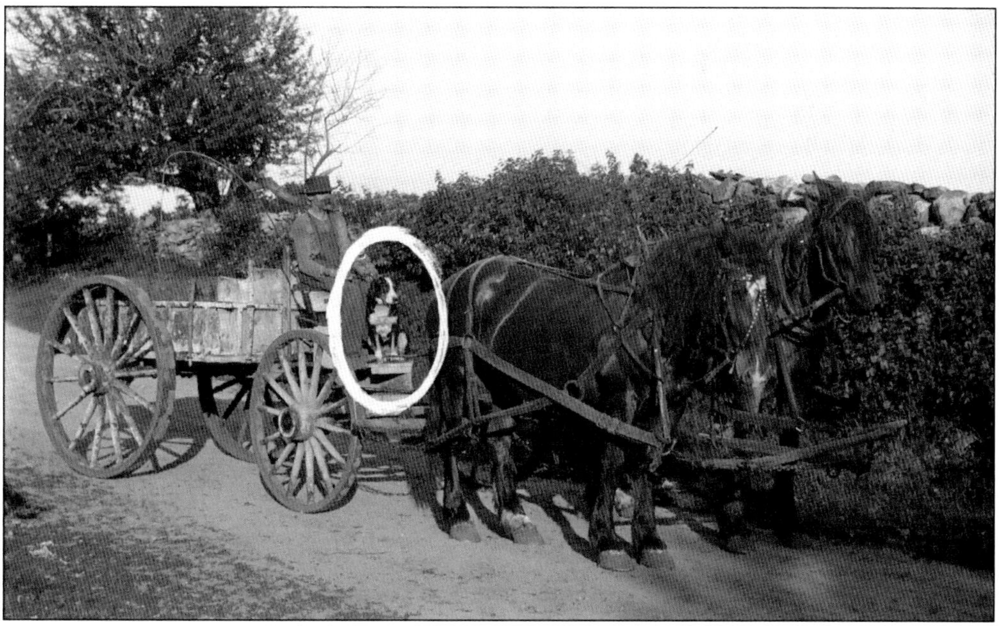

Walter Winning from 19 Elm Street was driving with his daughter Gladys (behind circle) and a dog when Arthur Emerson took this photograph around 1900. Henry R. Hodson of 243 Westford Street owned a similar heavy-duty wagon, and while on lunch break at a gravel pit in October 1903, sliding gravel spooked the team, and Henry tragically lost his life trying to stop them. (Chelmsford Historical Society Collection.)

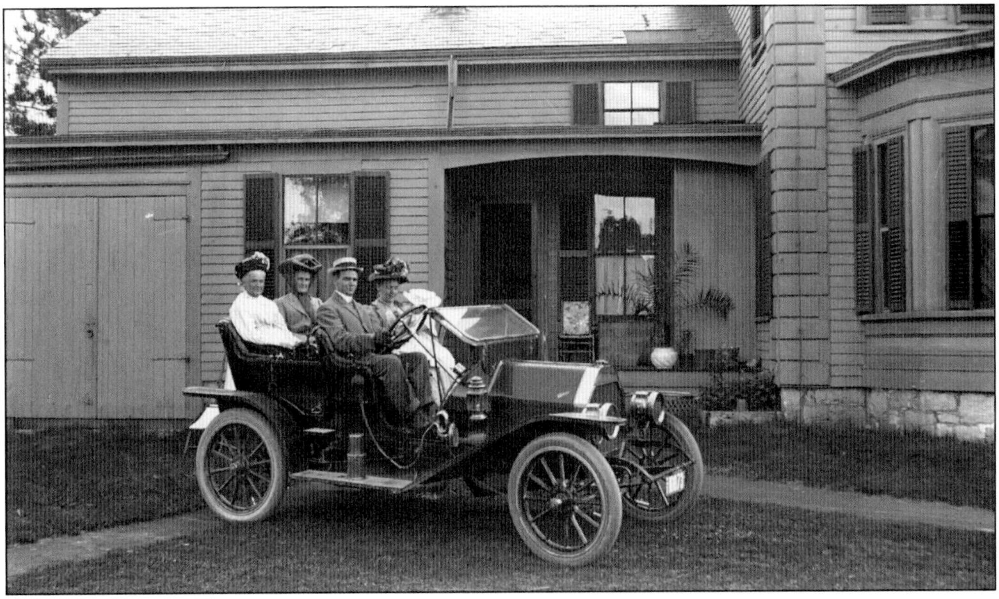

G. Thomas Parkhurst is showing off his new Simplex Model 50 automobile in August 1911. In the car are, from left to right, Martha D., Emma L., G. Thomas, Ednah B., and Eleanor Parkhurst (in Ednah's lap). The Simplex Model 50 was one of the most expensive and well-built luxury cars available at the time and, in racing circles, had a reputation for durability. (Chelmsford Historical Society Collection.)

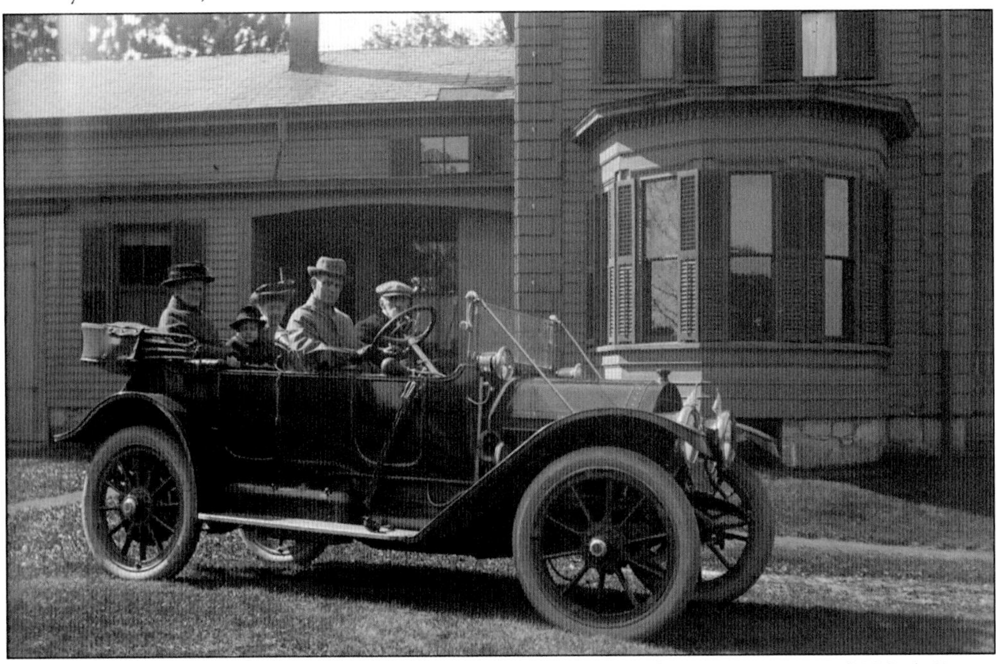

In 1913, G. Thomas drove another automobile, this time a Simplex touring car, to 78 High Street to take the family out for a drive. His mother, Martha, had died the year before, and the people in the car are, from left to right, Emma L., Eleanor, Ednah B., G. Thomas, and S. Waldo Parkhurst. Note that Simplex cars, even though American-made, had right-hand drive. (Chelmsford Historical Society Collection.)

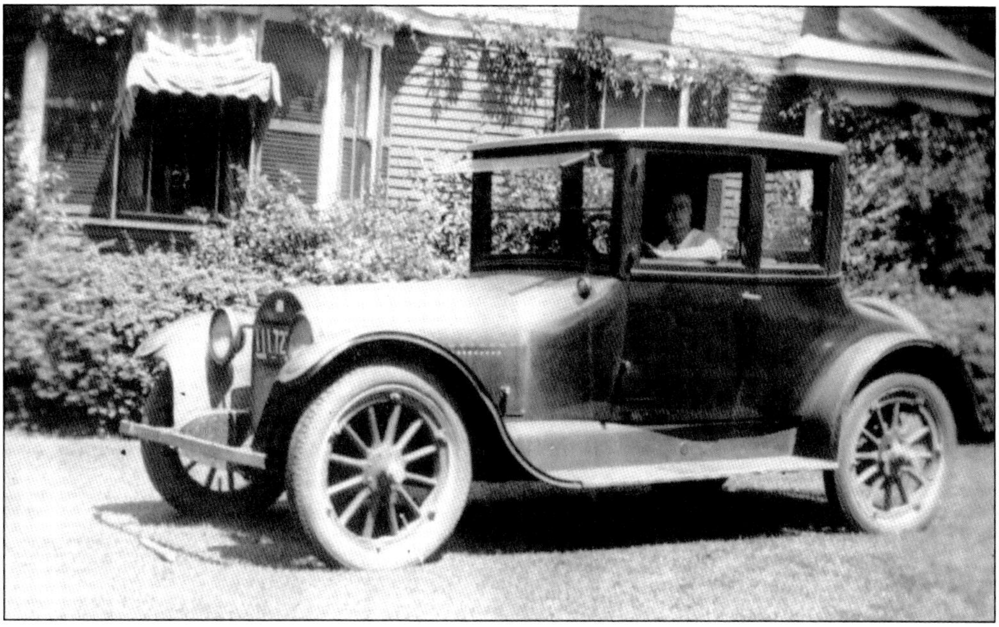

Eleanor Parkhurst is pictured here in the family's new 1927 Plymouth after her 18th birthday. She became interested in the Chelmsford Girl Scouts in 1919, joining Troop No. 1 as a Tenderfoot, and took part in all that the Scouts had to offer. In April 1928, Eleanor received the highest honor, the Golden Eaglet award, and continued scouting with the Wellesley College Girl Scout Club. (John Crawford III.)

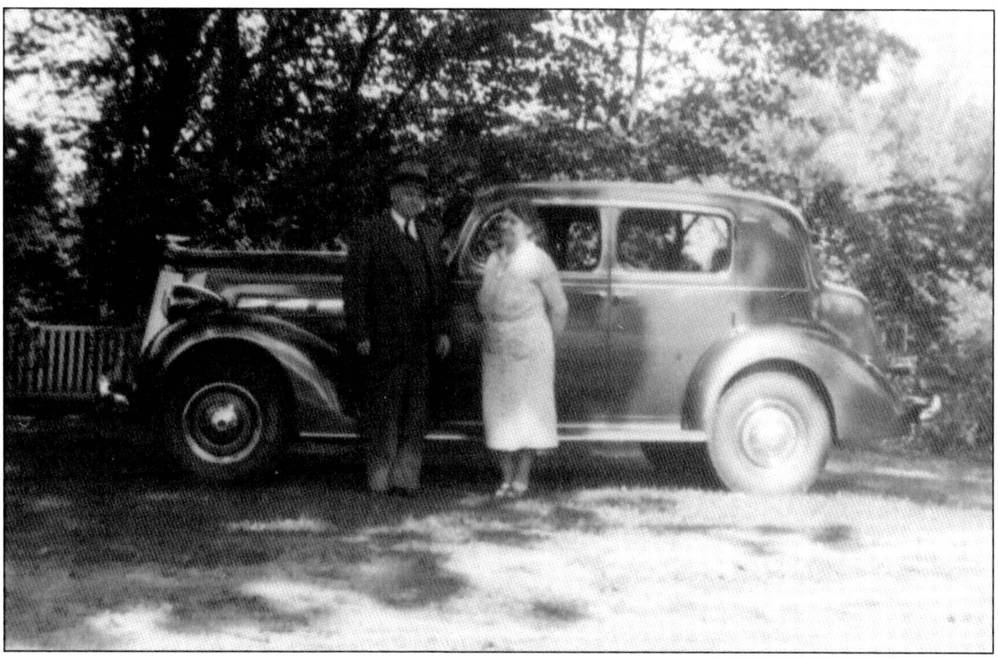

G. Thomas and Ednah Parkhurst are proud of their brand-new 1937 Packard. Eleanor's parents died in 1955 and 1961, and she stored the Packard in the barn at 78 High Street. When the vehicle was sold around 1967, the carburetor was cleaned and a battery installed, and the car started and was driven onto the trailer, according to the present owners of 78 High Street. (John Crawford III.)

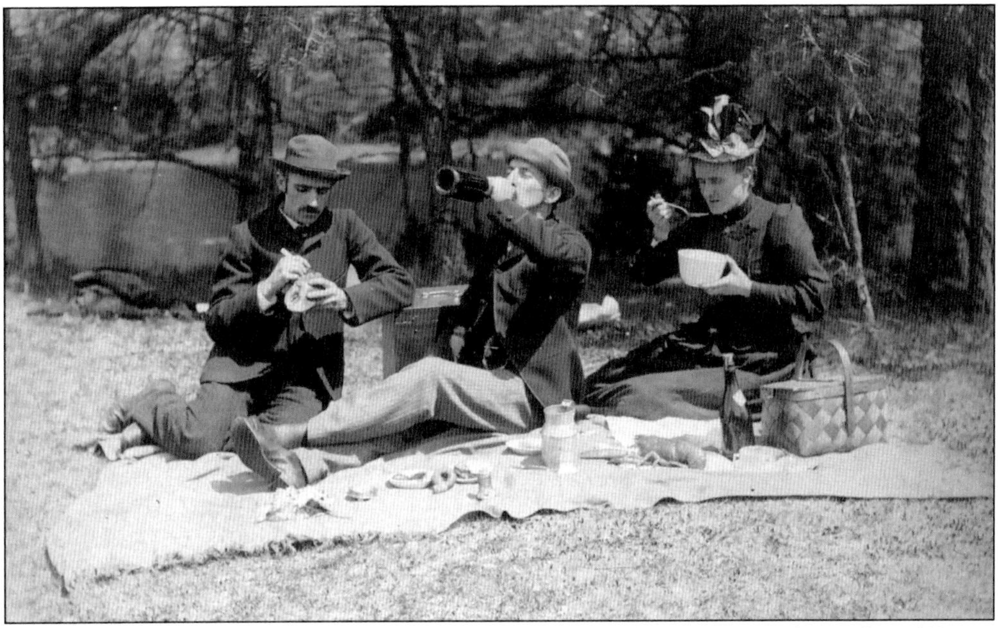

Picnics were a popular pastime. Willis B. Parkhurst (left), Arthur I. Emerson (center), and Emma L. Parkhurst are polishing off shrimp and a lobster on a riverbank, possibly the Merrimack River, with some Moxie or wine to drink. Arthur and Emma, 10 years younger, had been coworkers at the S.W. Parkhurst store and spent a lot of their leisure time together, based on numerous photographs, but never married. (Linda Prescott.)

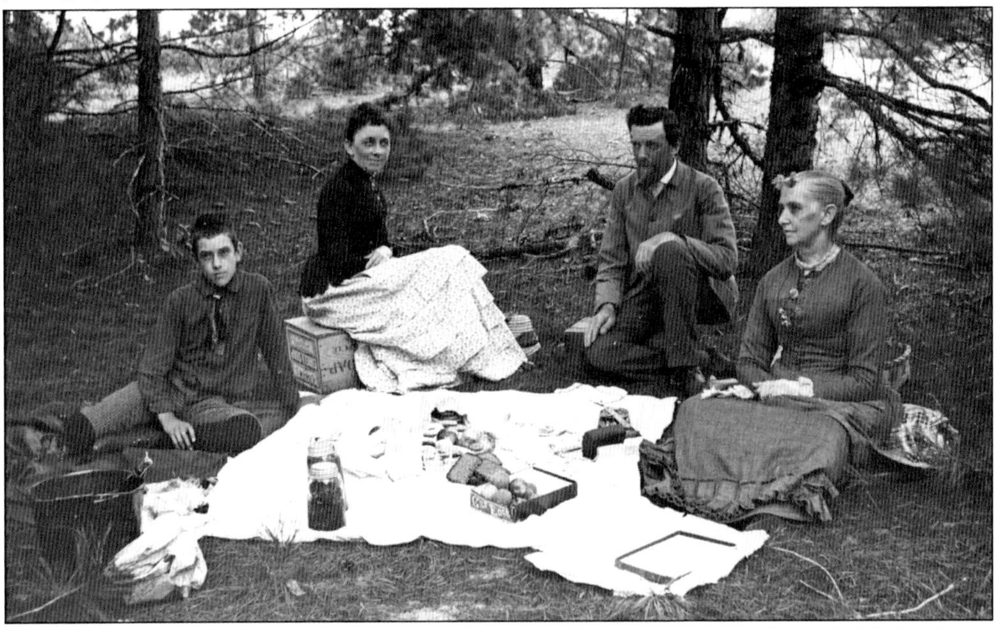

From left to right, Arthur and Malvina Hodgman and George A. and Clorinda H. Parkhurst are having a picnic lunch in a pine grove around 1890. Malvina was Clorinda's younger sister, and after 1878, she became the housekeeper for Dr. John C. Bartlett's widow, Maria J. Bartlett, at 15 Bartlett Street. She stayed on with the Bartlett family as a boarder until she died in 1907. (Chelmsford Historical Society Collection.)

Nine

CHURCHES

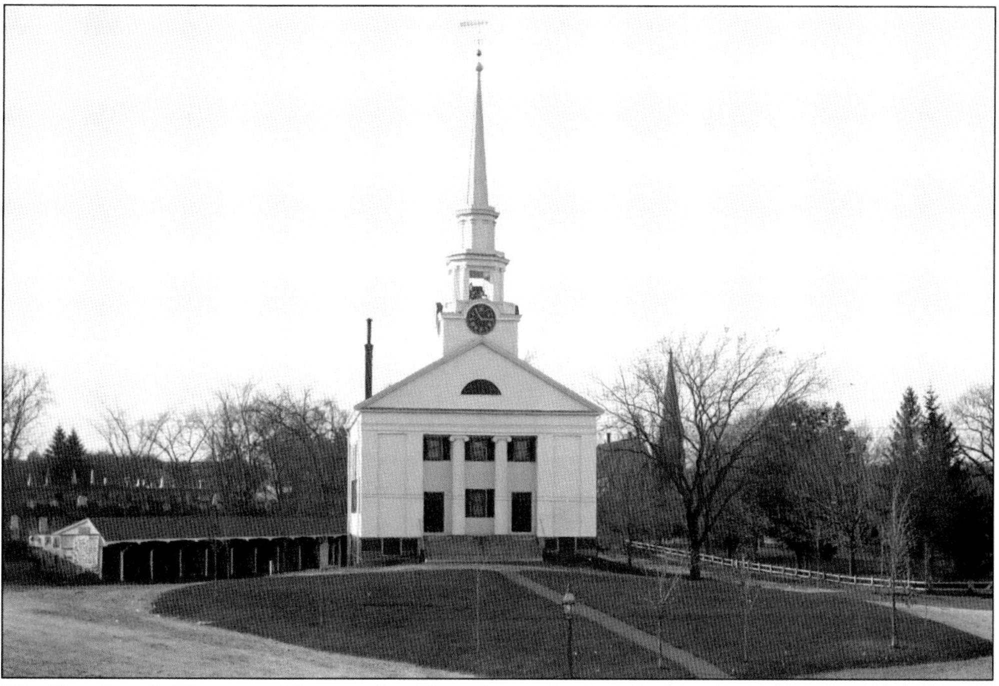

The First Parish Unitarian Universalist Church was the fourth church on this site and dedicated on April 19, 1843. The area in front of the church was described as a wasteland in 1876 with no lawns, shrubbery, walks, or roadbeds. The Village Improvement Association took up a public subscription to make the improvements seen here around 1890. The church voted to remove the horse sheds in 1917. (Chelmsford Historical Society Collection.)

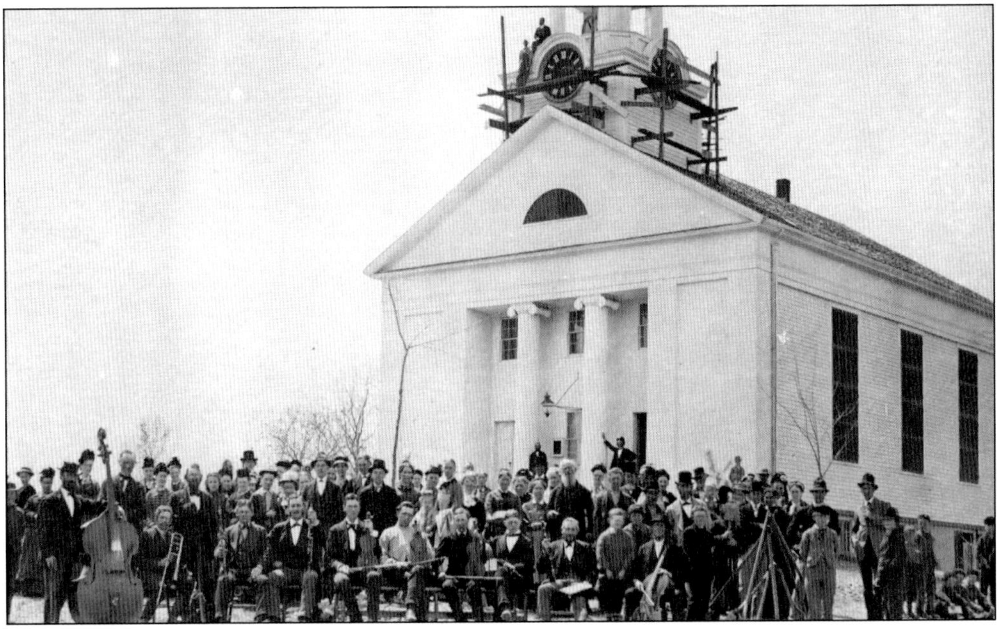

On March 21, 1876, a high wind toppled the steeple of the First Parish Church, and a group of citizens raised money to install a clock in the base of the steeple as part of the repairs. The dedication ceremony shown took place on May 17, 1876, and in January 1877, the Village Clock Association was formed to maintain the clock. The town took responsibility in 1892. (Chelmsford Historical Society Collection.)

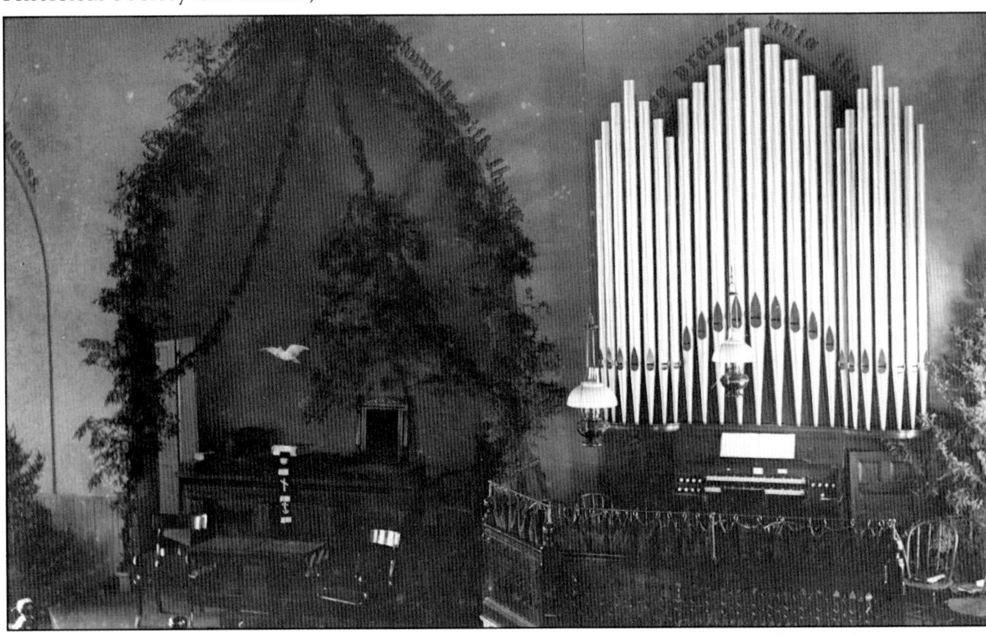

The interior of the First Parish Church was renovated in 1888, as seen here. The pews were rearranged, an aisle was added, the pulpit platform was lowered and enlarged, the choir loft was relocated, rooms were added on each side of the desk, and wallpaper was applied to both the walls and ceiling. The interior was renovated yet again in Colonial style in 1915. (Chelmsford Historical Society Collection.)

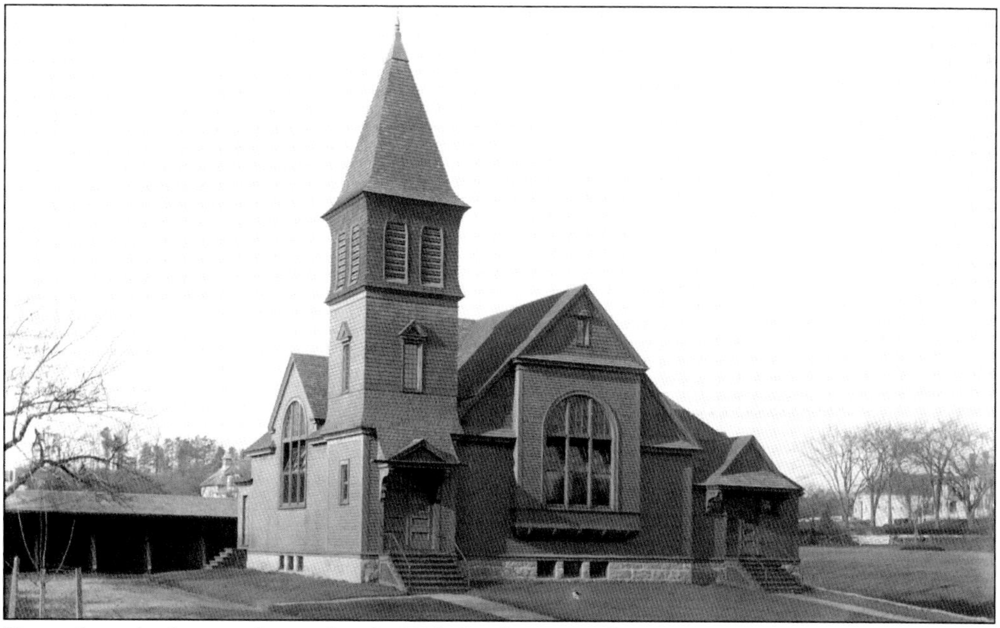

Ground was broken on September 2, 1887, for the Central Congregational Church on a North Road building lot gifted by the Winn sisters, who lived at 1 Academy Street. Additional land was purchased from Lyman S. Gale for outbuildings. The church was dedicated on May 9, 1888, and is seen here in November 1891. The 30-seat sanctuary and vestry below were soon outgrown. (Chelmsford Historical Society Collection.)

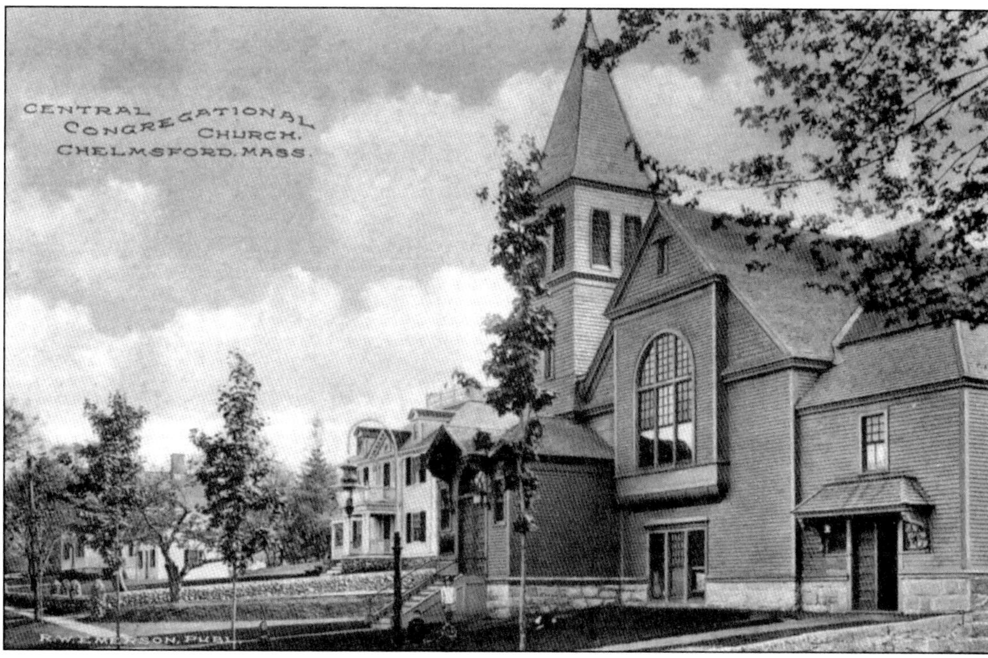

Starting in June 1893, the Central Congregational Church was remodeled by raising the building five feet; making room for a parlor, kitchen, bathroom, and steam-heating system; adding a porch in front of the tower; and increasing the sanctuary seating. Ralph W. Emerson, who also published this postcard, built the 10 North Road house on the left of the church in 1908. (Brad Perham.)

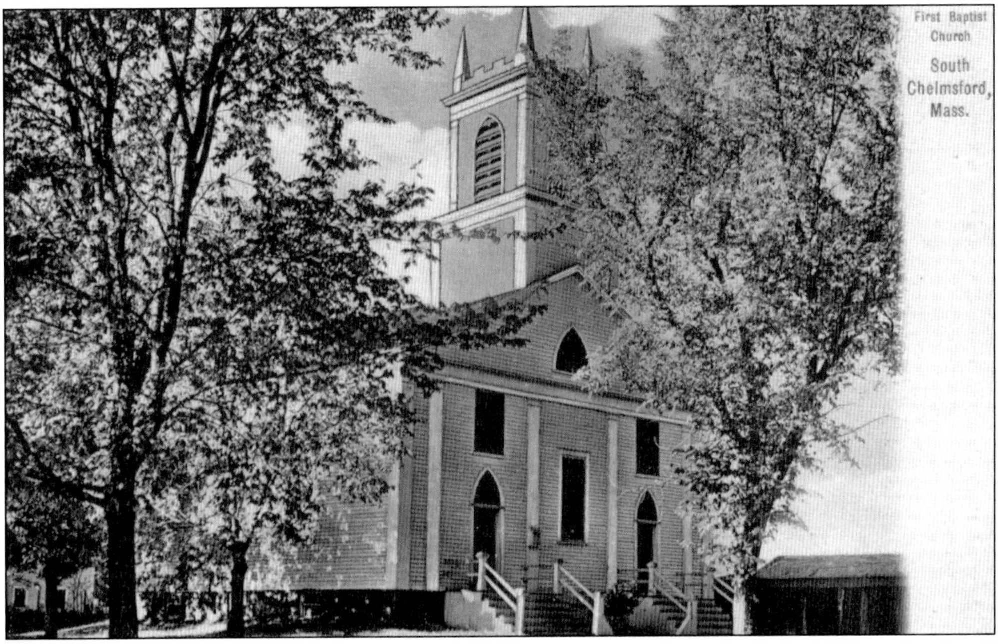

The First Baptist Church, seen here around 1910 on a postcard, was built in 1836 on land at 2 Maple Road, given by William Byam, and was the first church in Chelmsford that was separate from town government. In 1957, a change from Baptist to a community church was considered, but a restriction was discovered that would have voided the deed, so the congregation continued as Baptists. (Brad Perham.)

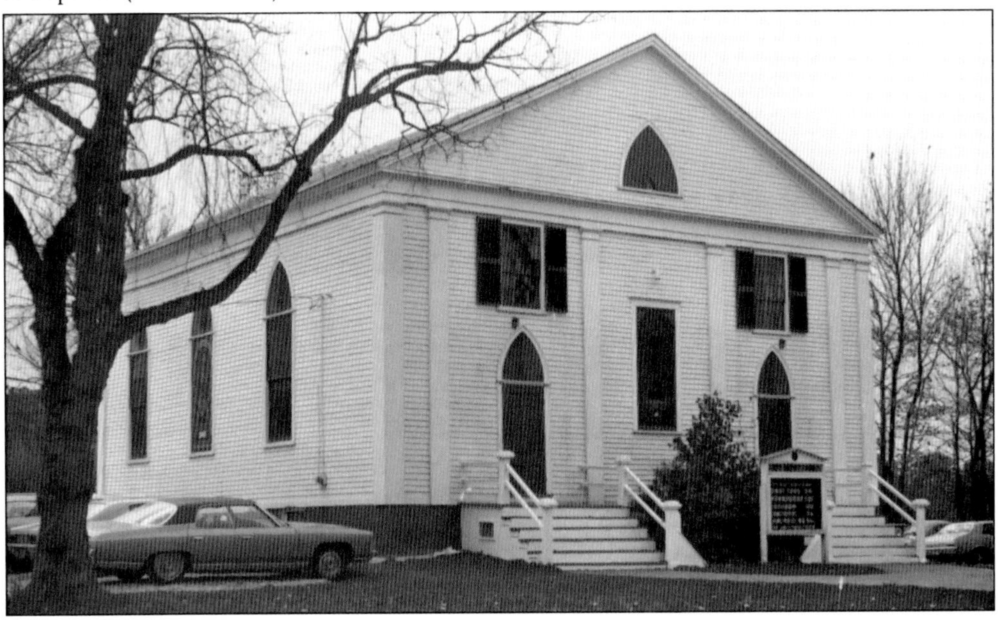

In 1871, the First Baptist Society celebrated its 100th anniversary, and to commemorate the occasion, the society added a cast bell to its steeple. In 1964, during extensive interior remodeling, it was discovered that the steeple and bell had become an unsafe load on the church, and on August 16, 1967, they were removed with a crane. This December 1973 photograph shows the result. (Chelmsford Historical Commission.)

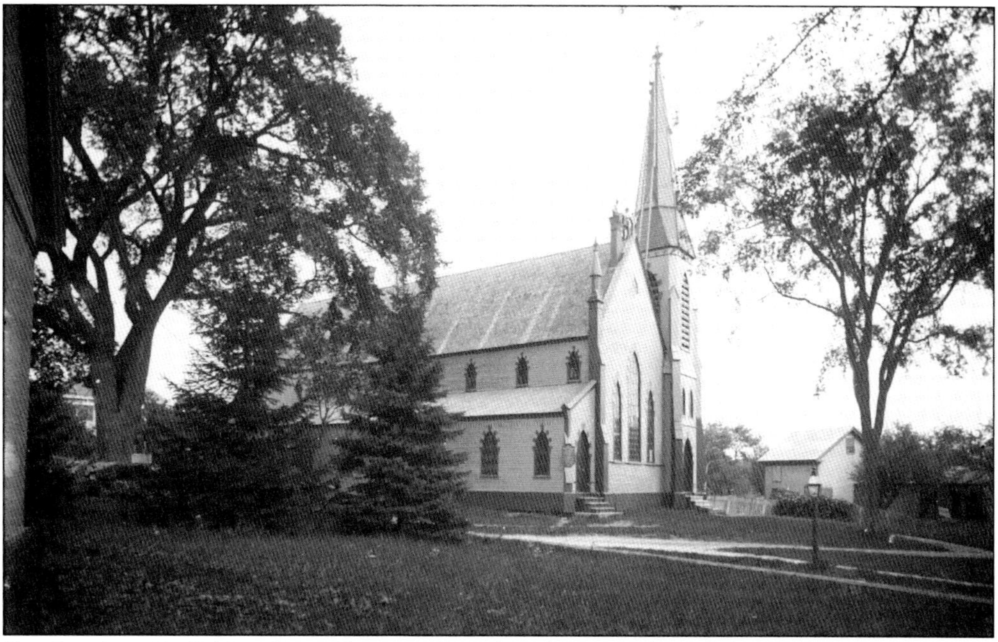

On October 17, 1866, cider mill owner David Perham purchased the Stoddard house at 11 Academy Street. On July 10, 1869, he sold at a discount the land with a newly built church on it to the deacons of the Central Baptist Church. In this c. 1900 photograph, taken from in front of the 1802 schoolhouse, there are steeplejacks at work on the church. (Chelmsford Historical Society Collection.)

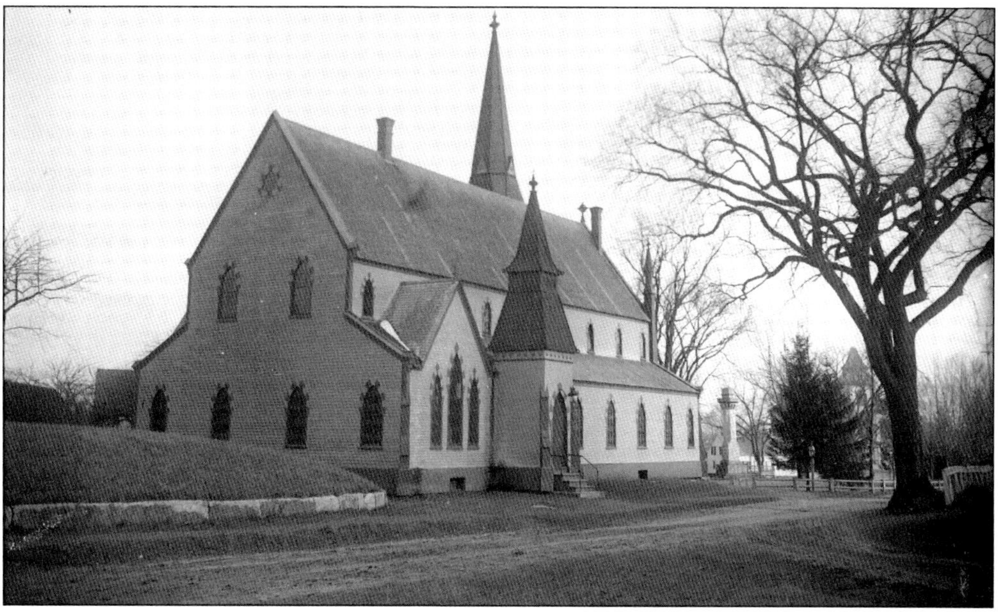

This view from Bridge Street shows the Central Baptist Church, the Revolutionary War Monument, the common, and town hall. On July 4, 1903, a wayward ember from a fire, which destroyed Minot A. Bean's house on Littleton Road, landed on the roof of this church and smoldered. After midnight, Stewart Redman and Roy Allen spotted the fire in time for fire crews to put it out. (Chelmsford Historical Society Collection.)

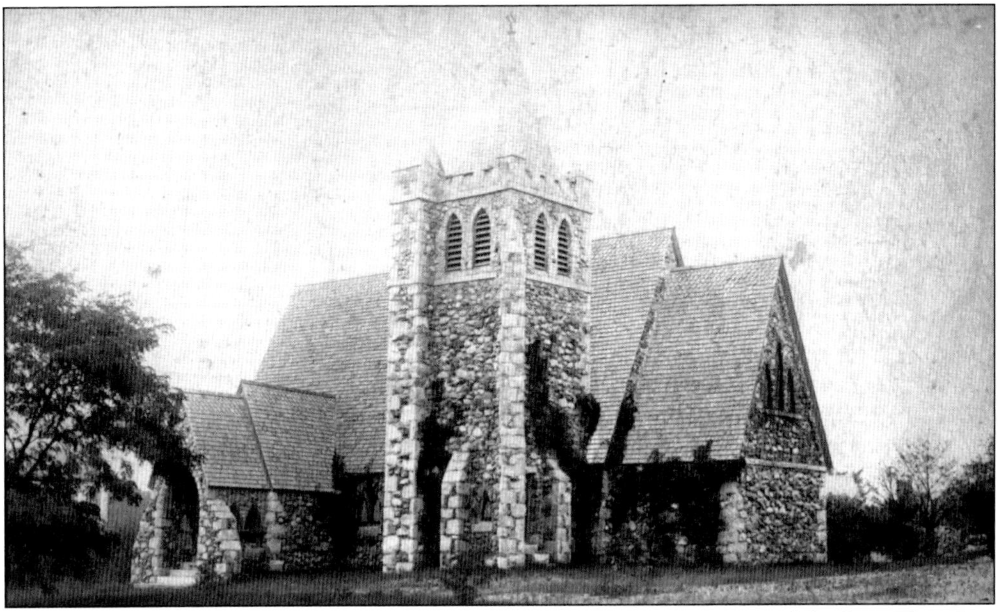

The cornerstone for the Parish of St. Anne's Church, a missionary project of the Rev. Theodore Edson, DD, of Lowell, was laid on November 5, 1879, and the dedication was held on December 20, 1882. The name was changed from the Parish of St. Anne to All Saints' Church in 1888—the same year this tower was completed in memory of Dr. Edson, partly funded by his daughter. (Chelmsford Historical Society Collection.)

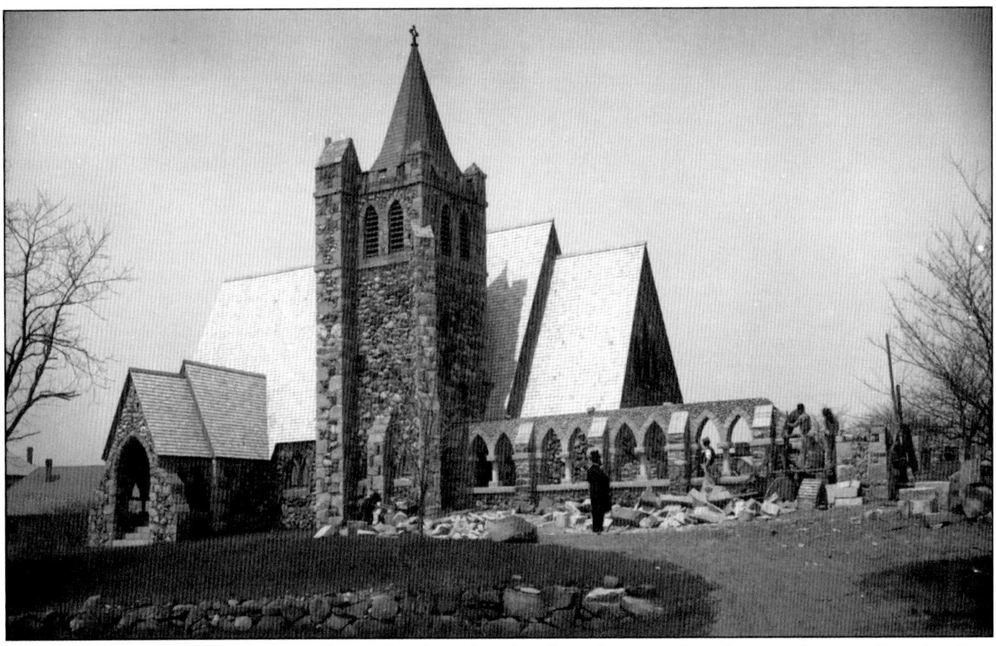

On September 21, 1896, ground was broken for the foundation of a cloister designed to lead to a study and porch and erected in memory of the mothers of the donors. Amos F. Adams was a contributor to the construction of the cloister. Rev. Wilson Waters is seen here with his top hat in 1897, checking up on construction by a team of stonemasons. (Chelmsford Historical Society Collection.)

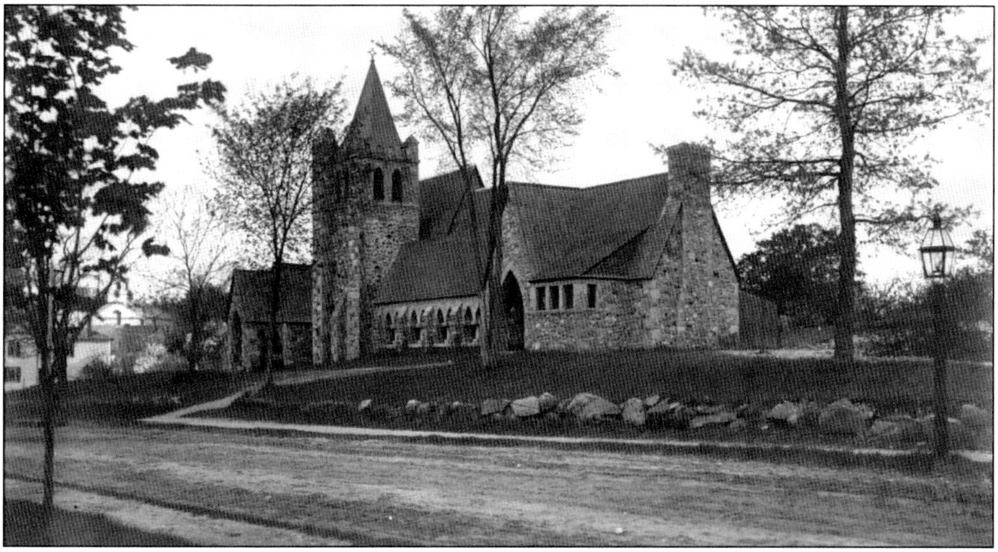

The church, as seen in this c. 1900 photograph, enjoyed a period of stability with Rev. Wilson Waters as rector until his death on June 13, 1933. As the town expanded in the 1950s, so did the church. A parish hall was dedicated in November 1952 to serve as a center of social life, and a new sanctuary was built behind the study in 1960. (Chelmsford Historical Society Collection.)

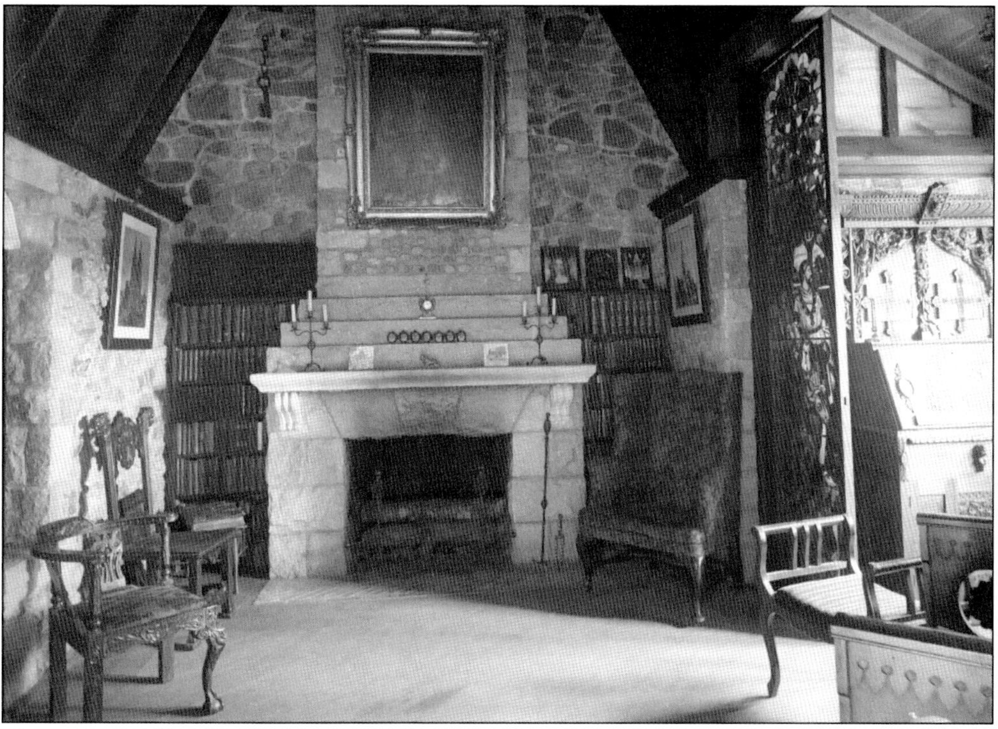

The study and library served as Rev. Wilson Waters' rectory. Henry S. Perham had been preparing an updated history of Chelmsford when he died on February 25, 1906. In 1907, Reverend Waters was, in his words, "asked by the Town to take up the work interrupted by the lamented death of Mr. Perham." This is the room where he researched and wrote the *History of Chelmsford Massachusetts*, published in 1917. (Chelmsford Historical Society Collection.)

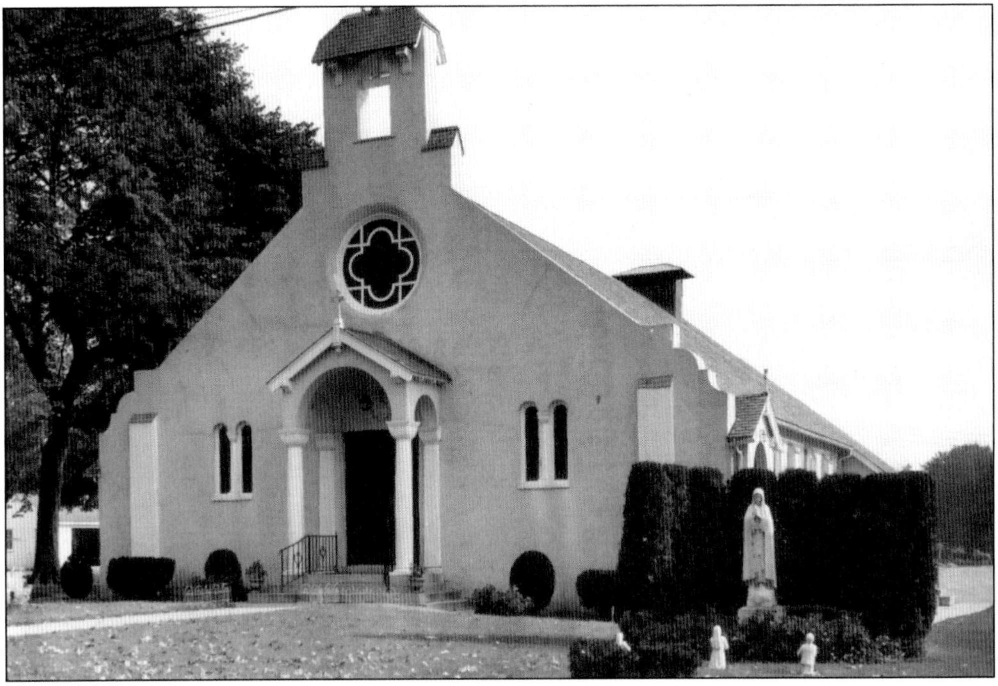

Early Catholic churchgoers in Chelmsford had to trek to Lowell or St. John's Church in North Chelmsford to attend Mass until 1921, when services were held upstairs in the Odd Fellows hall. In 1924, the estate of Lottie L. Adams on North Road was purchased, which included land and a house later used as a rectory. The stucco structure shown here was completed in 1926. (St. Mary Parish.)

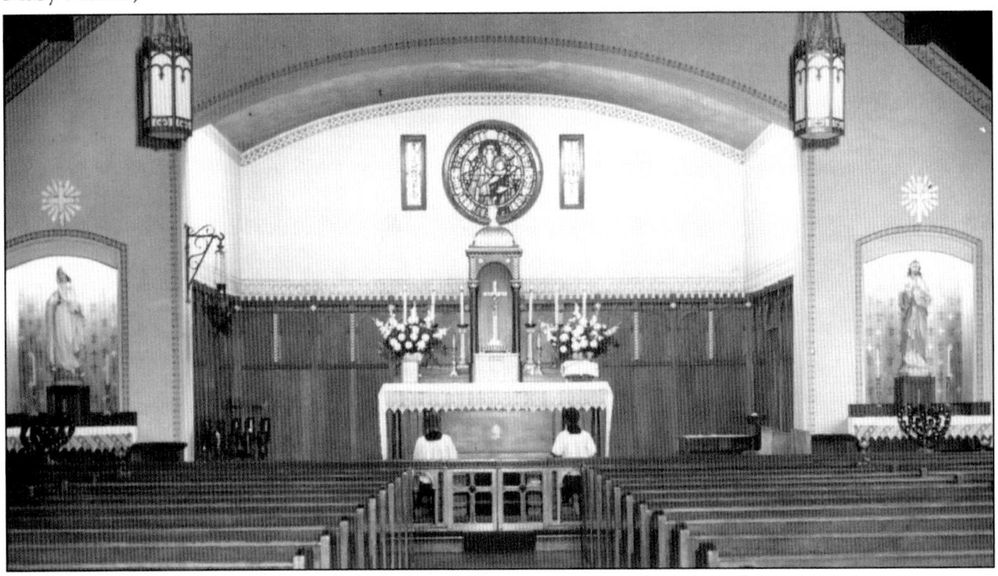

This is the interior of the 1926 church. For five years, St. Mary Parish operated as a mission under the direction of St. John's pastors Fr. John Crane and Fr. Joseph Curtin. In November 1931, Cardinal William O'Connell decreed that St. Mary become a separate parish. Authentic records could now be kept at St. Mary Parish, and the first baptism and marriage occurred that same month. (St. Mary Parish.)

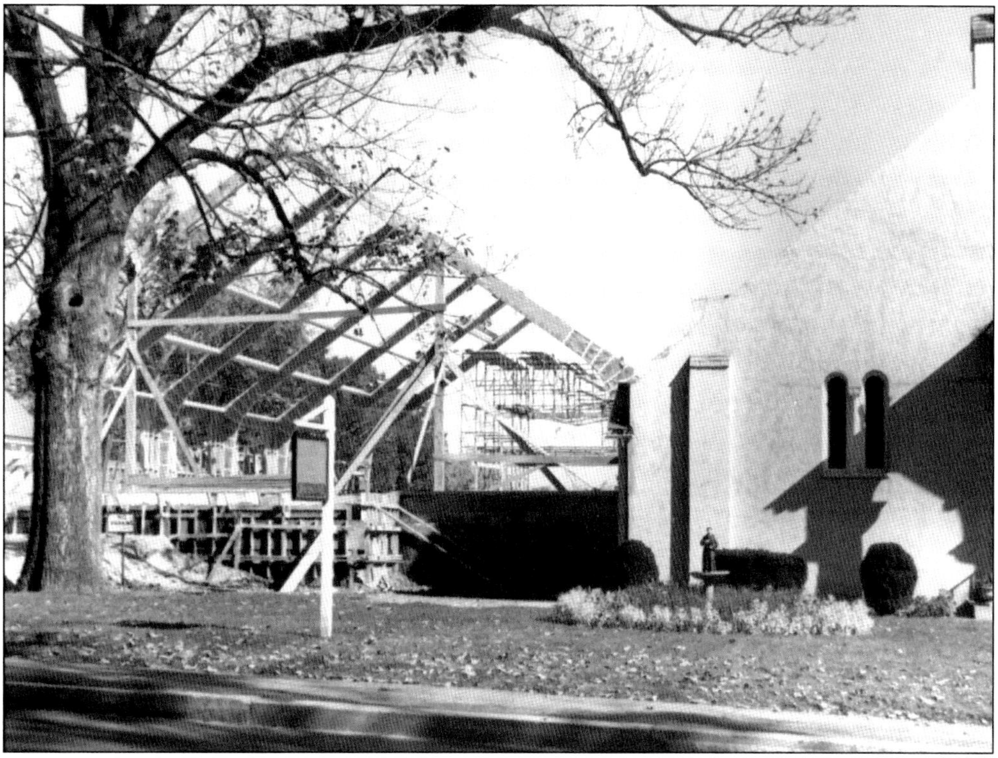

In 1961, ground was broken for a new church, seen here next to the original. The statuary from the Our Lady of Fatima story from the 1926 church was placed on the lawn of the new building. In 2012, to highlight the statues, a stone Marian Grotto was initiated by Chelmsford High School senior Danielle Lapierre and, later, beautifully constructed by a team of volunteers. (St. Mary Parish.)

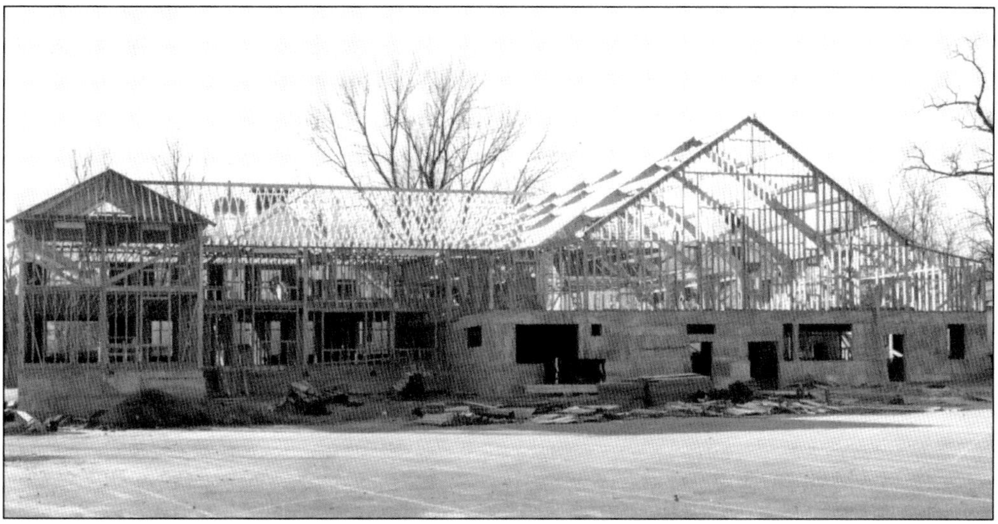

In this photograph taken from the Fletcher Street parking lot, the rectory office and residence wing and parish hall buildings are framed, and the rear of the old church can be seen through the rectory framing. The new church of St. Mary was dedicated on October 5, 1962, and the first Mass was celebrated on October 7, 1962, the Feast of the Most Holy Rosary. (St. Mary Parish.)